An Introduction
to Utilitarianism

From Theory to Practice

An Introduction to Utilitarianism

From Theory to Practice

Richard Yetter Chappell

Darius Meissner

William MacAskill

Hackett Publishing Company, Inc.
Indianapolis/Cambridge

27 26 25 24   1 2 3 4 5 6 7

For further information, please address
        Hackett Publishing Company, Inc.
        P.O. Box 44937
        Indianapolis, Indiana 46244-0937

        www.hackettpublishing.com

Cover and interior designs by E.L. Wilson
Composition by Aptara, Inc.

Cataloging-in-Publication data can be accessed via the Library of Congress Online Catalog at
https://lccn.loc.gov/2024024695.
LCCN: 2024024695

ISBN-13: 978-1-64792-200-9 (pbk.)
ISBN-13: 978-1-64792-201-6 (PDF ebook)
ISBN-13: 978-1-64792-202-3 (epub)

The paper used in this publication meets the minimum requirements of American National Standard for Information Sciences—Permanence of Paper for Printed Library Materials, ANSI Z39.48–1984.

∞

Contents

Foreword

Katarzyna de Lazari-Radek and Peter Singer

This introduction to utilitarianism appears at a propitious moment. Utilitarians have long strived to bring about practical changes to promote happiness and relieve suffering, criticizing practices that most people accepted as natural and inevitable conditions of human existence. Yet, not since the Philosophical Radicals, inspired by Jeremy Bentham, campaigned to extend voting rights and reform prisons in the early nineteenth century has utilitarianism attracted as much public attention as it does today. Nor has it ever been as prominent in discussions of ethics among teachers and researchers of philosophy.

Even in its nineteenth-century heyday, however, utilitarianism was widely ridiculed, and the reforms urged by leading utilitarians were vehemently opposed. Conservative defenders of the status quo succeeded in delaying, for several decades, reforms such as votes for women, the legalization of same-sex relationships, medical aid in dying, and laws to adequately protect the welfare of animals. In many countries, that opposition continues to block reforms that would reduce suffering. Nevertheless, thinking that is broadly utilitarian, even if not explicitly so, is having greater worldwide impact than it has ever had before.

That impact became apparent when the COVID-19 pandemic swept the world in 2020. Governments almost everywhere, faced with a new virus for which there was initially no vaccine, instituted lockdowns—depriving their citizens of the rights to freedom of movement and freedom of association. Did the citizens rise up, proclaiming that these rights are sacrosanct and not to be overridden by the goal of achieving the most well-being for all? No. Overwhelmingly, they accepted and supported suppressing these rights for the greater good. They may not have conceived of this greater good as sweepingly as utilitarians do—concerns for their own good or the good of their parents, children, or other loved ones may have moved them—but their governments usually did profess to be acting for the greater good of the community as a whole. That was true even of the United States, a country that began with a declaration of a supposedly self-evident and unalienable right to liberty. When it came to the crunch, rights yielded to the calculus of what government action would bring about the greatest benefit based on the best available evidence in that situation of uncertainty. This is exactly what utilitarians would do.

Several other twenty-first-century changes in ethical thinking and practice, consistent with utilitarian views, have overcome the opposition of institutions that follow inflexible non-utilitarian ethical doctrines, especially hardline religious teachings. During the past two or three decades, we have seen major shifts in public morality on issues like same-sex relationships. In several countries, these shifts culminated in the legalization of homosexual marriage and voluntary eutha-nasia or medically assisted dying, allowing the terminally ill to die peacefully at a time of their own choosing, without further suffering. The movement to protect animals from suffering has also gained strength and, as utilitarians would urge, is increasingly—though still insufficiently—focused on reducing the vast quantity of suffering we inflict on billions of intensively confined chickens, pigs, and fish rather than on the much smaller number of abused dogs and cats.

The newest and perhaps most promising example of the influence of util-itarian thinking is the effective altruism movement, which began in the first decade of the present century. It is a social movement and a philosophical outlook that emphasizes doing the most good we can, with the resources we have available, for all sentient beings, whether they are close at hand or on the other side of the planet, and whether they are living now or are yet to be con-ceived. While effective altruism and utilitarianism are different in important respects—the former being more ecumenical and making fewer controversial assumptions than the latter—the effective altruism movement takes seriously and seeks to implement key utilitarian principles, like beneficence, impartiality, welfarism, and aggregation.

Utilitarianism, then, is an ethical view whose time has come with the oppor-tunity to do far more good than it has ever done. It pushes us to examine the boundaries of our moral thinking and consider the interests of those who we often leave out of our concern—such as the global poor, non-human animals, and future generations.

Yet, utilitarianism remains contested. To make up our minds about it, we need to start by stating clearly what it is, examining its main varieties, and consid-ering the reasons for holding or rejecting these varieties. This is the purpose of the book you are now reading. It discusses, thoughtfully and clearly, what makes utilitarianism distinctive from other ethical theories, alongside key questions like *What even is the "well-being" that utilitarians seek to promote? How demanding is utilitarianism? How should we think about actions affecting future generations, such as having children? How much does utilitarianism diverge from commonsense morality?* And many more.

Before we conclude, we want to mention two unusual aspects of this work. The first is that it is written by three authors who partially disagree about which is the best moral theory. There can be many theoretical disagreements, even among those sympathetic to utilitarianism. Richard Yetter Chappell—like the classical utilitarians, Jeremy Bentham, John Stuart Mill, and Henry Sidgwick—subscribes to consequentialism, the view that the right action is the one that has the best consequences. He parts from that trio, however, in rejecting hedonism, the view that the only intrinsic good to be promoted is happiness. Will MacAskill, on the other hand, thinks that hedonism offers the most plausible account of which consequences matter but has doubts about whether the right action is always the one that has the best consequences. We will put our cards on the table too: we are consequentialists and hedonists, so we differ from both Chappell and MacAskill and agree with the classical utilitarians—especially with Sidgwick, whose book *The Methods of Ethics* we rank as possibly the best ever written on ethics.[1]

Despite these theoretical disagreements, we all largely agree on the implications of utilitarianism in practice, for what it means to live an ethical life. This is the unusual feature of this book that we like best: it does not treat utilitarianism only as a theory, as so many books on ethics treat the ideas they present, but also as a live option for each of us to choose as a philosophy that guides our life. The presence of a chapter on what it is like to live as a utilitarian indicates something uniquely important about ethics but often neglected. Studying ethics can change your life.

---

1. We explain why we think this in Katarzyna de Lazari-Radek and Peter Singer, *The Point of View of the Universe: Sidgwick and Contemporary Ethics* (Oxford: Oxford University Press, 2014).

Preface

Utilitarianism is taught in introductory ethics classes around the world. But textbook presentations of utilitarianism often misconstrue the theory, failing to present either the strongest arguments in favor of it or its most sophisticated defenses against objections. They also fail to present utilitarianism's distinctive practical contributions: showing what a life lived in accordance with utilitarian ideals would really look like.

To help rectify this situation, we've written this textbook aiming to present utilitarianism in a clear and broadly sympathetic light. Ethics remains controversial, of course, and we certainly don't expect all readers to agree that utilitarianism is ultimately correct. But we hope to convey a better sense of why one might reasonably find it appealing and how it can address objections that you might otherwise have assumed were devastating.

We also discuss at length the real-life practical implications of utilitarian moral theory. Throughout the text, we emphasize the utilitarian case for striving to make the world a better place as effectively as possible while respecting commonsense norms against harming others.

The most practically important features of utilitarianism are its *impartial beneficence* and its focus on *effectiveness*. No other widely held moral view so emphasizes the importance of helping others, regardless of what groups they belong to or how they relate to the agent. As Chapter 6 (Utilitarianism and Practical Ethics) emphasizes, utilitarianism expands our moral circle of concern. Not only does it condemn racism, sexism, and other discrimination already widely condemned today, but it also equally values the well-being even of people in faraway countries, of non-human animals, and of future generations. And, as Chapter 7 (Acting on Utilitarianism) explains, utilitarianism directs us to *prioritize* our efforts and resources to do more good rather than less. Utilitarianism thus naturally supports *effective altruism*: the project of finding the best ways to help others and acting accordingly. This may include focusing on global rather than local poverty (as money goes further in the poorest countries, making a bigger difference to its beneficiaries), on relieving the suffering of factory-farmed animals (which is both immense in scale and significantly tractable), and on anticipating and addressing global catastrophic risks, which threaten the existence of all future generations. We may most effectively contribute to these causes via our charitable donations, career choice, or outreach that encourages others to join the effort.

One needn't accept utilitarianism in order to agree with these practical implications. Chapter 8 (Near-Utilitarian Alternatives) explores possible departures from utilitarianism, assessing which ones do or do not threaten its beneficent practical implications. Indeed, all three authors of this text are personally much more confident of the merits of doing good effectively than we are in utilitarianism as a moral theory.

Chapter 2 (Elements and Types of Utilitarianism) introduces the crucial distinction between using utilitarianism as a *criterion* for moral assessments versus using it as a *decision procedure* to directly guide our actions in practice. Many objections to utilitarianism rest on mistakenly believing that utilitarians use the theory not only as a criterion but also as a decision procedure. However, as we further emphasize in Chapter 6, utilitarians reject making every decision on the basis of a naive utilitarian calculus. This fact substantially weakens several of the objections discussed in Part II, including the concern that utilitarianism recommends wicked-seeming actions whenever the agent believes them likely to do more good than harm. Instead, utilitarian goals may be best achieved by following reliable rules and heuristics (such as commonsense moral virtues and respect for individual rights). So, we believe that utilitarians, in practice, should aspire to live in accordance with virtues like integrity, trustworthiness, and law-abidingness, as well as avoiding harming others unless under the most extreme circumstances.

While we are all broadly sympathetic to utilitarianism, our precise attitudes vary. For example, Richard outright rejects the hedonism of classical utilitarianism and is undecided about the extent to which desert-adjustments and partiality toward our loved ones may be intrinsically warranted. But he's very confident that some form of consequentialism is correct and most likely one that at least roughly approximates utilitarianism in important cases.

In contrast, Will thinks that classical utilitarianism is the most plausible version of utilitarianism. However, he's not very confident in utilitarianism itself: he puts significant credence on non-consequentialist moral views, too, and thinks it's likely that we haven't yet even conceived of the correct moral theory. He takes this *moral uncertainty* to further bolster the practical case for deontic constraints against violating rights and for making further inquiry into ethics a moral priority.

As philosophers, we would not wish for our readers to leave this text with the impression that utilitarianism is unassailable or obviously correct. We think the theory has a lot going for it, and we've tried to bring that out. But, like any philosophical view, it also faces serious challenges and objections. We encourage readers to critically assess our arguments, and reflect for themselves upon what they think ultimately matters and how best to live and act in light of those reflections.

A note on the source material

 This textbook is adapted from material we have published online at **utilitarianism.net**. The web edition contains supplemental resources that may be of interest to readers, including audio narrations, a glossary of key terms, biographies of key thinkers, and guest essays by leading academics on specific topics relating to utilitarianism. We're grateful to Hackett Publishing for working with us to produce this convenient book edition while the web edition remains, as always, free and open access. All author royalties from this book will be donated to charity.

Author contributions

Authors are listed in order of contribution, with chapter-specific details available on the web edition (as not all authors contributed to the writing of all chapters).

—**Richard Yetter Chappell,**
Darius Meissner,
and William MacAskill

Part I: Utilitarianism Explained

1

Introduction to Utilitarianism

The task of the benevolent is surely to diligently seek to promote the benefit of the world and eliminate harm to the world and to take this as a model throughout the world. Does it benefit people? Then do it. Does it not benefit people? Then stop.

—Mòzǐ[1]

What, morally, ought we to do? Utilitarianism gives an answer: we ought always to promote overall well-being. Compared to other ethical theories, utilitarianism is less deferential to ordinary thought and may tell us to make substantial changes to how we lead our lives. Perhaps more so than any other ethical theory, it has produced a fierce philosophical debate between its proponents and its critics.

Why Do We Need Moral Theories?

When we make moral judgments in everyday life, we often rely on our intuition. If you ask yourself whether or not it's wrong to eat meat, to lie to a friend, or to buy sweatshop goods, you probably have a strong gut moral view on the topic. But there are problems with relying merely on our moral intuition.

Historically, people held beliefs we now consider morally horrific. In Western societies, it was once firmly believed to be intuitively obvious that people of color and women have fewer rights than white men, that homosexuality is wrong, and that it was permissible to own slaves. We now see these moral intuitions as badly misguided. This historical track record gives us reason to be concerned that we, in the modern era, may also be unknowingly responsible for serious, large-scale

---

1. *Mòzǐ* 32:1, trans. C. Fraser, in *The Essential Mòzǐ*: https://global.oup.com/academic/product /the-essential-mz-9780198848103.

wrongdoing. It would be a very lucky coincidence if the present generation were the first generation whose intuitions were perfectly morally correct.[2]

Also, people have conflicting moral intuitions, and we need a way to resolve these disagreements. We see the project of moral philosophy as being to reflect on our competing moral intuitions and develop a theory that will tell us what we ought to do and why. This will then allow us to identify which moral judgments of today are misguided, enabling us to make moral progress and act more ethically.

One of the most prominent and influential attempts to create such a theory is *utilitarianism*. Utilitarianism was developed by the philosophers Jeremy Bentham and John Stuart Mill, who drew on ideas going back to the ancient Greeks. Utilitarianism has since been widely discussed and has significantly influenced economics and public policy.

Track Record

While history cannot directly tell us which moral theory is correct, utilitarian moral reasoning has a strong track record of contributing to humanity's collective moral progress—suggesting that there may at least be something morally salutary to these ideas. The classical utilitarians of the eighteenth and nineteenth centuries had many social and political attitudes that were far ahead of their time: as a progressive social reformer, Jeremy Bentham advocated for the separation of church and state, the abolition of slavery and capital punishment, legal regulations to protect criminals and non-human animals from cruel treatment,[3] and the

---

2. For more details, see Evan G. Williams, "The Possibility of an Ongoing Moral Catastrophe," *Ethical Theory and Moral Practice* 18, no. 5 (February 2015): 971–82, https://doi.org/10.1007/s10677-015-9567-7.

3. For instance, Bentham commented on the issue of animal protection: "The question is not, Can they reason? nor, Can they talk? but, Can they suffer? Why should the law refuse its protection to any sensitive being? The time will come when humanity will extend its mantle over everything which breathes. We have begun by attending to the condition of slaves; we shall finish by softening that of all the animals which assist our labors or supply our wants." Bentham, *An Introduction to the Principles of Morals and Legislation*, ed. Jonathan Bennett (London, 1789; Early Modern Texts, 2017), 143–44, https://www.earlymoderntexts.com/assets/pdfs/bentham1780.pdf.

decriminalization of homosexuality.[4] Indeed, his manuscripts on homosexuality were so liberal that his editor hid them from the public after Bentham's death. They were only published two centuries later.

John Stuart Mill defended the provision of social welfare for the poor and of freedom of speech. He was the second MP in the UK Parliament to call for women's suffrage[5] and advocated for gender equality more generally. In his essay, *The Subjection of Women*,[6] Mill argued that

> the principle which regulates the existing social relations between the two sexes—the legal subordination of one sex to the other—is wrong itself, and now one of the chief hindrances to human improvement; and that it ought to be replaced by a principle of perfect equality, admitting no power or privilege on the one side, nor disability on the other.[7]

In a similar vein, Henry Sidgwick advocated for women's education and the freedom of education from religious doctrines. Modern utilitarians like Peter Singer are outspoken advocates against pressing moral problems such as extreme poverty and factory farming.[8]

The early proponents of utilitarianism were still far from getting everything right. (For example, Mill disappointingly shared the unsavory colonialist attitudes common among his compatriots.) But their utilitarian reasoning led them to escape many of the moral prejudices of their time and reach more enlightened

---

4. Cf. Bentham, *Introduction to the Principles of Morals*; L. Campos Boralevi, *Bentham and the Oppressed* (Berlin: De Gruyter, 2012).

5. UK Parliament, The 1866 Women's Suffrage Petition: The First Mass Votes for Women Petition, https://www.parliament.uk/about/living-heritage/transformingsociety/electionsvoting/womenvote/parliamentary-collections/1866-suffrage-petition/.

6. Mill attributes many of the ideas in *The Subjection of Women* to his wife, Harriet Taylor Mill. See Mill, *Autobiography*, ed. Jonathan Bennett (London, 1873; Early Modern Texts, 2017), 166, https://www.earlymoderntexts.com/assets/pdfs/bentham1780.pdf.

7. Mill, *The Subjection of Women*, ed. Jonathan Bennett (London, 1869; Early Modern Texts, 2017), 1, https://www.earlymoderntexts.com/assets/pdfs/mill1869.pdf.

8. On extreme poverty, see Singer, *The Life You Can Save: Acting Now to End World Poverty*, 2nd ed. (Bainbridge Island, WA: The Life You Can Save, 2019), available free at http://www.thelifeyoucansave.org/the-book. On factory farming, see Singer, *Animal Liberation Now: The Definitive Classic Renewed* (New York: HarperCollins, 2023).

moral and political positions. Those of us living today are, of course, still fallible, just as our forebears were. To help overcome our own biases, our moral and political views may similarly benefit from being checked against utilitarian principles.

What Is Utilitarianism?

We can define utilitarianism in simple terms:

> **Utilitarianism is the view that one ought always to promote overall well-being.**

The core idea is that we should want all lives to go as well as possible,[9] with no one's well-being counting for more or less than anyone else's.

Sometimes philosophers talk about "welfare" or "utility" rather than "well-being," but these words are typically used to mean the same thing.[10] (Others sometimes use "well-being" and "happiness" interchangeably, though we'll take "happiness" to be a narrower concept.)[11] Utilitarianism is most commonly applied to evaluate the rightness of actions, but the theory can also evaluate other things, like rules, policies, motives, virtues, and social institutions. It is perhaps unfortunate that the clinical-sounding term "utilitarianism" caught on as a name, especially since, in common speech, the word "utilitarian" is easily confused with joyless functionality or even outright selfishness.

All ethical theories in the utilitarian family share four defining elements: consequentialism, welfarism, impartiality, and aggregationism, which we'll define as follows:

1. **Consequentialism:** one ought always to promote overall value.
2. **Welfarism:** the value of an outcome is wholly determined by the well-being of the individuals in it.

---

9. This is most clear-cut in a fixed-population setting, where one's actions do not affect the number or identity of people. For more complex cases, see the discussion of population ethics in Chapter 5.

10. However, when economists use the term "utility," they typically refer, instead, to the numerical representation of an individual's preferences. (See Chapter 4.)

11. We use "happiness" to refer to pleasant, conscious experiences. Chapter 4 (Theories of Well-Being) explores whether well-being may involve more than this.

3. **Impartiality:** a given quantity of well-being is equally valuable no matter *whose* well-being it is.

4. **Aggregationism:** the value of an outcome is given by the *sum* value of the lives it contains.[12]

Utilitarianism's rivals (see Chapter 8) are theories that deny one or more of the above four elements. For example, they might hold that actions can be inherently right or wrong regardless of their consequences, or that things other than well-being can contribute to an outcome's value, or that morality allows us to be partial toward our friends and families, or that we should do whatever will most benefit the worst-off member of society.

Road Map

We cover the four elements of utilitarianism in greater depth, along with further theoretical distinctions, in Chapter 2: Elements and Types of Utilitarianism.

Chapter 3 explains reflective equilibrium as a moral methodology and presents several arguments for utilitarianism (and similar consequentialist views) over competing approaches to ethics. This includes a discussion of the veil of ignorance, the expanding moral circle, and the argument that utilitarianism offers an especially compelling account of *what fundamentally matters*. This chapter also explains the paradox of deontology, evolutionary debunking arguments, and other objections to non-consequentialist ethics.

Specific theories of well-being and of population ethics are explored in Chapters 4 and 5, respectively. While utilitarianism is often associated with *hedonism* about well-being and the *total view* of population ethics (a combination known as *classical utilitarianism*), other options are also worth considering. It's especially worth bearing in mind that objections to hedonism or to the total view may yet leave other forms of utilitarianism untouched. (Note that Chapter 5 on population

---

12. This definition applies to a fixed-population setting, where one's actions do not affect the number or identity of people. There are aggregationist theories that differ in how they deal with variable-population settings. This is a technical issue relevant to the discussion of population ethics in Chapter 5. Further note that non-welfarists might take things other than lives to contribute value to the world, which would then need to be included in the sum. We bracket this possibility for ease of exposition.

ethics is the most difficult and technical of the book, and some readers may prefer to skip it.)

Chapters 6 and 7 explore the practical applications of utilitarianism and its implications for how we should live our lives. We argue that, in practice, a utilitarian should try to do as much good as possible while still abiding by common-sense moral virtues like integrity, trustworthiness, and law-abidingness in order to advance social cooperation and mitigate the downside risk of miscalculation.

Chapter 8 examines how robust these practical recommendations are to various departures from strict utilitarian theory. While some alternative theories may yield radically divergent practical implications, we argue that a wide range of reasonable views ultimately converge on the core practical recommendation of utilitarian ethics—namely, to use a significant fraction of your time and/or money to help others, and to try to do so as effectively as possible, without violating commonsense moral constraints.

Prominent objections to utilitarianism are addressed in Part II. We introduce a "toolkit" of general maneuvers available to utilitarians to address a wide range of objections and then show how this toolkit can be used to address concerns about rights, demandingness, cluelessness, and more.

Conclusion

What matters most for utilitarianism is improving the well-being of all individuals, regardless of their gender, race, species, or geographical or temporal location.

All utilitarian theories share four key elements: consequentialism, welfarism, impartiality, and aggregationism. Classical utilitarianism includes two further elements: hedonism and totalism. Hedonism is the view that one's well-being is determined by the balance of one's positive and negative conscious experiences. The total view holds that the value of adding an additional person to an outcome is equal to the value of that person's lifetime well-being, together with whatever effects they have on others' well-being.

Utilitarian ethics has an intellectual tradition spanning centuries, during which it has prompted many heated debates. Critics of utilitarianism accuse the theory of disregarding rights and being overly demanding, among other objections. Advocates counter that the theory has attractive theoretical virtues and offers a compelling account of what fundamentally matters. If difficult trade-offs were settled behind a veil of ignorance to minimize risk of bias, it would be rational for everyone involved to endorse utilitarian recommendations. Close examination of these competing arguments is required to come to an informed view of this controversial theory.

The next chapter discusses the four elements of utilitarian theories in greater depth and introduces several variants of utilitarianism.

For additional resources
and study aids, see
https://utilitarianism.net/

Elements and Types of Utilitarianism

2

Introduction

As explained in Chapter 1 (Introduction to Utilitarianism), the core idea of utilitarianism is that we should want to improve the well-being of everyone by as much as possible. Utilitarian theories share four elements: consequentialism, welfarism, impartiality, and aggregationism. Classical utilitarianism is distinctive because it accepts two additional elements: first, hedonism as a theory of well-being; second, the total view of population ethics. There are several further important distinctions between utilitarian theories: we can distinguish scalar from maximizing or satisficing utilitarianism, expectational from objective utilitarianism, multi-level from single-level utilitarianism, and global from hybrid utilitarianism.

The Definition of Utilitarianism

Utilitarian theories share four defining elements:

1. Consequentialism
2. Welfarism
3. Impartiality
4. Aggregationism

Combining these, we can define utilitarianism as follows:

> **Utilitarianism is the view that one ought always to promote overall well-being.**

Sometimes philosophers talk about "welfare" or "utility" rather than "well-being," but they typically mean the same thing.

The Four Elements of Utilitarianism

Consequentialism

Utilitarianism is a form of *consequentialism*, which we define as follows:

> **Consequentialism is the view that one ought always to promote overall value.**

Consequentialism claims that the value of the outcome is what ultimately matters from a moral perspective. So, to evaluate whether to perform an action, we should look at its overall consequences rather than any of its other features (such as the *type* of action that it is). For instance, when breaking a promise has bad consequences—as it usually does—consequentialists oppose it. However, breaking a promise is not considered wrong in itself. In exceptional cases, breaking a promise could be the morally best action available, such as when it's necessary to save a life. The ends in this case justify the means.

Consequentialism's rivals offer alternative accounts of what one morally ought to do that depend on features other than the value of the resulting outcome. For example, according to deontology, morality is about following a system of rules, like "Do Not Lie" or "Do Not Steal." And according to virtue ethics, morality is fundamentally about having a virtuous character. Much of consequentialism's appeal may stem from the conviction that *making the world a better place* is simply more important than any of these competing moral goals.

Even some who think that morality is fundamentally about following the right rules might appreciate a consequentialist account of *which* rules are the right ones to follow.

Direct and Indirect Consequentialism: Explaining The Difference between Act Utilitarianism and Rule Utilitarianism

When offering a consequentialist account of rightness, a common distinction in the philosophical literature is between two views called *direct consequentialism* and *indirect consequentialism*.

According to the direct view, the rightness of an action (or rule, policy, etc.) depends only on its consequences. On this view, to determine the right action from among a set of feasible options, we should directly evaluate which option has the best consequences. Act utilitarianism (or act consequentialism, more generally) directly assesses the moral rightness of actions.

According to indirect consequentialism, we should instead evaluate the moral status of an action *indirectly*, based on its relationship to something else (such as a rule), which is, in turn, assessed in terms of its consequences. The most famous indirect view is known as *rule utilitarianism* (or *rule consequentialism* more generally). According to rule utilitarianism, what makes an action right is that it conforms to the set of rules that would have the best utilitarian consequences if they were generally accepted or followed. Since an action's morality depends on its conformity to a rule rather than its own consequences, rule utilitarianism is a form of indirect consequentialism.

On our definition of consequentialism, only the direct view is a genuinely consequentialist position, and rule consequentialism, despite the name, is not a type of consequentialism.[1] As Brad Hooker, a prominent rule consequentialist, argues, rule consequentialism is not plausibly motivated by a consequentialist commitment to outcomes being as good as possible: the case for rule consequentialism is instead that it impartially justifies intuitively plausible moral rules.[2] This marks an important difference from foundationally consequentialist theories.

Though act utilitarianism assesses only actions (rather than rules) in terms of "rightness," it nevertheless also recognizes the importance of having strong commitments to familiar moral rules. Rules such as "don't lie" and "don't kill" are

---

1. Some other cases where labels can be misleading: herbal tea is not a type of tea, a plastic flower is not a type of flower, and the flying lemur is not a lemur and does not fly.

2. For instance, Hooker writes: "The viability of this defense of rule-consequentialism against the incoherence objection may depend in part on what the argument for rule-consequentialism is supposed to be. The defense seems less viable if the argument for rule-consequentialism starts from a commitment to consequentialist assessment. For starting with such a commitment seems very close to starting from an overriding commitment to maximize the expected good. The defense against the incoherence objection seems far more secure, however, if the argument for rule-consequentialism is that this theory does better than any other moral theory at specifying an impartial justification for intuitively plausible moral rules." Brad Hooker, "Rule Consequentialism," *The Stanford Encyclopedia of Philosophy*, ed. Edward N. Zalta, Winter 2016 Edition, https://plato.stanford.edu/archives/win2016/entries/consequentialism-rule/.

regarded as useful guidelines that we should almost always follow in practice—precisely so that our actions better achieve good outcomes and avoid harm. For further discussion and clarification, see the section on "multi-level utilitarianism," below.

Welfarism

Consequentialists differ in what they take to be the *good* to be promoted. Utilitarians endorse *welfarism*, which we define as follows:

> **Welfarism is the view that the value of an outcome is wholly determined by the well-being of the individuals in it.**[3]

Specifically, welfarism holds that positive well-being is the only intrinsic good, and negative well-being is the only intrinsic bad. Philosophers use the term "well-being" to refer to what's good *for a person*, as opposed to what's good per se, or "from the point of view of the Universe" (to use Henry Sidgwick's poetic phrase). So, for example, one might coherently think that the punishment of an evil person is good, and moreover, it's good precisely because that punishment is bad *for him*. But that would be to reject the kind of welfarism that utilitarianism accepts, on which positive well-being is always intrinsically good, and negative well-being is always intrinsically bad.

Different theories of well-being regard different things as the basic constituents of well-being. The three main theories are *hedonism*, *desire theories*, and *objective list theories*. Chapter 4 explains these different theories of well-being in more detail.

While every plausible view recognizes that well-being is important, some philosophers reject welfarism by claiming that other things matter in addition. For example, egalitarians may hold that inequality is intrinsically bad, even when it benefits some and harms none. Others might hold that environmental and

---

3. Assigning further value to (for instance, more equal) distributions of well-being goes beyond welfarism by treating something other than well-being itself as intrinsically valuable.

aesthetic value must be considered in addition to well-being. Welfarists claim that these other things matter only insofar as they contribute to someone's well-being.

Impartiality and the Equal Consideration of Interests

Utilitarianism is committed to a conception of *impartiality* that builds in the *equal consideration of interests*:

> **Impartiality is the view that a given quantity of well-being is equally valuable no matter *whose* well-being it is.**

As utilitarian philosopher Henry Sidgwick states: "The good of any one person is no more important from the point of view . . . of the universe than the good of any other."[4] Utilitarians value the well-being of all individuals equally, regardless of their nationality, gender, where or when they live, or even their species. According to utilitarianism, *in principle*, you should not even privilege the well-being of yourself or your family over the well-being of distant strangers (though there may be good *practical* reasons to do so).[5]

Not all philosophers agree that impartiality is a core feature of morality. They might hold that we are allowed, or even required, to be *partial* toward a particular group, such as our friends and family. Or they might advance an alternative conception of "impartiality" that does not require the equal consideration of interests. For example, *prioritarianism* gives extra weight to the interests of the worst off, whoever they might be.

Aggregationism

The final common element of utilitarianism is *aggregationism*, which we define as follows:

---

4. Sidgwick, *The Methods of Ethics*, ed. Jonathan Bennett (London, 1874; Early Modern Texts, 2017), 186, https://www.earlymoderntexts.com/assets/pdfs/sidgwick1874.pdf.
5. See Chapter 15 (The Special Obligations Objection) for further discussion.

Aggregationism is the view that the value of an outcome is given by the *sum*[6] value of the lives it contains.[7]

When combined with welfarism and impartiality, this implies that we can meaningfully "add up" the well-being of different individuals and use this total to determine which trade-offs are worth making. For example, utilitarianism claims that improving five lives by some amount is five times better than improving one life by the same amount.

Some philosophers deny any form of aggregationism. They may believe, for instance, that small benefits delivered to many people cannot outweigh large benefits to a few people. To illustrate this belief, suppose you face the choice between saving a given person's life or preventing a large group of people from experiencing mild headaches. An anti-aggregationist might hold that saving the life is more morally important than preventing the headaches, *regardless of the number of headaches prevented*. Utilitarians would reason that if there are enough people whose headaches you can prevent, then the total well-being generated by preventing the headaches is greater than the total well-being of saving the life, so you should prevent the headaches.[8] The number of headaches we have to relieve for it to be better than saving a life might be, in practice, *extremely* high—but utilitarians, nonetheless, believe there is *some* number of headaches at which this trade-off should be made.

In practice, many individuals and policymakers appear to endorse these kinds of trade-offs. For example, allowing cars to drive fast on roads increases the number of people who die in accidents. Imposing extremely low-speed limits would

---

6. In principle, other aggregation methods (like multiplication or something more complex) are conceivable. But we focus here on the additive form of aggregationism, since that is by far the most common view.

7. This definition applies to a fixed-population setting, where one's actions do not affect the number or identity of people. Aggregationist theories differ in how they deal with variable-population settings. This is a technical issue, relevant to the discussion of population ethics in Chapter 5.

8. Derek Parfit further argues that anti-aggregative principles implausibly endorse choices that, when iterated sufficiently many times across the population, would make everyone worse off. Parfit, "Justifiability to Each Person," *Ratio* 16, no. 4 (November 2003): 368–90, https://doi .org/10.1046/j.1467-9329.2003.00229.x.

save lives at the cost of inconveniencing many drivers. Most people demonstrate an implicit commitment to aggregationism when they judge it worse to impose these many inconveniences for the sake of saving a few lives.

The Two Elements of Classical Utilitarianism

Above, we have explained the four elements all utilitarian theories accept: consequentialism, welfarism, impartiality, and aggregationism. While this is useful for distinguishing utilitarian from non-utilitarian moral theories, there are also important distinctions between utilitarian theories. Depending on how a utilitarian theory is spelled out, it might have widely differing practical implications and may be more or less compelling.

The oldest and most prominent utilitarian theory is *classical utilitarianism*, which can be defined as follows:

> **Classical utilitarianism is the view that one ought always to promote the sum total of happiness minus suffering.**

Classical utilitarianism can be distinguished from the wider utilitarian family of views because it accepts two additional elements: first, *hedonism*, the view that well-being consists only of conscious experiences; and second, the *total view* of population ethics, on which one outcome is better than another if and only if it contains a greater sum total of well-being, where well-being can be increased either by making existing people better off or by creating new people with good lives.

Theories of Well-Being: Hedonism

Classical utilitarianism accepts *hedonism* as a theory of well-being, which we define as follows:

> **Hedonism is the view that well-being consists in, and only in, the balance of positive minus negative conscious experiences.**

Ethical hedonists believe that the only things good in themselves are the experiences of positive conscious states, such as enjoyment and pleasure, and the only things bad in themselves are the experiences of negative conscious states, such as misery and pain. *Happiness* and *suffering* are commonly used by philosophers as shorthand for the terms *positive conscious experience* and *negative conscious experience*, respectively.

We discuss the arguments for and against hedonism—and its two major rivals, *desire theories* and *objective list theories*—in Chapter 4 (Theories of Well-Being).

Population Ethics: The Total View

Classical utilitarianism accepts a population ethical theory known as the *total view*, which holds that

> **One outcome is better than another if and only if it contains greater total well-being.**

The total view implies that we can improve the world in two ways:[9] either we can improve the quality of life of existing people, or we can increase the number of people living positive lives.[10] In practice, there are often trade-offs between making existing people happier and creating additional happy people. On a planet with limited resources, adding more people to an already large population may at some point diminish the quality of life of everyone else severely enough that total well-being decreases.

---

9. Technically, a third possibility would be to reduce the number of negative lives. Indeed, many utilitarians support (voluntary) euthanasia based on the recognition that a life of suffering may be worse than no life at all. See, e.g., Peter Singer, "Taking Life: Humans," chap. 7 in *Practical Ethics*, 3rd ed. (Cambridge: Cambridge University Press, 2011).

10. The notion of a positive life, crucial for the total view, only makes sense relative to a zero point on the well-being scale. This zero point is the threshold above which life becomes "worth living." A "neutral life," at well-being level 0, is neither "worth living" nor "not worth living." This may be either a life with no value or disvalue, or a life with exactly as much value as disvalue. For discussion of the subtleties surrounding the concept of a life "worth living," see John Broome, *Weighing Lives* (Oxford: Oxford University Press, 2004), 66–68.

The total view's foremost practical implication is giving great importance to ensuring the long-term flourishing of civilization. Since the total well-being enjoyed by all future people is potentially enormous, according to the total view, the mitigation of existential risks—which threaten to destroy this immense future value—is one of the principal moral issues facing humanity.

Alternatives to the total view in population ethics include the *average view*, *variable value theories*, *critical level (and range) theories*, and *person-affecting views*. We explain and discuss these theories in Chapter 5 (Population Ethics).

Further Distinctions among Utilitarian Theories

After selecting your preferred theory of well-being and population ethics view, you should also consider

1. how (or whether) to construct a conception of rightness;
2. whether to focus on *actual* or *expected* consequences;
3. the role of simple heuristics, derived from utilitarianism, to guide our actions in everyday life; and
4. what forms of moral evaluation apply to rules, motives, character, and other objects of moral interest beyond actions.

Reconstructing Rightness: Maximizing, Satisficing, and Scalar Utilitarianism

Utilitarianism is most often stated in its maximizing form: that, within any set of options, the action that produces the most well-being is right, and all other actions are wrong.

Though this is the most common statement of utilitarianism,[11] it may be misleading in some respects. Utilitarians agree that you *ideally* ought to choose

---

11. But note that it does not straightforwardly match what Jeremy Bentham and John Stuart Mill meant by utilitarianism. For example, Bentham said that actions should be evaluated "according to the tendency" by which they increase or decrease well-being. Similarly, Mill argued that "actions are right in proportion as they tend to promote happiness, wrong as they tend to produce the reverse of happiness." Bentham, *An Introduction to the Principles of Morals and Legislation*, ed. Jonathan Bennett (London, 1789; Early Modern Texts, 2017), 7, https://www.earlymoderntexts.com/assets/pdfs/bentham1780.pdf; Mill, *Utilitarianism*, ed. Jonathan

whatever action would best promote overall well-being. That's what you have the *most* moral reason to do. But they do not recommend *blaming* you every time you fall short of this ideal.[12] As a result, many utilitarians consider it misleading to take their claims about what *ideally ought* to be done as providing an account of moral "rightness" or "obligation" in the ordinary sense.[13]

To further illustrate this, suppose that Sophie could save no one, save 999 people at great personal sacrifice, or save 1,000 people at even greater personal sacrifice. From a utilitarian perspective, the most important thing is that Sophie saves either the 999 people or the 1,000 people rather than saving no one; the difference between Sophie's saving 999 people and 1,000 people is comparatively small. However, on the maximizing form of utilitarianism, both saving no one and saving the 999 people would simply be labeled as "wrong." While we might well accept a maximizing account of what agents *ideally ought* to do, there are further moral claims to make in addition.

Satisficing utilitarianism instead holds that, within any set of options, an action is right if and only if it produces *enough* well-being.[14] This proposal has its own problems and has not yet found wide support.[15] In the case given in the previous

---

Bennett (London, 1863; Early Modern Texts, 2017), 5, https://www.earlymoderntexts.com/assets/pdfs/mill1863.pdf.

12. Blame can be thought of as either an attitude (of moral disapproval) or an action (expressing such disapproval). Blaming actions are, for utilitarians, like any other action in that they should only be performed if they serve to promote well-being. Excessive blame would likely have bad consequences, because it discourages people from even trying. Instead, we should usually praise people who take steps in the right direction. On the moral assessment of attitudes, see the discussion of global versus hybrid utilitarianism below.

13. Peter Railton, "How Thinking about Character and Utilitarianism Might Lead to Rethinking the Character of Utilitarianism," *Midwest Studies in Philosophy* 13, (1) (September 1988): 407 https://doi.org/10.1111/j.1475-4975.1988.tb00135.x; Alastair Norcross, *Morality by Degrees: Reasons Without Demands* (Oxford: Oxford University Press, 2020).

14. For a discussion of this view, see Michael Slote and Philip Pettit, "Satisficing Consequentialism," *Proceedings of the Aristotelian Society*, Supplementary vol. 58 (1984): 139–63, 165–76, https://www.princeton.edu/~ppettit/papers/1984/SatisficingConsequentialism.pdf.

15. In particular, traditional satisficing accounts struggle to offer a non-arbitrary specification of the threshold for doing "enough" good and are vulnerable to the objection that they permit the gratuitous prevention of goodness above this threshold. Both objections are addressed in Richard Y. Chappell, "Willpower Satisficing," *Noûs* 53, no. 2 (June 2019): 251–65, https://doi.org/10.1111/nous.12213.

paragraph, we still want to say there is good reason to save the 1,000 people over the 999 people; labeling both actions as *right* would risk ignoring the important moral difference between these two options. So, while we may be drawn to a satisficing account of what agents are *obliged* to do in order to meet minimal moral standards,[16] this view, too, requires supplementation.

Instead, it's more popular among leading utilitarians today to endorse a form of *scalar utilitarianism*, which may be defined as follows:

> **Scalar utilitarianism is the view that moral evaluation is a matter of degree: the more that an act would promote well-being, the more moral reason one has to perform that act.**[17]

On this view, there is no fundamental, sharp distinction between "right" and "wrong" actions, just a continuous scale from morally better to worse.[18]

Philosophers have traditionally conceived of maximizing, satisficing, and scalar utilitarianism as competing views. But more recently, one of the authors (Chappell) has argued that utilitarians could fruitfully accept all three by constructing *multiple* different senses of "should" or "right."[19] On Chappell's "deontic pluralism" view (i) maximizers are correct to hold that Sophie *ideally* should save all 1,000 people; (ii) satisficers may be correct to hold that saving 999 is *minimally acceptable* in a way that saving no one is not; and (iii) scalar utilitarians are correct to hold that it's ultimately a matter of degree and that the gain from saving 999 rather than zero dwarfs the gain from saving 1,000 rather than 999.

---

16. See, e.g., Richard Y. Chappell, "Deontic Pluralism and the Right Amount of Good," in *The Oxford Handbook of Consequentialism*, ed. Douglas W. Portmore (New York: Oxford University Press, 2020), 498–512.

17. Norcross, *Morality by Degrees*.

18. Neil Sinhababu advances a form of scalar consequentialism that takes right and wrong to be themselves matters of degree, but the boundary point between the two is determined by conversational context rather than anything morally fundamental (or indeed genuinely significant in any way). As a result, this seems to be a merely verbal variant on the definition that we use here. Sinhababu, "Scalar Consequentialism the Right Way," *Philosophical Studies* 175 (December 2018): 3131–44, https://doi.org/10.1007/s11098-017-0998-y.

19. Chappell, "Deontic Pluralism and the Right Amount of Good," 498–512.

Expectational Utilitarianism versus Objective Utilitarianism

Given our cognitive and epistemic limitations, we cannot foresee all the consequences of our actions. Many philosophers have held that what we ought to do depends on what we (should) believe at the time of action. The most prominent example of this kind of account is *expectational utilitarianism.*[20]

> **Expectational utilitarianism is the view we should promote** *expected* **well-being.**

Expectational utilitarianism states we should choose the actions with the highest *expected value.*[21] The expected value of an action is the sum of the value of each of the potential outcomes multiplied by the probability of that outcome occurring. This approach follows expected utility theory, the most widely accepted theory of rational decision-making under uncertainty. So, for example, according to expectational utilitarianism, we should choose a 10 percent chance of saving 1,000 lives over a 50 percent chance of saving 150 lives because the former option saves an expected 100 lives (= 10% × 1,000 lives), whereas the latter option saves an expected 75 lives (= 50% × 150 lives). This provides an account of *rational* choice from a moral point of view.

Objective utilitarianism, by contrast, takes the extent to which we ought to perform an action to depend on the well-being it would *in fact* produce. The contrast between the two views may be illustrated using a thought experiment:

> **The Risky Treatment:** A patient has a chronic runny nose that will leave her, if untreated, with a mildly lower well-being for the rest of her life. The only treatment for her condition is very risky, with only a 1 percent chance of success. If successful, the treatment will cure her completely, but otherwise, it will lead to her death. Her doctor gives her the treatment, it succeeds, and she is cured.

---

20. Frank Jackson, "Decision-Theoretic Consequentialism and the Nearest and Dearest Objection," *Ethics* 101, no. 3 (April 1991): 461–82, https://doi.org/10.1086/293312.

21. In line with the above explanation of welfarism, utilitarians of any type understand "value" in terms of well-being.

The doctor's action has—as a matter of pure chance and against overwhelming odds—led to the best outcome for the patient, and not treating the patient would have left her worse off. Thus, according to objective utilitarianism, the doctor has acted rightly. However, the action was wrong from the perspective of expectational utilitarianism. The expected value of giving the treatment, with its overwhelming odds of killing her, is much worse for the patient than not treating her at all. The doctor's decision turned out to be immensely fortunate, but it was extremely reckless and irrational given their available information.

When there is a conflict in this way between which act would be *actually* best versus which would be *expectably* best, is there a fact of the matter as to which act is "really" right? Many philosophers are drawn to the view that this is merely a verbal dispute. We can talk about the actually best option as being "objectively right," and the expectably best option as "subjectively right," and each of these concepts might have a legitimate theoretical role.[22] For example, subjective rightness seems more apt to guide agents since in real life we are often uncertain what consequences will actually result from our actions. Subjective rightness is also relevant to assessing the quality of an agent's decision-making. (We think poorly of the reckless doctor, for example.) But we should presumably *prefer* that the actually best outcome be realized, and so will be *glad* that the doctor did as they "objectively ought," even if they acted subjectively wrongly. Objective rightness thus tracks *what a fully informed, morally ideal spectator would want you to do.*

On this understanding, objective and expectational utilitarianism aren't truly *rival* views at all. Objective utilitarianism tells us which choices are objectively preferable, and expectational utilitarianism tells us how to make *rational* moral decisions under conditions of uncertainty.[23] Their respective claims are mutually compatible.

---

22. Compare the analogous distinction between what is prudentially rational versus what is objectively best for you. Obviously, both of these normative concepts have a role to play in philosophical reflections about the perspective of self-interest. There's no inherent barrier to using the term "ought" in relation to *either* normative role, subjective or objective, so long as one is clear about which meaning is intended.

23. These are both genuine normative properties. We can ask which option has the normative property of being *what a fully informed, morally ideal spectator would want the agent to do.* And we can ask which option has the normative property of being *instrumentally rational, relative to the correct moral goals, given the evidence available to the agent.* Someone who thinks there is a

Multi-Level Utilitarianism versus Single-Level Utilitarianism

In the literature on utilitarianism, a useful distinction is made between a *criterion of rightness* and a *decision procedure*. A criterion of rightness tells us what it takes for an action (or rule, policy, etc.) to be right or wrong. A decision procedure is something that we use when deciding what to do.[24]

Utilitarians believe that their moral theory is the correct criterion of rightness (at least in the sense of what "ideally ought" to be done, as discussed above). However, they almost universally discourage using utilitarianism as a decision procedure to guide our everyday actions. This would involve deliberately trying to promote aggregate well-being by constantly calculating the expected consequences of our day-to-day actions. But it would be absurd to figure out what breakfast cereal to buy at the grocery store by thinking through all the possible consequences of buying different cereal brands to determine which one best contributes to overall well-being. The decision is low stakes and not worth spending a lot of time on.

The view that treats utilitarianism as both a criterion of rightness and a decision procedure is known as *single-level utilitarianism*. Its alternative is *multi-level utilitarianism*, which only takes utilitarianism to be a criterion of rightness, not a decision procedure. It is defined as follows:

> **Multi-level utilitarianism is the view that individuals should usually follow tried-and-tested rules of thumb, or *heuristics*, rather than trying to calculate which action will produce the most well-being.**

real dispute between the two must think that there is some *third* normative property, of being *what you really ought to do*, that might coincide with just one of the above two properties. If we doubt that there is any such third property, then there is nothing more to dispute. We just need to be clear about which of the above two properties we mean to pick out with our "ought" talk.
24. R. Eugene Bales, "Act-Utilitarianism: Account of Right-Making Characteristics or Decision-Making Procedure?," *American Philosophical Quarterly* 8, no. 3 (July 1971): 257–65, https://www.jstor.org/stable/20009403. For a discussion of the multi-level view in the context of Mill's *Utilitarianism*, see Roger Crisp, *Routledge Philosophy Guidebook to Mill on Utilitarianism* (Abingdon: Routledge, 1997), 105–12.

According to multi-level utilitarianism, we should, under most circumstances, follow a set of simple moral heuristics—do not lie, steal, kill, etc.—expecting that this will lead to the best outcomes overall. Often, we should use the commonsense moral norms and laws of our society as rules of thumb to guide our actions. Following these norms and laws usually leads to good outcomes because they are based on society's experience of what promotes overall well-being. The fact that honesty, integrity, keeping promises, and sticking to the law generally have good consequences explains why in practice, utilitarians value such things highly and use them to guide their everyday actions, as further discussed in Chapter 6 (Utilitarianism and Practical Ethics).[25]

In contrast, to our knowledge, no one has ever defended single-level utilitarianism, including the classical utilitarians.[26] Deliberately calculating the expected consequences of our actions is error-prone and risks falling into decision paralysis.

Sometimes, philosophers claim that multi-level utilitarianism is incoherent. But this is not true. Consider the following metaphor provided by Walter Sinnott-Armstrong: The laws of physics govern the flight of a golf ball, but a golfer does not need to calculate physical forces while planning shots.[27] Similarly, multi-level utilitarians regard utilitarianism as governing the rightness of actions, but they do not need to calculate expected consequences to make decisions. To the extent that following the heuristics recommended by multi-level utilitarianism results in better outcomes, the theory succeeds.

---

25. Richard M. Hare, *Moral Thinking: Its Levels, Method, and Point* (Oxford: Oxford University Press, 1981; Peter Railton, "Alienation, Consequentialism, and the Demands of Morality," *Philosophy and Public Affairs* 13, no. 2 (Spring 1984): 134–71, https://www.jstor.org/stable/2265273.

26. Jeremy Bentham rejected single-level utilitarianism, writing that "it is not to be expected that this process [of calculating expected consequences] should be strictly pursued previously to every moral judgment." Bentham, *Introduction to the Principles of Morals*, 23. Henry Sidgwick concurs, writing that "the end that gives the criterion of rightness needn't always be the end that we consciously aim at; and if experience shows that general happiness will be better achieved if men frequently act from motives other than pure universal philanthropy, those other motives are preferable on utilitarian principles." Sidgwick, *Methods of Ethics*, 201.

27. Sinnott-Armstrong, "Consequentialism," *The Stanford Encyclopedia of Philosophy*, ed. Edward N. Zalta and Uri Nodelman, Summer 2019 Edition, https://plato.stanford.edu/archives/sum2019/entries/consequentialism/.

A common objection to multi-level utilitarianism is that it is *self-effacing*. A theory is said to be (partially) self-effacing if it (sometimes) directs its adherents to follow a different theory. Multi-level utilitarianism often forbids using the utilitarian criterion when making decisions and instead recommends acting in accordance with non-utilitarian heuristics. However, there is nothing inconsistent about saying that your criterion of moral rightness comes apart from the decision procedure it recommends, and it does not mean that the theory fails.

The Difference between Multi-Level Utilitarianism and Rule Utilitarianism

Multi-level utilitarianism sounds similar to the position known as rule utilitarianism, which we discussed above, and it's easy to confuse the two. Yet, the two theories are distinct, and it's important to understand how they differ.

Multi-level utilitarianism takes utilitarianism to be the criterion of moral rightness. This means it does not regard recommended heuristics as the ultimate ethical justification of any action, which is instead determined by the action's tendency to increase well-being. In contrast, for rule utilitarianism, conformity to a set of rules is the criterion of moral rightness: the reason an action is right or wrong is because it does or does not conform to the right set of rules.

Insofar as you share the fundamental utilitarian concern with promoting well-being, and you simply worry that deliberate pursuit of this goal would prove counterproductive, this should lead you to accept multi-level utilitarianism rather than any kind of rule utilitarianism.

Global Utilitarianism and Hybrid Utilitarianism

Most discussions of utilitarianism revolve around act utilitarianism and its criterion of right action. But we can just as well consider the tendency of other things—like motives, rules, character traits, policies, and social institutions—to promote well-being. Since utilitarianism is fundamentally concerned with promoting well-being, we should not merely want to perform those *actions* that promote well-being. We should also want the motives, rules, traits, policies, institutions, etc., that promote well-being.

This aspect of utilitarianism has sometimes been overlooked, so those who seek to highlight its applicability to things besides just actions sometimes adopt the label "global utilitarianism" to emphasize this point:[28]

> **Global utilitarianism is the view that the utilitarian standards of moral evaluation apply to anything of interest.**

Global utilitarianism assesses the moral nature of, for example, a particular character trait, such as kindness or loyalty, based on the consequences that trait has for the well-being of others—just as act utilitarianism morally evaluates actions. This broad focus can help the view to explain or accommodate certain supposedly "non-consequentialist" intuitions. For instance, it captures the understanding that morality is not just about choosing the right acts but is also about following certain rules and developing a virtuous character.

All utilitarians should agree with this much. But there is a further question regarding whether this direct utilitarian evaluation is *exhaustive* of moral assessment or whether there is a role for other (albeit less important) kinds of moral evaluation to be made in addition. For example, must utilitarians understand *virtue* directly as a matter of character traits that tend to promote well-being,[29] or could they appeal to a looser but more intuitive connection (such as representing a positive orientation toward the good)?[30]

---

28. Advocates of global consequentialism have framed it as marking a departure from traditional act consequentialism, but there has been subsequent dispute over this claim. For advocacy of global consequentialism as a distinct view, see Philip Pettit and Michael Smith, "Global Consequentialism," in *Morality, Rules and Consequences: A Critical Reader*, ed. Brad Hooker, Elinor Mason, and Dale Miller (Edinburgh: Edinburgh University Press, 2000); Toby Ord, "Beyond Action: Applying Consequentialism to Decision Making and Motivation" (DPhil thesis, University of Oxford, 2009), http://files.tobyord.com/beyond-action.pdf. For criticism, see Brian McElwee, "The Ambitions of Consequentialism," *Journal of Ethics and Social Philosophy* 17, no. 2 (2020): https://doi.org/10.26556/jesp.v17i2.528; Richard Y. Chappell, "Fittingness: The Sole Normative Primitive," *Philosophical Quarterly* 62, no. 249 (June 2012): 684–704, https://doi.org/10.1111/j.1467-9213.2012.00075.x. The latter argues that global consequentialism is best understood as a merely verbal variant of act consequentialism.

29. Julia Driver, "A Consequentialist Theory of Virtue," chap. 4 in *Uneasy Virtue* (Cambridge: Cambridge University Press, 2001), 63–83.

30. Thomas Hurka, *Virtue, Vice, and Value* (New York: Oxford University Press, 2001).

A challenge for *pure* global utilitarianism is that it fails to capture all of the moral evaluations that we intuitively want to be able to make. For example, imagine a world in which moral disapproval was reliably counterproductive: if you blamed someone for doing X, that would just make them stubbornly do X even more in the future. Since we only want people to do more good acts, would it follow that only good acts, and not bad ones, were blame-*worthy*?

Here it's important to distinguish two claims. One is the direct utilitarian assessment that it would be good to blame people for doing good acts and not for doing bad ones since that would yield the best results (in the imagined scenario). But a second—distinct—claim is that only bad acts are truly blame-*worthy* in the sense of intrinsically *meriting* moral disapproval.[31] Importantly, these two claims are compatible. We may hold *both* that gratuitous torture (for example) warrants moral disapproval *and* that it would be a bad idea to express such disapproval if doing so would just make things worse.

This argument may lead one to endorse a form of *hybrid utilitarianism*, which we define as follows:

> **Hybrid utilitarianism is the view that, while one ought always to promote overall well-being, the moral quality of an aim or intention can depend on factors other than whether it promotes overall well-being.**

In particular, hybrid utilitarians may understand virtue and praise-worthiness as concerning whether the target individual *intends* good results, in contrast to global utilitarian evaluation of whether the target's intentions *produce* good results. When the two come into conflict, we should prefer to achieve good results than to merely intend them—so in this sense, the hybrid utilitarian agrees with much that the global utilitarian wants to say. Hybridists just hold that there is more to say in addition.[32] For example, if someone is unwittingly anti-reliable at achieving their goals (that is, they reliably achieve the *opposite* of what they intend, without

---

31. This mirrors Parfit's distinction between "state-given" versus "object-given" reasons. See Parfit, *On What Matters*, vol. 1 (Oxford: Oxford University Press, 2011), 50.

32. For further defense of this view, see Richard Y. Chappell, "Consequentialism: Core and Expansion," in *The Oxford Handbook of Normative Ethics*, ed. David Copp, Connie Rosati, and Tina Rulli (Oxford: Oxford University Press, forthcoming).

realizing it), it would clearly be *unfortunate* were they to sincerely aim at promoting the general good, and we should stop them from having this aim if we can. But their good intentions may be genuinely *virtuous* and admirable nonetheless.

Purists may object that hybrid utilitarianism is not "really" a form of utilitarianism. And indeed, it's a hybrid view, combining utilitarian claims (about what matters and what ought to be done) with claims about virtue, praise- and blame-worthiness that go beyond direct utilitarian evaluation. But as long as these further claims do not conflict with any of the core utilitarian claims about what matters and what ought to be done, there would seem no barrier to combining both kinds of claims into a unified view. This may prove a relief for those otherwise drawn to utilitarianism but who find pure global utilitarian claims about virtue and blame-worthiness to be intuitively implausible or incomplete.

Conclusion

All ethical theories belonging to the utilitarian family share four defining characteristics: they are consequentialist, welfarist, impartial, and aggregationist. As a result, they assign supreme moral importance to promoting overall well-being.

Within this family, there are many variants of utilitarian theories. The most prominent of these is classical utilitarianism. This theory is distinguished by its acceptance of hedonism as a theory of well-being and the total view of population ethics.

There are several further distinctions between utilitarian theories: we can distinguish scalar from maximizing and satisficing utilitarianism, expectational from objective utilitarianism, multi-level from single-level utilitarianism, and hybrid from pure global utilitarianism. These distinctions can make a significant difference to how plausible one finds the resulting view and how vulnerable it is to various objections.

The next chapter discusses arguments for utilitarianism and for consequentialism more broadly.

For additional resources
and study aids, see
https://utilitarianism.net/

Arguments for Utilitarianism

Introduction: Moral Methodology and Reflective Equilibrium

You cannot *prove* a moral theory. Whatever arguments you come up with, it's always possible for someone else to reject your premises—if they are willing to accept the costs of doing so. Different theories offer different advantages. This chapter will set out some of the major considerations that plausibly count in favor of utilitarianism. A complete view also needs to consider the costs of utilitarianism (or the advantages of its competitors), which are addressed in Part II (Objections and Responses). You can then reach an all-things-considered judgment as to which moral theory strikes you as overall best or most plausible.

To this end, moral philosophers typically use the methodology of *reflective equilibrium*.[1] This involves balancing two broad kinds of evidence as applied to moral theories:

1. Intuitions about specific cases (thought experiments)
2. General theoretical considerations, including the plausibility of the theory's *principles* or systematic claims about what matters

General principles can be challenged by coming up with putative *counterexamples* or cases in which they give an intuitively incorrect verdict. In response to such putative counterexamples, we must weigh the force of the case-based intuition against the inherent plausibility of the principle being challenged. This could lead you to *either* revise the principle to accommodate your intuitions about cases *or*

---

1. Norman Daniels, "Reflective Equilibrium," *The Stanford Encyclopedia of Philosophy*, ed. Edward N. Zalta, Summer 2020 Edition, https://plato.stanford.edu/archives/sum2020/entries /reflective-equilibrium/.

to reconsider your verdict about the specific case if you judge the general principle to be better supported (especially if you are able to "explain away" the opposing intuition as resting on some implicit mistake or confusion).

As we will see, the arguments in favor of utilitarianism rest overwhelmingly on general theoretical considerations. Challenges to the view (see Part II) can take either form, but many of the most pressing objections involve thought experiments in which utilitarianism is held to yield counterintuitive verdicts.

There is no neutral, non-question-begging answer to how one ought to resolve such conflicts.[2] It takes judgment, and different people may be disposed to react in different ways depending on their philosophical temperament. As a general rule, those of a temperament that favors *systematic theorizing* are more likely to be drawn to utilitarianism (and related views; see Chapter 8), whereas those who hew close to commonsense intuitions are less likely to be swayed by its theoretical virtues. Considering the arguments below may thus do more than just illuminate utilitarianism; it may also help you to discern your own philosophical temperament!

While our presentation focuses on utilitarianism, it's worth noting that many of the arguments below could also be taken to support other forms of welfarist consequentialism (just as many of the objections to utilitarianism also apply to these related views). This chapter explores arguments for utilitarianism and closely related views over non-consequentialist approaches to ethics.

Arguments for Utilitarianism

What Fundamentally Matters

Moral theories serve to specify *what fundamentally matters*, and utilitarianism offers a particularly compelling answer to this question.

Almost anyone would agree with utilitarianism that suffering is bad and well-being is good. What could be more obvious? If anything matters morally, human well-being surely does. And it would be arbitrary to limit moral concern to our own species, so we should instead conclude that well-being generally is

---

2. That is not to say that either answer is in fact equally good or correct, but just that you should expect it to be difficult to *persuade* those who respond to the conflicts differently than you do.

what matters. That is, we ought to want the lives of sentient beings to go as well as possible (whether that ultimately comes down to maximizing happiness, desire satisfaction, or other welfare goods, as the next chapter will address).

Could anything else be *more* important? Such a suggestion can seem puzzling. Consider: it is (usually) wrong to steal.[3] But that is plausibly because stealing tends to be *harmful*, reducing people's well-being.[4] By contrast, most people are open to redistributive taxation, if it allows governments to provide benefits that reliably raise the overall level of well-being in society. So it's not that individuals just have a natural right to not be interfered with no matter what. When judging institutional arrangements (such as property and tax law), we recognize that what matters is coming up with arrangements that tend to secure *overall good results* and that the most important factor in what makes a result *good* is that it *promotes well-being*.[5]

Such reasoning may justify viewing utilitarianism as the default starting point for moral theorizing.[6] If someone wants to claim that there is some other moral consideration that can override *overall well-being* (trumping the importance of saving lives, reducing suffering, and promoting flourishing), they face the challenge of explaining *how* that could possibly be so. Many common moral rules (like those that prohibit theft, lying, or breaking promises), while not explicitly utilitarian in content, nonetheless have a clear utilitarian rationale. If they did not

---

3. Of course, there may be exceptional circumstances in which stealing is beneficial overall and hence justified, for instance, when stealing a loaf of bread is required to save a starving person's life.

4. Here it is important to consider the indirect costs of reducing social trust, in addition to the obvious direct costs to the victim.

5. Compare our defense of aggregationism in Chapter 2, showing how, in practice, almost everyone endorses allowing sufficiently many small benefits to outweigh great costs to a few: "For example, allowing cars to drive fast on roads increases the number of people who die in accidents. Imposing extremely low-speed limits would save lives at the cost of inconveniencing many drivers. Most people demonstrate an implicit commitment to aggregationism when they judge it worse to impose these many inconveniences for the sake of saving a few lives." See also Robert Goodin, *Utilitarianism as a Public Philosophy* (Cambridge: Cambridge University Press, 1995).

6. Peter Singer argues, relatedly, that "we very swiftly arrive at an initially preference utilitarian position once we apply the universal aspect of ethics to simple, pre-ethical decision making." Singer, *Practical Ethics*, 3rd ed. (Cambridge: Cambridge University Press, 2011), 14.

generally promote well-being—but instead actively harmed people—it's hard to see why we would still want people to follow them. To follow and enforce *harmful* moral rules (such as rules prohibiting same-sex relationships) would seem like a kind of "rule worship," and not truly ethical at all.[7] Since the only moral rules that seem plausible are those that tend to promote well-being, that's some reason to think that moral rules are, as utilitarianism suggests, purely *instrumental* to promoting well-being.

Similar judgments apply to hypothetical cases in which you somehow know for sure that a typically reliable rule is, in this particular instance, counterproductive. In extreme cases, we all recognize that you ought to lie or break a promise if lives are on the line. In practice, as Chapter 6 argues, the best way to achieve good results over the long run is to respect commonsense moral rules and virtues while seeking opportunities to help others. (It's important not to mistake the hypothetical verdicts utilitarianism offers in stylized thought experiments with the practical guidance it offers in real life.) The key point is just that utilitarianism offers a seemingly unbeatable answer to the question of *what fundamentally matters*: protecting and promoting the interests of all sentient beings to make the world as good as it can be.

The Veil of Ignorance

Humans are masters of self-deception and motivated reasoning. If something benefits us personally, it's all too easy to convince ourselves that it must be okay. We are also more easily swayed by the interests of more salient or sympathetic individuals (favoring puppies over pigs, for example). To correct for such biases, it can be helpful to force impartiality by imagining that you are looking down on the world from behind a "veil of ignorance." This veil reveals the facts about each individual's circumstances in society—their income, happiness level, preferences, etc.—and the effects that each choice would have on each person while hiding from you the knowledge of *which of these individuals you are*.[8] To more fairly

---

7. J. J. C. Smart, "Extreme and Restricted Utilitarianism," *The Philosophical Quarterly* 6, no. 25 (1956): 344–54.

8. The Veil of Ignorance thought experiment was originally developed by Vickrey and Harsanyi, though nowadays, it is more often associated with John Rawls, who coined the term and

determine *what ideally ought to be done*, we may ask what everyone would have most personal reason to prefer from behind this veil of ignorance. If you're equally likely to end up being anyone in the world, it would seem prudent to maximize overall well-being, just as utilitarianism prescribes.[9]

How much weight should we give to the verdicts that would be chosen, on self-interested grounds, from behind the veil? The veil thought experiment highlights how utilitarianism gives equal weight to everyone's interests in an unbiased fashion. That is, utilitarianism is just what we get when we are *beneficent to all*: extending to everyone the kind of careful concern that prudent people have for their *own* interests.[10] But it may seem question-begging to those who reject welfarism, and so deny that *interests* are all that matter. For example, the veil thought experiment clearly doesn't speak to whether non-sentient life or natural beauty has intrinsic value. It's restricted to that sub-domain of morality that concerns *what we owe to each other*, where this includes just those individuals over whom our veil-induced uncertainty about our identity extends: presently existing sentient beings, perhaps.[11] Accordingly, any verdicts reached based on the veil of ignorance

---

tweaked the thought experiment to arrive at different conclusions. Specifically, Rawls appealed to a version in which you are additionally ignorant of the relative probabilities of ending up in various positions, to block the utilitarian implications and argue instead for a "maximin" position that gives lexical priority to raising the well-being of the worst off. W. Vickrey, "Measuring Marginal Utility by Reactions to Risk," *Econometrica* 13, no. 4 (1945): 329; John C. Harsanyi, "Cardinal Utility in Welfare Economics and in the Theory of Risk-Taking," *Journal of Political Economy* 61, no. 5 (1955): 434–35; John Rawls, *A Theory of Justice* (Cambridge, MA: Belknap Press, 1971).

9. This assumes a fixed-population setting. Variable population ethics is covered in Chapter 5. For related formal proofs, see John C. Harsanyi, "Bayesian Decision Theory and Utilitarian Ethics," *The American Economic Review* 68, no. 2 (May 1978): 223–28, http://www.jstor.org/stable/1816692. For discussion of Harsanyi's proof, see Hilary Greaves, "A Reconsideration of the Harsanyi–Sen–Weymark Debate on Utilitarianism," *Utilitas* 29, no. 2 (August 2017): 175–213, https://doi.org/10.1017/S0953820816000169.

10. Caspar Hare, "Should We Wish Well to All?," *Philosophical Review* 125, no. 4 (2016): 451–72, http://doi.org/10.1215/00318108-3624764.

11. It's notoriously unclear how to apply the veil of ignorance to "different number" cases in population ethics, for example. If the agent behind the veil is guaranteed to exist, it would naturally suggest the average view. If they might be a merely possible person—and so have some incentive to want more (happy) lives to get to exist—it would instead suggest the total view.

will still need to be weighed against what we might yet owe to any excluded others (such as future generations, or non-welfarist values).

Still, in many contexts, other factors will not be relevant, and the question of what we morally ought to do will be reduced to the question of how we should treat each other. Many of the deepest disagreements between utilitarians and their critics are concerned precisely with this question. And the veil of ignorance seems relevant here. The fact that some action is what *everyone affected would personally prefer* from behind the veil of ignorance seems to undermine critics' claims that any individual has been *mistreated* by, or has grounds to complain about, that action.

Ex Ante Pareto

A *Pareto* improvement is better for some people and worse for none. When outcomes are uncertain, we may instead assess the *prospect* associated with an action—the range of possible outcomes, weighted by their probabilities. A prospect can be assessed as better for you when it offers you greater well-being *in expectation*, or *ex ante*.[12] Putting these concepts together, we may formulate the following principle:

> **Ex ante Pareto:** in a choice between two prospects, one is morally preferable to another if it offers a better prospect for some individuals and a worse prospect for none.

This bridge between personal value (or well-being) and moral assessment is further developed in economist John Harsanyi's aggregation theorem.[13] But the

---

12. *Ex post* interests, by contrast, concern the actual outcomes that result. Interestingly, theories may combine ex post welfare evaluations with a broader "expectational" element. For example, ex post prioritarianism assigns extra social value to avoiding bad *outcomes* (rather than bad *prospects*) for the worst-off individuals but can still assess prospects by their *expected social value*.
13. See Harsanyi, "Cardinal Welfare, Individualistic Ethics, and Interpersonal Comparisons of Utility," *The Journal of Political Economy* 63, no. 4 (August 1955): 312–14, https://www.jstor .org/stable/1827128; and Harsanyi, *Rational Behavior and Bargaining Equilibrium in Games and Social Situations* (Cambridge University Press, 1977), 64–68. See also John Broome's interpretation of Harsanyi in Broome, "Utilitarianism and Expected Utility," *The Journal of Philosophy* 84, no. 8 (August 1987): 410–11, https://doi.org/10.2307/2026999; and Broome,

underlying idea that *reasonable beneficence* requires us to *wish well to all*, and prefer prospects that are in *everyone's* ex ante interests, has also been defended and developed in more intuitive terms by philosophers.[14]

A powerful objection to most non-utilitarian views is that they sometimes violate ex ante Pareto, such as when choosing policies from behind the veil of ignorance. Many rival views imply, absurdly, that prospect *Y* could be morally preferable to prospect *X*, even when *Y* is worse in expectation for everyone involved.

Caspar Hare illustrates the point with a Trolley case in which all six possible victims are stuffed inside suitcases: one is atop a footbridge, five are on the tracks below, and a train will hit and kill the five unless you topple the one on the footbridge (in which case the train will instead kill this one and then stop before reaching the others).[15] As the suitcases have recently been shuffled, nobody knows which position they are in. So, from *each* victim's perspective, their prospects are best if you topple the one suitcase off the footbridge, increasing their chances of survival from one in six to five out of six. Given that this is in everyone's ex ante interests, it's deeply puzzling to think that it would be morally preferable to override this unanimous preference, shared by *everyone* involved, and instead let five of the six die; yet that is the implication of most non-utilitarian views.[16]

Expanding the Moral Circle

When we look back on past moral atrocities—like slavery or denying women equal rights—we recognize that they were often sanctioned by the dominant societal norms at the time. The perpetrators of these atrocities were grievously

---

Weighing Goods: Equality, Uncertainty, and Time (London: Wiley-Blackwell, 1991), 165, 202–9. For further explanation, keep an eye out for our forthcoming guest essay on "Formal Arguments for Utilitarianism," by Johan E. Gustafsson and Kacper Kowalczyk, to appear at www.utilitarianism.net/guest-essays/.

14. For example: Hare "Should We Wish Well to All?," 451–72.

15. Hare, "Should We Wish Well to All?," 454–55.

16. Hare discusses some philosophers' grounds for skepticism about the moral significance of *ex ante justifiability to all*, and supports the principle with further arguments from *presumed consent*, *dirty hands*, and *composition*. Hare, "Should We Wish Well to All?"

wrong to exclude their victims from their "circle" of moral concern.[17] That is, they were wrong to be indifferent toward (or even delight in) their victims' suffering. But such exclusion seemed normal to people at the time. So we should question whether we might likewise be blindly accepting of some practices that future generations will see as evil, but that seem "normal" to us.[18] The best protection against making such an error ourselves would be to deliberately expand our moral concern outward, to include *all* sentient beings—anyone who can suffer—and so recognize that we have strong moral reasons to reduce suffering and promote well-being wherever we can, no matter *who* it is that is experiencing it.

While this conclusion is not yet all the way to full-blown utilitarianism, since it's compatible with, for example, holding that there are side-constraints limiting one's pursuit of the good, it is likely sufficient to secure agreement with the most important practical implications of utilitarianism (stemming from cosmopolitanism, anti-speciesism, and longtermism), as discussed in Chapters 6, 7, and 8.

The Poverty of the Alternatives

We've seen that there is a strong presumptive case in favor of utilitarianism. If no competing view can be shown to be superior, then utilitarianism has a strong claim to be the "default" moral theory. In fact, one of the strongest considerations in favor of utilitarianism (and related consequentialist views) is the deficiencies of the alternatives. Deontological (or rule-based) theories, in particular, seem to rest on questionable foundations.[19]

Deontological theories are explicitly *non-consequentialist*: instead of morally assessing actions by evaluating their consequences, these theories tend to take

---

17. Peter Singer, *The Expanding Circle: Ethics, Evolution, and Moral Progress* (Princeton, NJ: Princeton University Press, 2011).

18. Cf. Evan G. Williams, "The Possibility of an Ongoing Moral Catastrophe," *Ethical Theory and Moral Practice* 18, no. 5 (February 2015): 971–82, https://doi.org/10.1007/s10677 -015-9567-7.

19. The following arguments should also apply against virtue ethics approaches, if they yield non-consequentialist verdicts about what *acts* should be done.

certain types of action (such as killing an innocent person) to be *intrinsically wrong*.[20] There are reasons to be dubious of this approach to ethics, however.

The Paradox of Deontology

Deontologists hold that there is a *constraint* against killing: that it's wrong to kill an innocent person, even if this would save five *other* innocent people from being killed. This verdict can seem puzzling on its face.[21] After all, given how terrible killing is, should we not want there to be *less* of it? Rational choice in general tends to be goal-directed, a conception that fits poorly with deontic constraints.[22] A deontologist might claim that their goal is simply to avoid violating moral constraints *themselves*, which they can best achieve by not killing anyone, even if that results in more individuals being killed. While this explanation can render deontological verdicts coherent, it does so at the cost of making them seem awfully narcissistic, as though the deontologist's central concern was just to maintain their own moral purity or "clean hands."

Deontologists might push back against this characterization by instead insisting that moral action need not be goal-directed at all.[23] Rather than only seeking to promote value (or minimize harm), they claim that moral agents may sometimes be called upon to *respect* another's value (by not harming them, even as a

---

20. Absolutist deontologists hold such judgments to apply *no matter the consequences*. Moderate deontologists instead take the identified actions to be *presumptively* wrong, and not *easily* outweighed, but allow that this may be outweighed if a *sufficient* amount of value was on the line. So, for example, a moderate deontologist might allow that it's permissible to lie to save someone's life or to kill one innocent person to save a million.

21. Samuel Scheffler noted that "either way, someone loses: some inviolable person is violated. Why isn't it at least permissible to prevent the violation of five people by violating one?" Scheffler, *The Rejection of Consequentialism: A Philosophical Investigation of the Considerations Underlying Rival Moral Conceptions*, rev. ed. (Oxford: Clarendon Press, 1994), 88.

22. Samuel Scheffler, "Agent-Centred Restrictions, Rationality, and the Virtues," *Mind* 94, no. 375 (July 1985): 409–19, https://doi.org/10.1093/mind/XCIV.375.409.

23. See, e.g., Timothy Chappell, "Intuition, System, and the 'Paradox' of Deontology," in *Perfecting Virtue: New Essays on Kantian Ethics and Virtue Ethics*, ed. Lawrence Jost and Julian Wuerth (Cambridge: Cambridge University Press, 2011), 271–88.

means to preventing greater harm to others), which would seem an appropriately outwardly directed, non-narcissistic motivation.

The challenge remains that such a proposal makes moral norms puzzlingly divergent from other kinds of practical norms. If morality sometimes calls for respecting value rather than promoting it, why is the same not true of prudence? (Given that pain is bad for you, for example, it would not seem prudent to refuse a painful operation now if the refusal commits you to five comparably painful operations in the future.) Deontologists may offer various answers to this question, but insofar as we are inclined to think, pre-theoretically, that ethics ought to be continuous with other forms of rational choice, that gives us some reason to prefer consequentialist accounts.

Deontologists also face a tricky question of where to draw the line. Is it at least okay to kill one person to prevent a hundred killings? Or a million? *Absolutists* never permit killing, no matter the stakes. But such a view seems too extreme for many. *Moderate* deontologists allow that sufficiently high stakes may justify violations. But how high? Any answer they offer is apt to seem arbitrary and unprincipled. Between the principled options of consequentialism or absolutism, many will find consequentialism to be the more plausible of the two.

The Hope Objection

Impartial observers should want and hope for the best outcome. Non-consequentialists claim, nonetheless, that it's sometimes wrong to bring about the best outcome. Putting the two claims together yields the striking result that you should sometimes hope others act wrongly.

Suppose it would be wrong for some stranger—call him Jack—to kill one innocent person to prevent five other (morally comparable) killings. Non-consequentialists may claim that Jack has a special responsibility to ensure that *he* does not kill anyone, even if this results in more killings by others. But *you* are not Jack. From your perspective as an impartial observer, Jack's killing one innocent person is no more or less intrinsically bad than any of the five other killings that would thereby be prevented. You have most reason to hope that there is only one killing rather than five. So you have reason to hope that Jack acts "wrongly" (killing one to save five). But that seems odd.

More than merely being odd, this might even be taken to undermine the claim that deontic constraints *matter*, or are genuinely *important* to abide by. After all, to be important is just to be worth caring about. For example, we should care if others are harmed, which validates the claim that others' interests are morally important. But if we should not care more about Jack's abiding by the moral constraint against killing than we should about his saving five lives, that would seem to suggest that the constraint against killing is *not* in fact more morally important than saving five lives.

Finally, since our moral obligations ought to track what is genuinely morally important, if deontic constraints are not in fact important then we cannot be obligated to abide by them.[24] We cannot be obliged to prioritize deontic constraints over others' lives, if we ought to care more about others' lives than about deontic constraints. So deontic constraints must not accurately describe our obligations after all. Jack really ought to do whatever would do the most good overall, and so should we.

Skepticism about the Distinction between Doing and Allowing

You might wonder: If respect for others requires not harming them (even to help others more), why does it not equally require not *allowing* them to be harmed? Deontological moral theories place great weight on distinctions such as those between doing and allowing harm, killing and letting die, or intended versus merely foreseen harms. But *why* should these be treated so differently? If a victim ends up equally dead either way, whether they were killed or "merely" allowed to die would not seem to make much difference to them—surely what matters to them is just their death. Consequentialism accordingly denies any fundamental significance to these distinctions.[25]

---

24. It's open to the deontologist to insist that it should be more important *to Jack*, even if not to anyone else. But this violates the appealing idea that the moral point of view is impartial, yielding verdicts that reasonable observers (and not just the agents themselves) could agree on.
25. Though it remains open to consequentialists to accommodate nearby intuitions by noting ways in which these distinctions sometimes *correlate* with other features that may be of moral interest. For example, someone who goes out of their way to *cause* harm is likely to

Indeed, it's far from clear that there *is* any robust distinction between "doing" and "allowing." Sometimes, you might "do" something by remaining perfectly still.[26] Also, when a doctor unplugs a terminal patient from life support machines, this is typically thought of as "letting die"; but if a mafioso, worried about an informant's potentially incriminating testimony, snuck into the hospital and unplugged the informant's life support, we are more likely to judge it to constitute "killing."[27] Jonathan Bennett argues at length that there is no satisfactory, fully general distinction between doing and allowing—at least, none that would vindicate the moral significance that deontologists want to attribute to such a distinction.[28] If Bennett is right, then that might force us toward some form of consequentialism (such as utilitarianism) instead.

Status Quo Bias

Opposition to utilitarian trade-offs—that is, benefiting some at a lesser cost to others—arguably amounts to a kind of status quo bias, prioritizing the *preservation of privilege* over promoting well-being more generally.

Such conservatism might stem from the Just World fallacy: the mistake of assuming that the status quo is just, and that people naturally get what they deserve. Of course, reality offers no such guarantees of justice. What circumstances one is born into depends on sheer luck, including one's endowment of physical and cognitive abilities that may pave the way for future success or failure. Thus, even later in life, we never manage to fully wrest back control from the whimsies of fortune, and, consequently, some people are vastly better off than

---

pose a greater threat to others than someone who merely *allows* harms to occur that they could prevent.

26. For example, you might gaslight your spouse by remaining hidden in camouflage when they could have sworn that you were just in the room with them. Or, as Philippa Foot suggests, "An actor who fails to turn up for a performance will generally spoil it rather than allow it to be spoiled." Foot, "The Problem of Abortion and the Doctrine of the Double Effect," in *Virtues and Vices and Other Essays in Moral Philosophy* (Berkley: University of California Press, 1978), 26.

27. Tom L. Beauchamp, "Justifying Physician-Assisted Deaths," in *Ethics in Practice: An Anthology*, ed. Hugh LaFollette, 5th ed. (Hoboken, NJ: Wiley Blackwell, 2020), 78–85.

28. Bennett, *The Act Itself* (Oxford: Oxford University Press, 1998).

others despite being no more deserving. In such cases, why should we not be willing to benefit one person at a lesser cost to privileged others? They have no special entitlement to the extra well-being that fortune has granted them.[29] Clearly, it's good for people to be well-off, and we certainly would not want to harm anyone unnecessarily.[30] However, if we can increase overall well-being by benefiting one person at the lesser cost to another, we should not refrain from doing so merely due to a prejudice in favor of the existing distribution.[31] It's easy to see why traditional elites would want to promote a "morality" which favors their entrenched interests. It's less clear why others should go along with such a distorted view of what (and who) matters.

It can similarly be argued that there is no real distinction between imposing harms and withholding benefits. The only difference between the two cases concerns what we understand to be the status quo, which lacks moral significance. Suppose scenario A is better for someone than B. Then, to shift from A to B would be a "harm," while to prevent a shift from B to A would be to "withhold a benefit." But this is merely a descriptive difference. If we deny that the historically

---

29. In a similar vein, Derek Parfit wrote that "Some of us ask how much of our wealth we rich people ought to give to these poorest people. But that question wrongly assumes that our wealth is ours to give. This wealth is legally ours. But these poorest people have much stronger moral claims to some of this wealth. We ought to transfer to these people . . . at least ten per cent of what we earn." Parfit, *On What Matters*, vol. 3 (Oxford: Oxford University Press, 2017), 436–37.

30. On the topic of sacrifice, John Stuart Mill wrote that "The utilitarian morality does recognise in human beings the power of sacrificing their own greatest good for the good of others. It only refuses to admit that the sacrifice is itself a good. A sacrifice which does not increase, or tend to increase, the sum total of happiness, it considers as wasted." Mill, "What Utilitarianism Is," chap. 2 in *Utilitarianism* (London, 1863).

31. However, this does not mean that utilitarianism will strive for perfect equality in material outcomes or even well-being. Joshua Greene notes that "a world in which everyone gets the same outcome no matter what they do is an idle world in which people have little incentive to do anything. Thus, the way to maximize happiness is not to decree that everyone gets to be equally happy, but to encourage people to behave in ways that maximize happiness. When we measure our moral success, we count everyone's happiness equally, but achieving success almost certainly involves inequality of both material wealth and happiness. Such inequality is not ideal, but it's justified on the grounds that, without it, things would be worse overall." Greene, *Moral Tribes: Emotion, Reason, and the Gap between Us and Them* (New York: Penguin Books, 2013), 163. See also our discussion in Chapter 16 (The Equality Objection).

given starting point provides a morally privileged baseline, then we must say that the cost in either case is the same, namely the difference in well-being between A and B. In principle, it should not matter where we start from.[32]

Now, suppose that scenario B is vastly better for someone else than A: perhaps it will save their life, at the cost of the first person's arm. Nobody would think it okay to kill a person just to save another's arm (that is, to shift from B to A). So if we are to avoid status quo bias, we must similarly judge that it would be wrong to *oppose* the shift from A to B—that is, we should not object to saving someone's life at the cost of another's arm.[33] We should not care especially about preserving the privilege of whoever stood to benefit by default; such conservatism is not truly fair or just. Instead, our goal should be to bring about whatever outcome would be best *overall*, counting everyone equally, just as utilitarianism prescribes.

Evolutionary Debunking Arguments

Against these powerful theoretical objections, the main consideration that deontological theories have going for them is closer conformity with our intuitions about particular cases. But if these intuitions cannot be supported by independently plausible principles, that may undermine their force—or suggest that we should interpret them as good rules of thumb for practical guidance, rather than as indicating what *fundamentally* matters.

The force of deontological intuitions may also be undermined if it can be demonstrated that they result from an unreliable process. For example, evolutionary processes may have endowed us with an emotional bias favoring those who look, speak, and behave like ourselves; this, however, offers no justification for discriminating against those unlike ourselves. Evolution is a blind, amoral process whose only "goal" is the propagation of genes, not the promotion of well-being or moral rightness. Our moral intuitions require scrutiny, especially in scenarios

---

32. In practice, the psychological phenomenon of *loss aversion* means that someone may feel *more upset* by what they perceive as a "loss" rather than a mere "failure to benefit." Such negative feelings may further reduce their well-being, turning the judgment that "loss is worse" into something of a self-fulfilling prophecy. But this depends on contingent psychological phenomena generating *extra* harms; it's not that the loss is *in itself* worse.

33. Nick Bostrom and Toby Ord, "The Reversal Test: Eliminating Status Quo Bias in Applied Ethics," *Ethics* 116, no. 4 (July 2006): 656–79, https://doi.org/10.1086/505233.

very different from our evolutionary environment. If we identify a moral intuition as stemming from our evolutionary ancestry, we may decide not to give much weight to it in our moral reasoning—the practice of *evolutionary debunking*.[34]

Katarzyna de Lazari-Radek and Peter Singer argue that views permitting partiality are especially susceptible to evolutionary debunking, whereas impartial views like utilitarianism are more likely to result from undistorted reasoning.[35] Joshua Greene offers a different psychological debunking argument. He argues that deontological judgments—for instance, in response to trolley cases—tend to stem from unreliable and inconsistent emotional responses, including our favoritism of identifiable over faceless victims and our aversion to harming someone up close rather than from afar. By contrast, utilitarian judgments involve the more deliberate application of widely respected moral principles.[36]

Such debunking arguments raise worries about whether they "prove too much": after all, the foundational moral judgment that *pain is bad* would itself seem emotionally laden and susceptible to evolutionary explanation—physically vulnerable creatures would have powerful evolutionary reasons to want to avoid pain *whether or not* it was objectively bad, after all![37]

However, debunking arguments may be most applicable in cases where we feel that a principled explanation for the truth of the judgment is lacking. We do not

---

34. There are other types of debunking arguments not grounded in evolution. Consider that in most Western societies Christianity was the dominant religion for over one thousand years, which explains why moral intuitions grounded in Christian morality are still widespread. For instance, many devout Christians have strong moral intuitions about sex, which non-Christians do not typically share, such as the intuition that it's wrong to have sex before marriage or that it's wrong for two men to have sex. The discourse among academics in moral philosophy generally disregards such religiously contingent moral intuitions. Many philosophers, including most utilitarians, would therefore not give much weight to Christians' intuitions about sex.

35. de Lazari-Radek and Singer, "The Objectivity of Ethics and the Unity of Practical Reason," *Ethics* 123, no. 1 (October 2012): 9–31, https://doi.org/10.1086/667837.

36. Greene, "The Secret Joke of Kant's Soul," in *Moral Psychology*, vol. 3, ed. Walter Sinnott-Armstrong (Cambridge, MA: MIT Press, 2007).

37. Some utilitarians, including those cited above, try to argue that utilitarian verdicts are less susceptible to debunking. For another example, see Neil Sinhababu's essay offering an introspective argument for hedonism. Sinhababu, "Naturalistic Arguments for Ethical Hedonism," accessed May 23, 2024, https://www.utilitarianism.net/guest-essays/naturalistic-arguments-for-ethical-hedonism/.

tend to feel any such lack regarding the badness of pain—that is surely an intrinsically plausible judgment if anything is. Some intuitions may be *over-determined*: explicable *both* by evolutionary causes *and* by their rational merits. In such a case, we need not take the evolutionary explanation to undermine the judgment, because the judgment *also* results from a reliable process (namely, rationality). By contrast, deontological principles and partiality are far less *self-evidently* justified, and so may be considered more vulnerable to debunking. Once we have an explanation for these psychological intuitions that can explain why we would have them even if they were rationally baseless, we may be more justified in concluding that they are indeed rationally baseless.

As such, debunking objections are unlikely to change the mind of one who is drawn to the target view (or regards it as independently justified and defensible). But they may help to confirm the doubts of those who already felt there were some grounds for skepticism regarding the intrinsic merits of the target view.

Conclusion

Utilitarianism can be supported by several theoretical arguments, the strongest perhaps being its ability to capture *what fundamentally matters*. Its main competitors, by contrast, seem to rely on dubious distinctions—like "doing" versus "allowing"—and built-in status quo bias. At least, that is how things are apt to look to one who is broadly sympathetic to a utilitarian approach. Given the flexibility inherent in reflective equilibrium, these arguments are unlikely to sway a committed opponent of the view. For those readers who find a utilitarian approach to ethics deeply unappealing, we hope that this chapter may at least help you better understand what appeal *others* might see in the view.

However strong you judge the arguments in favor of utilitarianism to be, your ultimate verdict on the theory will also depend upon how well the view is able to counter the influential objections that critics have raised against it—discussed in Part II.

The next chapter discusses theories of well-being, or what counts as being good for an individual.

For additional resources
and study aids, see
https://utilitarianism.net/

4

Theories of Well-Being

To what shall the character of utility be ascribed, if
not to that which is a source of pleasure?

—Jeremy Bentham[1]

Introduction

A core element of utilitarianism is welfarism—the view that only the *welfare* (also called *well-being*) of individuals determines how good a particular state of the world is. While consequentialists claim that what is right is to promote the amount of good in the world, welfarists specifically equate the good to be promoted with well-being.

Philosophers use the term "well-being" to refer to what's good *for a person*, as opposed to what's good per se, or "from the point of view of the Universe" to use Sidgwick's poetic phrase. Utilitarianism holds that well-being is always good from the point of view of the universe and not *just* good for the individual. But other views may coherently deny this. For example, one might think that the punishment of an evil person is good, and moreover, it's good precisely because that punishment is bad *for him*.

In this chapter, we explore different accounts of the *intrinsic* or *basic* welfare goods—as opposed to things that are only *instrumentally* good for you. For example, happiness is (plausibly) intrinsically good for you; it directly increases your well-being. In contrast, money can buy many useful things and is thus

---

1. Bentham, *The Rationale of Reward*, trans. Richard Smith (London: J. & H. L. Hunt, 1825), book 3, chap. 1.

45

instrumentally good for you, but it does not *in itself* constitute well-being. (We can similarly speak of things that are intrinsically bad for you, like misery, as "welfare bads.")

However, there is widespread disagreement about what constitutes well-being.[2] What things are in themselves good for a person? The diverging answers to this question give rise to a variety of theories of well-being, each of which regards different things as the components of well-being. The three main theories of well-being are *hedonism, desire theories*, and *objective list theories*.[3] The differences between these theories are—in today's world, at least—of primarily theoretical interest; they overlap sufficiently in practice that the immediate practical implications of utilitarianism are unlikely to depend upon which of these, if any, turns out to be the correct view. But as we'll see, future technology could severely disrupt this practical overlap. It may then matter greatly which account of well-being we accept.

Hedonism

The theory of well-being that is built into classical utilitarianism is *hedonism*.[4]

> **Hedonism is the view that well-being consists in, and only in, the balance of positive minus negative conscious experiences.**[5]

---

2. For a more detailed overview of theories of well-being, see Roger Crisp, "Well-Being," *The Stanford Encyclopedia of Philosophy*, ed. Edward N. Zalta, Fall 2017 Edition, Section 4: Theories of Well-Being, https://plato.stanford.edu/entries/well-being/#TheWelBei.

3. This tripartite classification is widespread in the literature—following Derek Parfit, "What Makes Someone's Life Go Best," appendix I to *Reasons and Persons* (Oxford: Clarendon Press, 1984). It has, however, been criticized: cf. Woodard, "Classifying Theories of Welfare," *Philosophical Studies* 165 (2013): 787–803, https://doi.org/10.1007/s11098-012-9978-4.

4. For a more detailed account of and discussion of hedonism, see Andrew Moore, "Hedonism," *The Stanford Encyclopedia of Philosophy*, ed. Edward N. Zalta, Winter 2019 Edition, https://plato.stanford.edu/entries/hedonism/.

5. Hedonism about well-being should not be confused with *psychological hedonism*, the dubious empirical claim that humans always pursue what will give themselves the greatest happiness.

On this view, the only basic welfare goods are pleasant experiences such as enjoyment and contentment. Conversely, the only basic welfare bads are unpleasant experiences such as pain and misery. For the sake of readability, we refer to pleasant experiences as *happiness* and to unpleasant experiences as *suffering*.

The hedonistic conception of happiness is broad: it covers not only paradigmatic instances of sensory pleasure—such as the experiences of eating delicious food or having sex—but also other positively valenced experiences, such as the experiences of solving a problem, reading a novel, or helping a friend. Hedonists claim that all of these enjoyable experiences are intrinsically valuable. Other goods, such as wealth, health, justice, fairness, and equality, are also valued by hedonists, but they are valued instrumentally. That is, they are only valued to the extent that they increase happiness and reduce suffering.

When hedonism is combined with impartiality, as in classical utilitarianism, hedonism's scope becomes universal. This means that happiness and suffering are treated as equally important regardless of when, where, or by whom they are experienced. From this follows sentiocentrism, the view that we should extend our moral concern to all *sentient beings*, including humans and most non-human animals, since only they can experience happiness or suffering. Alternatively, non-utilitarian views may accept hedonism but reject impartiality, thus restricting hedonism's scope to claim that only the happiness of a specified group—or even a single individual[6]—should "count" morally.

The notion at the heart of hedonism, that happiness is good and suffering is bad, is widely accepted. The simple act of investigating our own conscious experiences through introspection appears to support this view: the goodness of happiness and the badness of suffering are self-evident to those who experience them.[7] Importantly, happiness seems good (and suffering bad) not simply because they help (or hinder) us in our pursuit of *other* goods, but because experiencing them is good (or bad) in itself.

---

6. This view is known as ethical egoism. See Robert Shaver, "Egoism," *The Stanford Encyclopedia of Philosophy*, ed. Edward N. Zalta and Uri Nodelman, Spring 2023 Edition, https://plato.stanford.edu/archives/spr2023/entries/egoism/.

7. Cf. Neil Sinhababu, "The Epistemic Argument for Hedonism," in *Human Minds and Cultures*, ed. Sanjit Chakraborty (Switzerland: Springer Nature Switzerland, 2024); and Sinhababu, "Naturalistic Arguments for Ethical Hedonism," accessed May 23, 2024, https://utilitarianism.net/guest-essays/naturalistic-arguments-for-ethical-hedonism/.

However, what makes hedonism controversial is that it implies that

1. *all* happiness is intrinsically good for you, and all suffering is intrinsically bad;
2. happiness is the *only* basic welfare good, and suffering is the only basic welfare bad.

Critics of hedonism dispute the first claim by pointing to instances of putative *evil pleasures*, which they claim are *not* good for you. And they often reject the second claim by invoking Robert Nozick's Experience Machine thought experiment to argue that there must be basic welfare goods other than happiness. We explain each objection, and how hedonists can respond, in turn.

The "Evil Pleasures" Objection

Critics often reject the hedonist claim that all happiness is good and all suffering is bad. Consider a sadist who takes pleasure in harming others without their consent. Hedonists can allow that nonconsensual sadism is typically *overall* harmful, as the sadist's pleasure is unlikely to outweigh the suffering of their victim. This clearly justifies disapproving of nonconsensual sadism in practice, especially with a multi-level utilitarian view. Under that view, we might assume that finding the rare exceptions to this rule would have little practical value. However, the risk of mistakenly permitting harmful actions means that we would be better off establishing a general prohibition on harming others without their consent.

Still, on a purely theoretical level, we may ask: What if there were *many* sadists collectively rejoicing in the suffering of a single tortured soul? If their aggregate pleasure outweighs the suffering of the one, then hedonistic utilitarianism implies that this is a good outcome, and the sadists act rightly in torturing their victim. But that seems wrong.

At this point, it's worth distinguishing a couple of subtly different claims that one might object to: (i) the sadists benefit from their sadistic pleasure, and (ii) the benefits to the sadists count as *moral goods*, or something that we should want to promote (all else equal).

To reject (i) means rejecting hedonism about well-being. But if sadistic pleasure does not benefit the sadist, then this implies that someone who wants to make the sadist worse off (for whatever reason) could not achieve that by means of blocking their sadistic pleasure. And that seems mistaken.

Alternatively, one might retain hedonism about well-being while respecting our intuitive opposition to "evil pleasures" by instead rejecting (ii) and denying that *benefiting sadists at the expense of their victims* is reasonable or good. This would involve rejecting utilitarianism, strictly speaking, though a closely related consequentialist view that merely gives equal weight to all *innocent* interests (while discounting illicit interests) remains available and overlaps with utilitarianism in the vast majority of cases.

Hedonistic utilitarians might seek to preserve both (i) and (ii) by offering an alternative explanation of our intuitions. For example, we may judge the sadists' *characters* to be bad insofar as they enjoy hurting others, and so they seem likely to act wrongly in many other circumstances.[8]

When "evil" pleasures are detached from their usual consequences, it becomes much less clear that they are still bad. Imagine a universe containing only a single sadist whose sole enjoyment in life comes from their false belief that there are other people undergoing significant torment. Would it really improve things if the sadist's one source of delight was taken away from them? If not, then it seems like sadistic pleasure is not intrinsically bad after all. (Though we can, of course, still disapprove of its *instrumental* badness in real-life circumstances.) Even so, if we think it would inherently improve things to replace the sole inhabitant's sadistic pleasure with an equal amount of non-sadistic pleasure instead, this might suggest the need for some minor tweaks to either hedonism or utilitarianism.[9]

---

8. To control for this, imagine a society of utilitarian sadists who are strictly morally constrained in their sadism: they would never allow harm to another unless it caused greater net benefits to others (including themselves). We might even imagine that they are willing to suffer the torture themselves if enough others would benefit from this. (Perhaps they draw lots to decide on a victim, in a sadistic analogue of John Harris's Survival Lottery.) When the sadists are stipulated to be morally conscientious in this way, it may be easier to accept that their sadistic pleasure counts as a good in itself. John Harris, "The Survival Lottery," *Philosophy* 50, no. 191 (1975): 81–87, https://doi.org/10.1017/S0031819100059118.

9. Unless we value the simplicity of hedonistic utilitarianism more highly than the accommodation of such intuitions.

The Experience Machine Objection

Robert Nozick disputed the view that happiness is the only basic good and suffering the only basic bad by providing a thought experiment intended to show that we value things other than conscious experiences. Specifically, Nozick argued that hedonists are committed, mistakenly, to plugging into an "experience machine":

> Suppose there were an experience machine that would give you any experience you desired. It could stimulate your brain so that you would think and feel you were writing a great novel, or making a friend, or reading an interesting book. All the time you would be floating in a tank, with electrodes attached to your brain. Should you plug into this machine for life, pre-programming your life experiences?[10]

Nozick suggests that you should not plug into the experience machine despite the machine promising a life filled with much more happiness than "real life."[11] Most of us do not merely want to passively experience "pre-programmed" sensations, however pleasant they might be; we also want to (i) make real choices, actively living our lives,[12] and (ii) genuinely interact with others, sharing our lives with real friends and loved ones.[13]

If happiness were the only basic welfare good, it would not matter whether our experiences were real or were generated by the experience machine without any input from us (or others). Consequently, if we would prefer not to plug into

---

10. This description was adapted from Nozick, *Anarchy, State, and Utopia* (New York: Basic Books, 1974), 42.

11. Of course, one might agree with Nozick's general point while regarding life in the experience machine as superior to at least *some* (e.g., miserable) "real" lives, such that "plugging in" could be advisable in some circumstances.

12. Nozick, *Anarchy, State, and Utopia*, 43.

13. Nozick further claimed that we want to live "in contact with reality," but it's not clear that there would be any loss of well-being in living and interacting with others in a shared virtual world like that depicted in *The Matrix*. A shared virtual world could, in contrast to the experience machine, fulfill many of our non-hedonic values and desires, such as having friends and loving relationships. Nozick, *Anarchy, State, and Utopia*, 45.

the machine, that suggests we value things other than just happiness, such as autonomy and relationships.

One way that hedonists have tried to resist this argument is to question the reliability of the intuitions evoked by the thought experiment. In some cases, reluctance to plug into the machine might stem from pragmatic concerns that the technology may fail.[14] Others might be moved by moral reasons to remain unplugged (for example, to help others in the real world), even if that means sacrificing their own happiness. Finally, many have argued that our responses to the thought experiment reflect status quo bias: if you tell people that they are *already* in the experience machine, they are much more likely to want to *remain* plugged in.[15]

Still, even after carefully bracketing these confounding factors, many will intuitively recoil from the suggestion that an experience machine could provide all that they truly want from life. Imagine that person A lives a happy and accomplished life in the real world, the subjective experience of which is somehow "recorded" and then "played back" to B (who is attached to an experience machine from birth), with just an extra jolt of mild pleasure at the end.[16] Hedonism implies that B has the better life of the two, but many will find this implausible. Note that this

---

14. Dan Weijers, "Nozick's Experience Machine Is Dead, Long Live the Experience Machine!," *Philosophical Psychology* 27, no. 4 (2014): 513–35, https://doi.org/10.1080/09515089.2012.7 57889. Puzzlingly, many respondents reported that they would favor plugging into the experience machine when choosing for another person, even when they would not choose this for themselves.

15. Among others, this suggestion has been made by: Adam J. Kolber, "Mental Statism and the Experience Machine," *Bard Journal of Social Sciences* 3 (Winter 1994/1995): 10–17, https://ssrn.com/abstract=1322059; J. D. Greene, "A Psychological Perspective on Nozick's Experience Machine and Parfit's Repugnant Conclusion" (Presentation at the Society for Philosophy and Psychology Annual Meeting, Cincinnati, OH, 2001); Felipe de Brigard, "If You Like It, Does It Matter If It's Real?," *Philosophical Psychology* 23, no. 1 (2010): 43–57, https://doi.org/10.1080/09515080903532290.

16. Adapted from Roger Crisp, "Hedonism Reconsidered," *Philosophy and Phenomenological Research* 73, no. 3 (November 2006): 635–36, https://doi.org/10.1111/j.1933-1592.2006.tb00551.x. The advantages of third-personal judgments about the relative values of lives inside and outside the experience machine, to better avoid objections, is also stressed by Eden Lin, "How to Use the Experience Machine," *Utilitas* 28, no. 3 (2016): 314–32, https://doi.org/10.1017/S0953820815000424.

intuition cannot easily be explained away as stemming from pragmatic or moral confounds or mere status-quo bias.

Roger Crisp advises hedonists to regard these intuitions as being *useful* rather than *accurate*:

> This is to adopt a strategy similar to that developed by "two-level utilitarians" in response to alleged counter-examples based on common-sense morality. The hedonist will point out the so-called "paradox of hedonism," that pleasure is most effectively pursued indirectly. If I consciously try to maximize my own pleasure, I will be unable to immerse myself in those activities, such as reading or playing games, which do give pleasure. And if we believe that those activities are valuable independently of the pleasure we gain from engaging in them, then we shall probably gain more pleasure overall.[17]

Someone committed to hedonism on other grounds may thus remain untroubled by our intuitions about the experience machine. Even so, they raise a challenge for the view: If a competing theory yields intuitively more plausible verdicts, why not prefer that view instead? To adequately assess the prospects for hedonism, we must first explore the challenges for these rival accounts.

Desire Theories

We saw that hedonism struggles to capture all people care about when reflecting on their lives. *Desire theories* avoid this problem by grounding well-being in each individual's own desires.

> **Desire theories hold that well-being consists in the satisfaction (minus frustration) of desires or preferences.**

According to desire theories, what makes your life go well for you is simply to get whatever you want, desire, or prefer. Combining utilitarianism with a desire

---

17. Crisp, "Well-Being," section 4.1 Hedonism, https://plato.stanford.edu/entries/well-being/#TheWelBei. See also Crisp, "Hedonism Reconsidered," 637.

theory of well-being yields *preference utilitarianism*, according to which the right action best promotes (everyone's) preferences overall.

Importantly, our preferences can be satisfied without our realizing it, so long as things in reality are as we prefer them to be. For example, many parents would prefer to:

(i) falsely believe their child has died when the child is actually alive and happy,

rather than to

(ii) falsely believe their child is alive and happy when the child is actually dead.

A parent who strongly desires a happy life for their child may be happier in scenario (ii), where they (falsely) believe this desire to be satisfied. But their desire is actually satisfied in (i), and that is what really benefits them, according to standard desire theories.[18]

As a result, desire theories can easily account for our reluctance to plug into the experience machine.[19] It offers happiness based on false beliefs. But if we care about anything outside of our own heads (as most of us seem to), then the experience machine will leave those desires unfulfilled. A "real" life may contain less happiness but more desire-fulfillment, and hence more well-being according to desire theories.

Desire theories may be either *restricted* or *unrestricted* in scope. Unrestricted theories count *all* of your desires without exception. On such a view, if you desire that our galaxy should contain an even number of stars, then you are better off if this is true and worse off if it is false. Restricted desire theories instead claim that only desires in some restricted class—perhaps those that are in some sense *about*

---

18. They probably also desire their own happiness, of course, which is better served in scenario (ii). But the fact that they nonetheless prefer the prospect of (i) over (ii) suggests that (i) is the outcome that better fulfills their desires *overall*.

19. By contrast, the "evil pleasures" objection to hedonism would seem to apply with equal force against desire theories, as these theories also imply that sadistic pleasure can benefit you (if you desire it).

your own life[20]—affect your well-being. Under a restricted theory, something can seem good *to* you without being good *for* you, and this kind of desire would not be seen as meaningfully affecting your well-being.

Desire theories may be motivated by the thought that what makes your life go well *for you* must ultimately be *up to you*. Other theorists might support anti-paternalistic policies in practice, supposing that individuals are typically the best judges of what is good for them,[21] but only desire theorists take an individual's preferences about their own life to *determine* what is good for them. By contrast, other theorists are more open to overruling an individual's self-regarding preferences as misguided if they fail to track what is objectively worthwhile.

Bizarre Desires

To test your intuitions about desire theories, it may help to imagine someone whose desires come apart from anything that is plausibly of objective value (including their own subjective happiness). Suppose that someone's strongest desire is to count blades of grass, even though this is a compulsive desire that brings them no pleasure.[22] Many of us would regard this preference as *pathological* and worth overriding or even extinguishing for the subject's own sake—at least if they would be happier as a result. But committed desire theorists will insist that however strange another's preferences may seem to us, it's each person's *own*

---

20. This is Parfit's suggestion in Parfit, *Reasons and Persons*. For an alternative restriction based on *genuine attraction*, see Chris Heathwood, "Which Desires Are Relevant to Well-Being?," *Noûs* 53, no. 3 (September 2019): 664–88, https://doi.org/10.1111/nous.12232.

21. As argued by John Stuart Mill in his 1859 book *On Liberty*, accessible at https://utilitarianism.net/books/on-liberty-john-stuart-mill/1/.

22. John Rawls, *A Theory of Justice* (Cambridge, MA: Belknap Press, 1971), 432. Some desire theorists might restrict their view to "hot" desires, which present their objects as being in some way appealing to the subject, in contrast to mere compulsive motivations. But the counterexample can be adapted to cover the "hot" desire view as follows: Further suppose that the agent suffers from severe memory loss, so they don't even appreciate when this desire is satisfied. Still, it is what they want to happen, so much so that they would prefer to count grass (without realizing it) than to pause to take medicine that would restore their cognitive functioning and ability to enjoy themselves (without generating stronger new desires). Again, this preference seems pathological and worth overriding for the subject's sake.

preferences that matter for determining what is in their interests.[23] How satisfying you find this response will likely depend on how strongly drawn to desire views you were in the first place.

Changing Preferences

One tricky question for desire theorists is how to deal with changing preferences. Suppose that, as a child, I unconditionally desire to be a firefighter when I grow up—that is, even in the event that my grown-up self wants a different career. Suppose that I will naturally develop to instead want to be a teacher, which would prove a more satisfying career for my adult self. But further, suppose that if I instead dropped out of school and became a drug addict, I would acquire stronger—and more easily satisfied—desires—although I currently view this prospect with distaste.[24] Given these stipulations, am I best off becoming a firefighter, a teacher, or a drug addict? Different desire theories will offer different answers to this question.

The simplest form of desire theory takes the well-being value of a life to be determined by the sum total of its satisfied desires minus its frustrated desires at each moment.[25] Such a view could easily end up rating the prospect of drug

---

23. Chris Heathwood additionally stresses the importance of looking at the agent's overall (whole-life) desire satisfaction. Sometimes, it will be worth thwarting one desire in order to better promote others. But we can build into the case that the person's actual desires are maximally satisfied by leaving them to forgetfully count the grass. Heathwood, "The Problem of Defective Desires," *Australasian Journal of Philosophy* 83, no. 4 (August 2006): 487–504, https://doi.org/10.1080/00048400500338690.
24. Adapted from Derek Parfit, *Reasons and Persons*, 497. Parfit stipulates that the agent is guaranteed a lifetime supply of the drug and that the drug in question poses no health risk or untoward side effects besides the extreme addiction.
25. Weighted by how strong each desire is. For example, you may be well-off overall if you have one very strong desire satisfied and two very weak ones frustrated.

addiction as providing the best future,[26] no matter my current preferences.[27] This would be an especially awkward implication for any who were drawn to desire views on the anti-paternalist grounds that each person gets to decide for themselves where their true interests lie.

To avoid this implication, one might decide to weigh present desires more heavily than potential future desires. A *necessitarian* approach, for example, only counts desires that exist (or previously existed) in *all* of the potential outcomes under consideration.[28] This nicely rules out induced desires, like those in the induced addiction scenario, but may also justify impeding natural desire change (such as between firefighting and teaching careers), which can seem counterintuitive.[29] So it's far from straightforward for desire theorists to give intuitive answers across a range of preference-change cases.

---

26. That is, the best future in terms of *this one individual's well-being*. They might still have moral reasons to choose a different future, as being a teacher or firefighter would surely help others more. But even the limited claim that drug addiction is what is best *for this individual* will seem counterintuitive to many.

27. One's past desires to avoid this outcome would weigh against it to some degree unless one builds in a "concurrence requirement" that only desires existing *at the same time* as their satisfaction count. Concurrence views thus have even more difficulty avoiding the implication that such induced desire satisfactions can easily override your present preferences.

28. This theory is temporally relative because once the relevant choice is made, the once-contingent future choice may no longer be contingent on any remaining decisions, in which case it will no longer be discounted. If you actually become a satisfied drug addict, for example, the necessitarian may *now* say that this outcome was for the best, even though *before* the choice was made, they would have advised against it (on the basis of your prior desires). This generates an awkward temporal inconsistency, as our theorist seems committed to claims like, "It would now be bad for you to become a drug addict, but if you go ahead and do it, it will instead be good for you."

29. It merely "may" because much depends on the details. It's entirely possible that becoming a well-satisfied teacher would also better serve *other* desires that one has (in both outcomes). In which case, even the necessitarian could conclude that this change would be in one's overall best interests, despite giving no intrinsic weight to the contingent desire to be a teacher (and giving full weight to the past, and hence non-contingent, desire to be a firefighter). But there will be at least some cases in which impeding the change counterintuitively wins out because of the discounting.

Objective List Theories

Both hedonism and desire theories are *monist*. They suggest that well-being consists of a single thing—either happiness or desire satisfaction. In contrast, while *objective list theorists* usually agree that happiness is an important component of well-being, they deny that it's the *only* such component; consequently, objective list theories are *pluralist*.[30]

> **Objective list theories hold that there are a variety of objectively valuable things that contribute to one's well-being.**

In addition to happiness, these lists commonly include loving relationships, achievement, aesthetic appreciation, creativity, knowledge,[31] and more. Crucially, these list items are understood as basic or intrinsic goods; they are valuable in themselves, not because of some instrumental benefit they provide. The list is called *objective* because its items are purported to be good for you regardless of how you feel about them. The same list applies to everyone, though different lives may end up realizing different goods from the list, so there may still be many different ways of living an excellent life. On this view, some things (such as love and happiness) are inherently more worth caring about than others (such as counting blades of grass), and it makes your life go better if you attain more of the things that are truly good or worth pursuing.

Objective list theories do not necessarily imply that people would benefit from being forced to pursue objective goods against their will. Autonomy could be a

---

30. Objective list theorists include: John Finnis, *Natural Law and Natural Rights* (Oxford: Clarendon Press, 1980); James Griffin, *Well-Being: Its Meaning, Measurement and Moral Importance* (Oxford: Clarendon Press, 1986); Guy Fletcher, "A Fresh Start for an Objective List Theory of Well-Being," *Utilitas* 25, no. 2 (2013): 206–20, https://doi.org/10.1017/S0953820812000453; Eden Lin, "Pluralism about Well-Being," *Philosophical Perspectives* 28, no. 1 (2014): 127–54, https://doi.org/10.1111/phpe.12038. For an overview and discussion of value pluralism, including objective list theories, see Elinor Mason, "Value Pluralism," *The Stanford Encyclopedia of Philosophy*, ed. Edward N. Zalta, Spring 2018, https://plato.stanford.edu/entries/value-pluralism/; Eden Lin, "Monism and Pluralism," in *The Routledge Handbook of Philosophy of Well-Being*, ed. Guy Fletcher (London: Routledge, 2015), 331–41.

31. Though memorizing the phonebook or other trivial data would not seem to have any value, so this is best restricted to *significant* knowledge or knowledge of *important* truths.

value on the list, and happiness certainly is; either of these is apt to be severely thwarted by such coercion. Still, one notable implication is that if you are able to *change* someone's preferences from worthless to worthwhile goals, this is likely to improve their well-being (even if they are no more satisfied, subjectively speaking, than before).

Objective list theories are thus in a good position to explain which preference-changes are good or bad for you (a potential advantage over desire theories). And the inclusion of values beyond just happiness yields more plausible verdicts than hedonism in Experience Machine cases.[32]

Is Objective Value "Spooky"?

Resistance to objective list theories may stem from the sense that there is something metaphysically extravagant, disreputable, or "spooky" about the objective values they posit—that they are a poor fit with a modern scientific worldview. But competing theories of well-being are arguably in no better position regarding such metaethical[33] concerns. Well-being is an inherently evaluative concept: it is that which is *worth pursuing for an individual's sake.*[34] (If you are not describing something that *matters* in this way, then whatever it is that you are giving an

---

32. Recall our contrast of person A (with the excellent life) and person B, who experiences a passive "replay" of A's life, with an extra jolt of pleasure at the end. Although B's life contains more pleasure, A's life will contain more overall value if we also count loving relationships, achievements, etc., as basic welfare goods. While B's life contains all the same experiences *as of* loving relationships, achievements, etc., as A's did, it is a passive "replay," involving no actual choices or interactions. Therefore, B's life includes none of A's actual achievements or relationships.

33. For a state-of-the-art exploration of the relations between theories of well-being and metaethical views, see Guy Fletcher, "Prudential Normativity," chap. 7 in *Dear Prudence: The Nature and Normativity of Prudential Discourse* (Oxford: Oxford University Press, 2021).

34. Note that to be *worth pursuing for an individual's sake* does not entail being worth pursuing *all things considered.* It's more of a conditional reason: *insofar* as you have reason to care about S's well-being, you have reason to care about what is desirable, or worth pursuing, for S's sake. Utilitarians think we always have reason to care about everyone's well-being. But others may disagree. So it remains an open conceptual possibility that you should not care about someone's well-being. If you think that S deserves to be punished, for example, you may see what is *undesirable for S's sake* as being *all things considered* desirable precisely *because* it is bad for S.

account of, it cannot truly be *well-being*. A thoroughgoing nihilist must deny that there is any such thing.)[35]

Utilitarians, especially, regard well-being as objectively valuable: if someone claims that others' interests do not matter, we think they are making a serious moral mistake. So we're already committed to moral facts that hold regardless of others' opinions. So what further cost is there to claiming that something may contribute to another's well-being regardless of their feelings or opinions? (In the Alienation section below, we consider the objection that this yields implausible verdicts. But for now, we're just considering the objection that there would be something "spooky" or unscientific about it.) Once you are on board with welfare value at all, it's not clear that there is any additional metaphysical cost to accepting an objective list theory in particular.[36]

On the other hand, it can be hard to shake the sense that there is *something* less mysterious-seeming about grounding value in what we want or what makes us happy. The challenge for the critic here is to develop an argument that makes clear what *metaphysical* difference follows from grounding value in our desires or feelings, so long as the resulting value is equally real and important no matter what it's grounded in. Otherwise, the intuitive force of the "spookiness" objection may just stem from mistakenly conflating feeling-based value with outright nihilism.[37]

A related (but importantly different) argument might start from the idea that there should be some *common explanation* for why the things on the objective list are good. Some critics may find objective list theories arbitrary or ad hoc, in contrast to hedonism and desire theories, which each offer a way to unify all welfare goods into a single kind (either happiness or desire satisfaction). Objective list theorists may respond by disputing the idea that any such common explanation is

---

35. Expressivists may give an anti-realist gloss on what "really mattering" amounts to. But then they can just as comfortably extend this gloss to the kind of first-order "objectivity" posited by objective list theories.

36. Cf. Matthew S. Bedke, "Might All Normativity Be Queer?," *Australasian Journal of Philosophy* 88, no. 1 (2010): 41–58, https://doi.org/10.1080/00048400802636445.

37. It would indeed be less "mysterious" to deny the reality of value and claim that subjective valuing is *all there is* in the vicinity. But this would be a form of nihilism: that S values *p* is a purely descriptive fact about S's psychology. There is nothing inherently value-laden about this unless we further claim that subjective valuation is something that actually *matters* in some way. And then we are back to attributing real value in all its mysterious glory.

necessary: Why could there not be several different kinds of things that can each enrich one's life in fundamentally different ways? (And why regard a list with just one item on it—whether happiness or desire satisfaction—as any less arbitrary?)[38] Whether or not you are inclined to assume that a "common explanation" is necessary (or even to be expected) here may thus have a significant impact on how plausible you find objective list theories.

Alienation

Perhaps the most powerful objection to objective list theories instead challenges it on its putative point of strength: its ability to accommodate our intuitive judgments about what makes one's life go well. If we imagine a subjectively miserable life, it's hard to believe that it could be a really good life for the person living it, no matter how highly they might score on all the *other* putative objective values (besides happiness). Someone who feels deeply alienated from the putative "goods" in their life would not seem to benefit from the goods in question.[39] A committed hermit, for example, might deny that having friends to interrupt his solitude would do him any good at all. So this casts doubt on the simple objective list theory that takes the items on the list to constitute welfare goods regardless of whether we want them or they make us happy.

This concern might move us toward a *hybrid* view, according to which well-being consists in *subjective appreciation of the objective candidate welfare goods*.[40] So unwanted friendships no longer count as a "benefit" to the hermit. However, if he

---

38. One advantage of only having one good on the list is that you avoid potential arbitrariness in *exchange rates* (between the different types of goods). But that's different from claiming that there's arbitrariness in which things get to count as good *at all*.

39. As Peter Railton writes, "What is intrinsically valuable for a person must have a connection with what he would find in some degree compelling or attractive, at least if he were rational and aware. It would be an intolerably alienated conception of someone's good to imagine that it might fail in any such way to engage him." Railton, "Facts and Values," in *Facts, Values and Norms: Essays Toward a Morality of Consequence* (Cambridge: Cambridge University Press, 2003), 47.

40. Perhaps the best-known hybrid view is found in Shelly Kagan, "Well-Being as Enjoying the Good," *Philosophical Perspectives* 23, no. 1 (December 2009): 253–72, https://doi.org/10.1111/j.1520-8583.2009.00170.x.

came to truly appreciate other people, this would be better for him than getting equal enjoyment from merely counting blades of grass. In this way, the alienation objection can be addressed while (i) rejecting the experience machine and (ii) maintaining the core objectivist idea that some ways of life are better for us than others, even if they would result in equal desire satisfaction and happiness.

Practical Implications of Theories of Well-Being

Hedonism, desire theories, and objective list theories of well-being all largely overlap in practice. This is because we tend to desire things that are (typically regarded as) objectively worthwhile, and we tend to be happier when we achieve what we desire. We may also tend to reshape our desires based on our experiences of what feels good. As a result, defenders of any given theory of well-being might seek to debunk their competitors by suggesting that competing values (be they pleasure, desire-fulfillment, or objective goods) are of merely *instrumental* value, tending to produce, or otherwise go along with, what *really* matters.

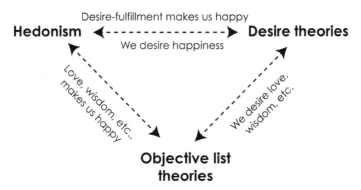

Theories of well-being

Still, by appealing to stylized thought experiments (involving experience machines, changing preferences, and the like), we can carefully pry apart the implications of the various theories of well-being and so form a considered judgment about which theory strikes us as most plausible.

Even if the theories *currently* coincide in practice, their differences could become more practically significant as technology advances and, with it, our ability to manipulate our own minds. If we one day face the prospect of engineering our descendants so that they experience bliss in total passivity, it will be important to determine whether we would thereby be doing them a favor or robbing them of much of what makes for a truly flourishing life.

Conclusion

While utilitarians agree about wanting to promote well-being, they may disagree about what *constitutes* well-being: what things are basic goods and bads for us. According to the most prominent theories of well-being, it may consist of either happiness, desire satisfaction, or a plurality of objective goods.

Hedonism, in holding happiness to be the only basic welfare good, achieves simplicity at the cost of counterintuitive implications in the Experience Machine thought experiment.

Desire theories avoid these implications but risk *other* counterintuitive implications in cases involving bizarre or changing desires.

Finally, objective list theories risk alienating individuals from their own welfare goods unless some concessions are made toward what the individual desires or what makes them happy. As a result, a more complex hybrid account may do the best job of capturing our myriad intuitions about well-being.

The competing theories of well-being mostly coincide in practice, but this may change as technology advances. Their implications may differ starkly in scenarios involving futuristic technology such as digital minds and virtual reality. Whether the future we build for our descendants is utopian or dystopian may ultimately depend on which theory of well-being is correct—and whether we can identify it in time.

The next chapter discusses *population ethics* and how to evaluate outcomes in which different numbers of people may exist.

5

Population Ethics

Introduction

Utilitarians agree that if the number of people that were ever to exist is held constant, we should promote the *sum total of well-being* in that fixed population.[1] But in reality, the population is not fixed. We have the option of bringing more people into existence, such as by having children. If these additional people were to have good lives, is that a way of making the world better? This question falls in the domain of *population ethics*, which deals with the moral problems that arise when our actions affect who and how many people are born and at what quality of life.

Population ethics is not just an academic exercise. It is relevant to many important practical questions, such as how many children we ought to have, if any; how much we should invest in climate change mitigation; and how much we should worry about near-term risks of human extinction.

This chapter will survey five major approaches to population ethics:

1. the *total view* that evaluates populations according to the total amount of well-being they contain;
2. the *average view* that instead focuses on the *average* well-being level in the population;
3. *variable value theories* that take both factors into account, approximating the total view for smaller populations and the average view for larger populations;

---

1. When we talk about populations, we mean total populations: not just how many people are alive at a specific time, but consideration of all people across all time.

4. *critical level* (and *critical range*) *theories* that tweak the total view to only count positive well-being above a critical baseline level (or range); and

5. *person-affecting views* that deny we have (non-instrumental) reason to add happy lives to the world.[2]

The Total View

According to the *total view* of population ethics:

> **One outcome is better than another if and only if it contains greater total well-being.[3]**

Importantly, one population may have greater total well-being than another by virtue of having more people. One way to calculate this total is to multiply the number of individuals (N) by their average quality of life (Q).[4] We can, therefore, represent the total view by the following value function:

$$\text{Value}_{totalview} = N * Q$$

Consider a hypothetical world A with 100 inhabitants (N_A) at an average well-being level 10 (Q_A) and another hypothetical world B with 200 inhabitants (N_B) at well-being level 5 (Q_B). On the total view, worlds A and B are equally good because they both have 1,000 units of well-being ($N_A * Q_A = N_B * Q_B = 1,000$).

---

2. Other writers, following Derek Parfit, sometimes speak of a "wide person-affecting view" that allows for (non-instrumental) reasons to add happy lives. For ease of expression, in this chapter, we use "person-affecting" in the more distinctive *narrow* sense that rejects this idea. Parfit, *Reasons and Persons* (Oxford: Clarendon Press, 1984).

3. Throughout this chapter, we use the terms "quality of life," "welfare," and "well-being" interchangeably. These terms are used to describe how well or poorly someone's entire life goes, not just how well-off someone is at a specific moment in time. Moreover, concepts such as "units of well-being" and "well-being levels" are simplifications used for illustrative purposes, and they do not imply that we can, in practice, precisely measure well-being.

4. An alternative method is to add up the well-being levels of all individuals.

When comparing hypothetical worlds in population ethics, these worlds are often illustrated graphically. The width of the following graphs represents the number of people, and the height represents their average well-being level. Consequently, the graphs' area—width times height—represents the total welfare in the hypothetical worlds. Illustrated graphically, worlds A and B are equally valuable, according to the total view, since their graphs have the same area.

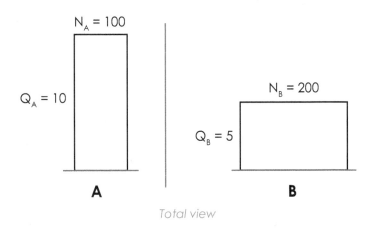

Total view

The total view implies that we can improve the world in two ways: either we can improve the quality of life of existing people, or we can increase the number of people living positive lives.[5] The total view makes no distinction between whether the additional well-being would come to people who already exist or to entirely new people. For example, the total view regards having a child who lives a happy and fulfilled life as something that makes the world better, all else equal, since it adds to the total well-being.[6] Importantly, the claim is not that having the child might make the world better in virtue of enriching the lives of others; instead, it's that having the child is good in itself. How good it is to bring a new person into

---

5. The notion of a positive life, which is critical for the total view, only makes sense relative to a zero point on the well-being scale. This zero point is the threshold above which life becomes "worth living." A "neutral life," at well-being level 0, is neither "worth living" nor "not worth living." This may be either a life with no value or disvalue, or a life with exactly as much value as disvalue. For discussion of the subtleties surrounding the concept of a life "worth living," see John Broome, *Weighing Lives* (Oxford: Oxford University Press, 2004), 66–68.

6. Stronger still: on the total view, it would be intrinsically *better* to create a new person at welfare level 100 than to improve an existing person's well-being from level 1 to 100.

existence depends on how much better or worse that person's life is than a "neutral life." According to this view, happy people are good, and having more of a good thing, other things being equal, makes an outcome better.

In practice, there might be trade-offs between making existing people happier and creating additional happy people. For example, you might think that, on a planet with limited resources, adding more people to an already large population may at some point diminish the quality of life of everyone else severely enough that total well-being decreases. It's an open empirical question whether our world has reached the population size at which adding a person increases or decreases overall well-being.[7]

The foremost practical implication of the total view is that it gives great importance to ensuring the long-term flourishing of civilization. This entails taking existential risk reduction very seriously as a moral priority.[8] Existential risks—such as all-out nuclear war, or extreme climate change, or an engineered global pandemic—threaten the survival of humankind. If humanity survives, civilization may flourish over billions of years, and an enormous number of future people may get to enjoy highly fulfilling lives. The total well-being across all future generations may be astronomically large, and an existential catastrophe would irreversibly deprive humanity of this potentially grand future. From the perspective of the total view and many other moral views, the stakes involved with existential risks are so immense that the mitigation of these risks becomes one of the principal moral issues facing humanity.

---

7. For an exploration of whether the world is overpopulated or underpopulated, see Toby Ord, "Overpopulation or Underpopulation?," chap. 3 in *Is the Planet Full?*, ed. Ian Goldin (Oxford: Oxford University Press, 2014).

8. Reducing existential risk is a priority not just for the total view but for a wide variety of moral views. However, for the total view there is an especially large amount of value at stake with preserving the long-term flourishing of civilization. Toby Ord, "Existential Risk," chap. 2 in *The Precipice: Existential Risk and the Future of Humanity* (London: Bloomsbury Publishing, 2020).

Objecting to the Total View: The Repugnant Conclusion

The most prominent objection to the total view is the *repugnant conclusion*, originally raised by Derek Parfit.[9] In its simplest form, the repugnant conclusion is that[10]

> **For any world A, there is a better world Z in which no one has a life that is more than barely worth living.**

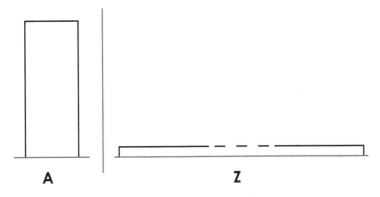

The repugnant conclusion

---

9. While Parfit deserves credit for raising the philosophical debate around the repugnant conclusion, arguably, Henry Sidgwick noticed it much earlier, writing that "the point up to which, on utilitarian principles, population ought to be encouraged to increase, is not that at which the average happiness is the greatest possible . . . but that at which the happiness reaches its maximum." Sidgwick, *The Methods of Ethics* (London, 1907; Hackett Publishing, 1981), 415.
10. This formulation is taken from Hilary Greaves, "Population Axiology," *Philosophy Compass* 12, no. 11 (November 2017): https://doi.org/10.1111/phc3.12442. Parfit's longer original formulation was as follows: "For any possible population of at least ten billion people, all with a very high quality of life, there must be some much larger imaginable population whose existence, if other things are equal, would be better even though its members have lives that are barely worth living." Parfit, *Reasons and Persons*, 342. The total view further implies the *Very Repugnant Conclusion*, according to which enough lives barely worth living can outweigh any number of additional arbitrarily miserable lives. Gustaf Arrhenius, "The Very Repugnant Conclusion," in *Logic, Law, Morality: Thirteen Essays in Practical Philosophy in Honour of Lennart Åqvist*, ed. Krister Segerberg and Ryszard Sliwinski (Uppsala: Uppsala University, 2003), 29–44.

All lives in world Z are positive, but they are only barely worth living. If the population in Z is sufficiently large, Z's total well-being—represented by the graph's area—is greater than A's. Consequently, the total view implies that world Z is better than world A: the repugnant conclusion.

On the total view, a sufficiently large increase in the quantity of a population can compensate for any loss in the average quality of lives in this population, as long as average well-being remains positive. Most people find some trade-offs between quantity and quality intuitive; for instance, almost everyone would agree that our world of about eight billion people is better than a world with only one person with a slightly higher average well-being level. However, many people find the repugnant conclusion counterintuitive and think that the total view takes quantity-quality trade-offs too far. Given that no one in world Z has a life more than barely worth living, it's tempting to think that Z must be worse than A, regardless of Z's population size.

Importantly, the total view need not imply that we should maximize population size *in practice*. It's an open empirical question how best to promote total well-being in real-life circumstances: blindly increasing population without also ensuring a high quality of lives is not guaranteed (or even likely) to be the best approach. But even if the total view avoids repugnant implications in practice, it remains important to assess whether its broader implications (for various hypothetical scenarios) are ones that we are willing to accept.

As such, proponents of the total view might respond to the challenge presented by the repugnant conclusion by debunking the intuition, biting the bullet, or attacking the alternatives. We will consider these in turn.

Debunking the Intuition

Our intuitions about these cases may be unreliable or based on subtle misunderstandings.[11]

First, the repugnant conclusion involves cases with extremely large numbers of individuals with low but positive welfare. Many philosophers argue that this is a situation where we should expect our intuitions to be unreliable: human brains struggle to intuitively grasp both very large numbers and how adding up lots of

---

11. Stéphane Zuber et al., "What Should We Agree on about the Repugnant Conclusion?," *Utilitas* 33, no. 4 (April 2021): 379–83, https://doi.org/10.1017/S095382082100011X.

small values results in a very large value.[12] So we may fail to understand on an intuitive level how the vast number of lives in world Z could ever compound to something more valuable than world A.

Second, we may not adequately appreciate that lives "barely worth living" are good rather than bad.[13] A life "barely worth living" *is* worth living, and a person with such a life has reason to be glad they exist. Misleading representations of lives "barely worth living" in the academic literature may contribute to this misunderstanding. While it's controversial how to determine which lives are worth living, it has been argued that influential examples in the literature—such as lives containing no goods besides "muzak and potatoes"[14]—are actually not worth living.[15]

Third, we may mistakenly imagine ourselves as part of the populations being compared in the repugnant conclusion. Consequently, an egoistic bias may push us to favor populations with a high quality of life.[16]

Tolerating the Intuition

Proponents of the total view may "bite the bullet" and simply accept that world Z is better than world A. They may point out that, while initially counterintuitive, this conclusion is based on the compelling goal of creating a world with as much total well-being as possible. On the total view, reductions in the average

---

12. John Broome, *Weighing Lives*; Michael Huemer, "In Defence of Repugnance," *Mind* 117, no. 468 (October 2008): 899–933, https://www.jstor.org/stable/20532700; Johan E. Gustafsson, "Our Intuitive Grasp of the Repugnant Conclusion," in *The Oxford Handbook of Population Ethics*, ed. Gustaf Arrhenius et al. (New York: Oxford University Press, 2022).

13. Jesper Ryberg, "Is the Repugnant Conclusion Repugnant?," *Philosophical Papers* 25, no. 3 (1996): 161–77, https://doi.org/10.1080/05568649609506547; Torbjörn Tännsjö, "Who Are the Beneficiaries?," *Bioethics* 6, no. 4 (October 1992): 288–96, https://doi.org/10.1111/j.1467-8519.1992.tb00207.x; J. L. Mackie, "Parfit's Population Paradox," in *Persons and Values*, ed. Joan Mackie and Penelope Mackie (Oxford: Oxford University Press, 1985).

14. This was how Parfit sometimes characterized the "repugnant" world Z, for example, in his "Overpopulation and the Quality of Life," in *Applied Ethics*, ed. Peter Singer (Oxford: Oxford University Press, 1986).

15. M. Hutchinson, "The Ethics of Extending and Creating Life" (DPhil diss., University of Oxford, 2014, unpublished).

16. Torbjörn Tännsjö, "Why We Ought to Accept the Repugnant Conclusion," *Utilitas* 14, no. 3 (November 2002): 339–59, https://doi.org/10.1017/S0953820800003642; Huemer, "In Defence of Repugnance," 899–933.

well-being level of a population can be more than compensated for by adding sufficiently many lives that are worth living. Since lives worth living are (one would naturally think) an inherently good thing, it seems rhetorically overblown to call this implication "repugnant."

Indeed, it turns out to be remarkably difficult to avoid the repugnant conclusion. Strong arguments, such as Parfit's Mere Addition Paradox,[17] entail the Repugnant Conclusion without assuming the total view to begin with. Consider the choice between the following three worlds: A, A+, and B.

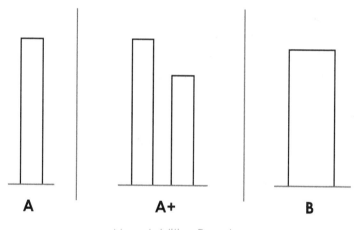

Mere Addition Paradox

In world A, everyone's well-being is very high. World A+ contains (i) one population group that is identical to the A population in terms of population size and average well-being, and (ii) a second group of the same size but with slightly lower well-being. Most people would agree that A+ is not worse than A (and may even be better) since, intuitively, merely adding people with lives worth living (without thereby harming anyone else) cannot make an outcome worse. Now consider world B, which has the same overall population size as A+. The average well-being in B is slightly higher than in A+ but lower than in A. When we compare worlds A+ and B, it seems that B must be better. Not only are the average *and* total welfare in B higher than in A+, but well-being is also more equally distributed. Yet, if B is better than A+, and A+ is not worse than A, it follows that B must

---

17. Parfit, "The Mere Addition Paradox," chap. 19 in *Reasons and Persons*.

be better than A.[18] Repeating this process—comparing world B with B+ and C, etc.—leads to world Z with an enormous number of people with lives barely worth living. Following the above reasoning, world Z must be better than world A: the repugnant conclusion.

Attacking the Alternatives

A final response is to note that counterintuitive implications are by no means unique to the total view. Several impossibility theorems prove that it's *logically impossible* for any population ethical theory to satisfy every intuitively desirable principle and axiom.[19] One such axiom is to avoid the repugnant conclusion. However, some philosophers argue that avoiding the repugnant conclusion is not worth the theoretical costs of giving up other axioms or fundamental principles. Accepting the repugnant conclusion provides an easy response to the impossibility theorems since the total view is consistent with all the other axioms of these theorems.[20] In light of this, a growing number of ethicists have come to accept and defend the repugnant conclusion and the total view.[21]

To evaluate this comparative claim, we must consider the merits (and demerits) of the competing views. Philosophers have proposed several alternatives to the total view that seek to avoid (at least the original version of) the repugnant

---

18. At least on standard assumptions. As we will see below, this no longer follows if, in addition to the standard trichotomy of value relations (being *greater than*, *lesser than*, and *precisely equal*), there is a fourth relation of being *on a par*. For then, B might be better than A+, while *both* A+ and B are merely on a par with A.

19. Gustaf Arrhenius, "An Impossibility Theorem for Welfarist Axiologies," *Economics and Philosophy* 16, no. 2 (November 2000): 247–66, https://doi.org/10.1017/S0266267100000249; Arrhenius, "The Impossibility of a Satisfactory Population Ethics," in *Descriptive and Normative Approaches to Human Behavior*, ed. Ehtibar N. Dzhafarov and Lacey Perry (Singapore: World Scientific Publishing Co., 2011), 1–26; Philip Kitcher, "Parfit's Puzzle," *Noûs* 34, no. 4 (December 2000): 550–77, https://doi.org/10.1111/0029-4624.00278; Erik Carlson, "Mere Addition and Two Trilemmas of Population Ethics," *Economics and Philosophy* 14, no. 2 (October 1998): 283–306, https://doi.org/10.1017/S0266267100003862; Yew-Kwang Ng, "What Should We Do about Future Generations? Impossibility of Parfit's Theory X," *Economics and Philosophy* 5, no. 2 (October 1989): 235–53, https://doi.org/10.1017/S0266267100002406.

20. Greaves, "Population Axiology."

21. Tännsjö, "Why We Ought to Accept the Repugnant Conclusion," 339–59; Huemer, "In Defence of Repugnance," 899–933.

conclusion. These theories include the *average view, variable value theories, critical level and range theories,* and *person-affecting views.*

The Average View

According to the *average view* of population ethics:

> **One outcome is better than another if and only if it contains greater average well-being.**

Since the average view aims only to improve the *average well-being level,* it disregards—in contrast to the total view—the number of individuals that exist.[22] Consequently, the average view is represented by a simple value function, with average well-being level Q:

$$\text{Value}_{\text{averageview}} = Q$$

The average view avoids the repugnant conclusion because it entails that reductions in the average well-being level can never be compensated for merely by adding more people to the population.

However, the average view has very little support among moral philosophers since it suffers from severe problems.

First, consider a world inhabited by a single person enduring excruciating suffering. The average view entails that we could improve this world by creating a million new people whose lives were also filled with excruciating suffering, if the suffering of the new people was ever-so-slightly less bad than the suffering of the original person.[23]

Second, the average view entails the (misleadingly named) *sadistic conclusion:*[24]

---

22. Note that the average and total views *always* agree on the ranking of outcomes when these outcomes contain the same number of individuals. In such cases, both theories are said to be "extensionally equivalent."

23. This is a variation on the Hell Three case from Derek Parfit, *Reasons and Persons,* 422.

24. Definition adapted from Arrhenius, "An Impossibility Theorem for Welfarist Axiologies," 247–66. Note that this label is misleading. Whereas the previous objection noted how the average view sometimes favors the addition of miserable lives (which does seem sadistic), the so-called "sadistic conclusion" instead objects to the claim that adding a small number of

> **It can sometimes be better to create lives with negative well-being than to create lives with positive well-being from the same starting point, all else equal.**

Adding a small number of tortured, miserable people to a population diminishes the average well-being less than adding a sufficiently large number of people whose lives are pretty good, yet below the existing average. To see this, consider the following graph where world A has lower average well-being than world B. Counterintuitively, the average view thus entails that we should prefer world B over world A.

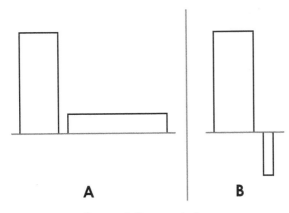

The sadistic conclusion

Third, the average view prefers arbitrarily small populations over very large populations as long as the average well-being is higher. For example, a world with a single, extremely happy individual would be favored to a world with ten billion people, all of whom are extremely happy but just ever-so-slightly less happy than that single person.

Variable Value Theories

To compromise between the total and average views, some philosophers have proposed *variable value theories*. According to these theories, the marginal value

---

negative-welfare lives may be *less bad* than adding a vast number of moderately positive ones to an otherwise very happy world. Insofar as this comparative judgment stems from evaluating (some) positive-welfare lives negatively rather than negative-welfare lives positively, the "sadism" label seems a misnomer.

of creating additional people diminishes—the larger the existing population, the smaller the value of adding another person.

The simplest variable value theories may be represented by the following value function, with number of individuals N and average quality of life Q:[25]

$$\textbf{Value}_{\text{variablevalue}} = \textbf{Q} * \textbf{f(N)}$$

This diminishing marginal value allows variable value theories to avoid some of the weaknesses of the total and average views. For instance, Hilary Greaves writes:

> Arguably, the average view is intuitively less plausible for small populations: if there are otherwise only ten persons who will ever live, for instance, it (perhaps) seems more worthwhile to add an additional person with a given positive well-being level than if there are already 100 billion persons.[26]

At first glance, it's an attractive feature of variable value theories that they approximate the total view at small population sizes and the average view at large population sizes since they may thereby avoid the repugnant conclusion.[27]

However, variable value theories face problems of their own. First, in approximating the average view at large population sizes, they risk susceptibility to the same objections. So, to avoid approving adding (above-average) negative lives to the world, variable value theorists must invoke an asymmetry according to which only the value of positive lives diminishes but not the disvalue of negative lives. Adding negative lives to a world always makes the world non-instrumentally worse, on such a view, even if it happens to improve the average. However, such an asymmetry leads to an analogue of what Parfit calls the *absurd conclusion*:[28]

---

25. Where **f** is a strictly increasing and strictly concave function with a horizontal asymptote. That is, as N increases, **f(N)** increases at a diminishing pace, and never surpasses a certain limit. Cf. Thomas Hurka, "Value and Population Size," *Ethics* 93, no. 3 (April 1983): 496–507, https://doi .org/10.1086/292462; Ng, "What Should We Do about Future Generations?," 235–53.
26. Greaves, "Population Axiology."
27. They may avoid the repugnant conclusion since the total value of a population is subject to an upper limit if the value of additional lives diminishes asymptotically. Cf. Greaves, "Population Axiology."
28. Parfit, "The Absurd Conclusion," chap. 18 in *Reasons and Persons*.

that a population considered to be good, with many happy and few miserable lives, can be turned into a population considered to be bad merely by proportionally increasing the number of both positive and negative lives.[29] To escape this objection, variable value theorists must allow additional good lives to sometimes *compensate* for additional bad lives, without introducing further unintended consequences that undermine their view. This is no easy task.[30]

Critical Level and Critical Range Theories

According to critical level theories:

> **Adding an individual makes an outcome better to the extent that their well-being exceeds some critical level.**

Consequently, an outcome can be made worse not only by bringing into existence an individual with negative well-being but also if their well-being is positive yet below the critical level.[31]

The total value of an outcome, according to critical level theories, can be represented by the following value function, with number of individuals N, average quality of life Q, and critical level a:

$$\textbf{Value}_{\text{criticallevel}} = \textbf{N} * (\textbf{Q} - a)$$

By looking at this value function, we may observe that the total view of population ethics is simply a critical level theory with a critical level of zero ($a = 0$). Critical level theories, including the total view, agree that the non-instrumental value of

---

29. Consider a good world with one billion happy people and a single miserable person. Imagine we repeatedly increase the numbers of happy and miserable people by the same factor—ten billion happy people and ten miserable people, one hundred billion happy people and one hundred miserable people, etc. For a sufficiently large population, every time we increase its size in this way, the world gets worse (according to these asymmetric theories) until we eventually reach an overall bad world.

30. For one such attempt, see Richard Y. Chappell, *Parfit's Ethics* (Cambridge: Cambridge University Press, 2021), section 7.2.2.

31. The critical level is generally assumed to be non-negative, that is, either positive or zero. A negative critical level would implausibly attribute positive value to (some) negative lives.

adding an individual to the world depends only on that individual's well-being level and—in contrast to the average view and variable value theories—not on the number of existing persons or their well-being levels.

Critical level theories avoid the repugnant conclusion if their critical level is greater than the well-being level that makes a life "barely worth living." This follows from the definition of critical level theories since only adding people whose welfare exceeds the critical level can compensate for reductions in the average quality of life.

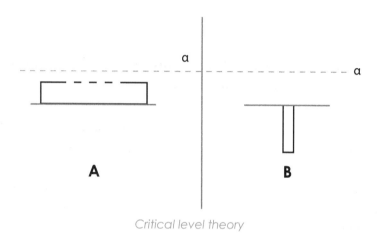

Critical level theory

However, a positive critical level entails an especially appalling version of the sadistic conclusion, which gets worse the higher the chosen critical level.[32] This is because it implies that it's preferable for a world to contain individuals with negative well-being—lives not worth living, such as lives of constant torture—than to contain vastly more individuals with lives that are worth living yet below the critical level. Graphically illustrated, critical level theories counterintuitively imply that world A (with a sufficiently large population) is *worse* than world B.

To avoid this unacceptable result, we may move to a *critical range* theory,[33] according to which:

---

32. Cf. Broome, *Weighing Lives*, 213–14.

33. Charles Blackorby, Walter Bossert, and David Donaldson, "Quasi-Orderings and Population Ethics," *Social Choice and Welfare* 13, no. 2 (April 1996): 129–50, https://doi.org/10.1007/BF00183348; Wlodek Rabinowicz, "Broome and the Intuition of Neutrality," *Philosophical Issues* 19, no. 1 (October 2009): 389–411, https://doi.org/10.1111/j.1533-6077.2009.00174.x;

> **Adding an individual makes an outcome better to the extent that their well-being exceeds the upper end of a *critical range*, and makes an outcome worse to the extent that their well-being falls below the lower limit of the critical range.**

By setting the lower limit of the critical range to include all neutral lives that are neither good nor bad for the person living them, critical range theories can avoid the sadistic conclusion. And by setting the upper limit of the range at the point where lives become clearly worthwhile, these theories avoid the repugnant conclusion.

What about lives that fall within the critical range? Life within this range may strike us as *meh*:[34] neither good nor bad, but also not precisely equal to *zero* in value, either. After all, some meh lives (those toward the upper end of the range) are better than others (those toward the lower end), so it cannot be that adding any life in this range results in an equally valuable outcome. Instead, the outcome's value must be *incomparable* or *on a par* with that of the prior state: neither better, nor worse, nor precisely equal in value.[35] Note that it may be better to add an upper-range meh life to the world than to add a lower-range meh life, even though adding *either* life is merely meh, or results in an outcome that is incomparable with the world in which neither life is added.[36]

Johan E. Gustafsson, "Population Axiology and the Possibility of a Fourth Category of Absolute Value," *Economics and Philosophy* 36, no. 1 (March 2020): 81–110, https://doi.org/10.1017/S0266267119000087.

34. While philosophers do not typically use this colloquial term, it may be helpful to imagine someone who, when asked whether the world is improved by adding a barely worth-living life, shrugs their shoulders and responds, "Meh."

35. Cf. Ruth Chang, "The Possibility of Parity," *Ethics* 112 no. 4 (July 2022): 659–88, https://doi.org/10.1086/339673.

36. One may, for example, get this result by thinking of the critical range as representing a range within which it's *indeterminate where the critical level lies*. Or one may consider it a range of *reasonable pluralism*, such that one could permissibly treat any point in this range as the critical level when forming personal preferences about which lives to add (or not) to the world. On either approach, we can then *supervaluate* and hold that population X is (truly, determinately, or objectively) better than Y just if this evaluation would follow from *all* critical level theories where the critical level falls within the specified range.

To further develop this view (along lines suggested by Johan Gustafsson), we may think of the value of a life as having two dimensions.[37] In addition to the familiar negative-versus-positive dimension, there is a second dimension of what we might call *value blur*. When there is zero blur, the resulting values are perfectly precise and comparable: any positive life, however barely so, then constitutes an intrinsic improvement to the world. But as we increase blur, the resulting value becomes increasingly meh, or *incomparable*. If life's value had infinite blur, then *all* lives would be meh. (We will consider such a view in the next section.) Alternatively, if we think that life's value admits of just moderate blur, then sufficient positive (or negative) value may overcome this blurriness to qualify the life in question as one that would be in itself good (or bad) to add to the world.

The key implication of this critical range theory (with moderate value blur) is that an intrinsically good life must contain *significantly* more welfare than an intrinsically bad life because, between these two levels, there is a moderate range of lives that are meh, as illustrated below:[38]

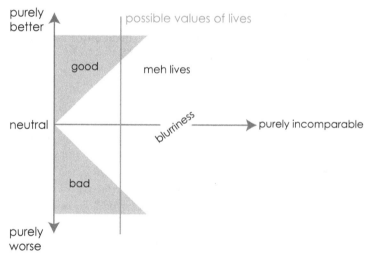

Critical range theory

<hr />

37. Gustafsson speaks of "undistinguishedness" in place of our term "value blur." See Gustafsson, "Population Axiology and the Possibility of a Fourth Category," 81–110.

38. The following illustration is adapted from Johan E. Gustafsson, "Population Axiology and the Possibility of a Fourth Category," 92.

The resulting view, while theoretically complex, seems less susceptible to severe objections than the other views we've surveyed. In particular, it can simultaneously avoid both the repugnant conclusion and the sadistic conclusion. But it cannot accommodate the strong "anti-repugnance" intuition that the idyllic world A is strictly *better* than the repugnant world Z.[39] Critical range theories instead regard the two worlds as incomparable due to the immense value blur introduced by all those meh lives in world Z.

Person-Affecting Views and the Procreative Asymmetry

All of the theories discussed above—the total view, the average view, variable value theories, and critical level and range theories—are *impersonal theories*.[40]

Impersonal Theories	Value Function (Value of a Particular State of the World)
Total view	$N * Q$
Average view	Q
Variable value theory	$f(N) * Q$
Critical level theory[41]	$N * (Q - a)$

N = number of persons; Q = average well-being level; a = critical level; $f()$ = strictly increasing and strictly concave function with a horizontal asymptote

---

39. This may prove especially problematic if the critical range is symmetric, such that slightly negative lives also qualify as meh (rather than bad). Most would think the idyllic world A should be strictly better than a world "Z-" containing a vast number of slightly negative lives, but symmetric critical range theories will struggle to deliver this verdict. Cf. Gustafsson, who claims that this is not a terrible bullet to bite if the personal/well-being value of such a life is also blurry, and so "meh" (in our terminology) rather than bad *for the person living it*. Gustafsson, "Population Axiology and the Possibility of a Fourth Category," 95.

40. Here we use the term "impersonal" simply to contrast with the (narrow) person-affecting view. So even an impersonal theory (on our usage) can take the value of a state of affairs to be grounded in facts about what is good for particular people, e.g., if one holds that a happy existence can constitute a non-comparative benefit, parallel to how a miserable existence constitutes a non-comparative harm.

41. The critical range theories we've discussed are more difficult to capture in a numerical formula. But if we put aside any lives that fall within the critical range, we might approximate the remaining overall value by separately summing the positive and negative welfare levels, to the extent that they exceed their respective ends of the critical range. So, using positive and negative subscripts to denote the respective numbers (N), averages (Q), and critical boundary points (a)

Impersonal theories imply that creating an additional person with a (sufficiently) good life makes the world better, other things being equal.[42] However, some people reject this implication. They say that there are no moral reasons to bring additional people into existence—at least no reasons based on the well-being these people would enjoy if created. Jan Narveson put this idea in slogan form: "We are in favor of making people happy, but neutral about making happy people."[43] *Person-affecting views* of population ethics attempt to capture this intuition of neutrality and are especially common among non-consequentialists.[44]

---

for these two subpopulations, we can write the value function as $N_+ * (Q_- - a_+) + N_- * (Q - a_-)$. Alternatively, we might think of the value of the world as itself indeterminate or corresponding to a numerical range, as given by all the possible critical level theories corresponding to the critical range, i.e., everything from $N * (Q - a_-)$ to $N * (Q - a_-)$. On this approach, the value of the repugnant world Z, for example, would be indeterminate across an immense range of values stemming from *extremely negative* to *extremely positive* because N is unimaginably huge, whereas the sign of $(Q - a)$ is indeterminate, given the range of candidate critical levels a.

42. On the total view, adding a person with positive well-being is always good, all else equal. The same is true for variable value theories, though for a large pre-existing population, the marginal value of an additional life being added may be low. On the average view, adding a person is good, other things being equal, if the person's well-being exceeds the existing average; similarly, it is good on critical level (and range) theories if the person's well-being exceeds the critical level (or range).

43. Jan Narveson, "Moral Problems of Population," *The Monist* 57, no. 1 (January 1973): 80, https://doi.org/10.5840/monist197357134. To put pressure on the slogan, consider the limited appeal of its negative-welfare analogue: "We are opposed to making people miserable, but neutral about making miserable people." As this section goes on to discuss, the viability of person-affecting approaches to population ethics crucially depends upon validating a radical asymmetry between positive and negative lives.

44. For instance, see Elizabeth Finneron-Burns, "What's Wrong with Human Extinction?," in "Ethics and Future Generations," ed. Rahul Kumar, special edition, *Canadian Journal of Philosophy* 47, no. 2–3 (2017): 327–43, https://doi.org/10.1080/00455091.2016.1278150; Jan Narveson, "Utilitarianism and New Generations," *Mind* 76, no. 301 (January 1967): 62–72, https://www.jstor.org/stable/2252027; Narveson, "Moral Problems of Population," 62–86; Melinda A. Roberts, "A New Way of Doing the Best That We Can: Person-Based Consequentialism and the Equality Problem," *Ethics* 112, no. 2 (January 2002): 315–50, https://doi.org/10.1086/324321; Roberts, "Person-Based Consequentialism and the Procreation Obligation," in *The Repugnant Conclusion*, ed. Jesper Ryberg and Torbjörn Tännsjö, vol. 15, *Library of Ethics and Applied Philosophy* (Dordrecht: Kluwer Academic Publishers, 2004), 99–128.

To this end, standard person-affecting views accept the *person-affecting restriction*:

> **An outcome cannot be better (or worse) than another unless it is better (or worse) *for* someone.**[45]

At first glance, this principle sounds eminently plausible. When considering only fixed-population cases, it amounts to an expression of *welfarism*: the view that well-being is the only value. But problems arise when comparing outcomes in which different people exist, especially if combined with the principle of *existence incomparability*:[46]

> **If a person exists in one outcome but not the other, it is not possible to compare their well-being across these outcomes.**

According to this principle, since the value of existence and non-existence are assumed to be incomparable, existing cannot be better (or worse) for you. When combined with the person-affecting restriction, we get the result that your existence likewise cannot make the outcome better (or worse). But we commonly think that lives of unrelenting suffering would be worse than not existing at all. And an outcome containing additional suffering lives would surely be, in that respect, a worse outcome.[47]

To accommodate these intuitions, person-affecting theorists must allow that *intrinsically bad states* (like undeserved suffering) can count as *non-comparative harms*. Even if, strictly speaking, we cannot compare existence to non-existence, we can certainly hold that a life of unrelenting suffering is *bad for you*. The person-affecting restriction can then be tweaked to specify that one outcome can be worse

---

45. At least, it cannot be better or worse in terms of well-being.

46. Cf. Gustaf Arrhenius, "Future Generations: A Challenge for Moral Theory" (PhD thesis, Uppsala University, 2000), chap. 8, http://uu.diva-portal.org/smash/get/diva2:170236/FULLTEXT01; David Heyd, "Procreation and Value: Can Ethics Deal with Futurity Problems?," *Philosophia* 18 (1988): 151–70, https://doi.org/10.1007/BF02380074.

47. Cf. Derek Parfit's Wretched Child case. Parfit, *Reasons and Persons*, 391.

than another if *either* it's worse for someone *or* it's bad for someone (while the alternative is not).

Generalizing this reasoning would lead us to similarly hold that intrinsically *good* states (or positive welfare) can count as a non-comparative benefit of existence.[48] But this result would rob the person-affecting view of its distinctiveness. It could easily end up coinciding with the total view, for example, and endorsing the repugnant conclusion on behalf of the multitudes in world Z who would each receive a tiny non-comparative benefit from getting to exist.

Many person-affecting theorists wish to avoid this result and instead endorse the *procreative asymmetry*, according to which:

> **It is bad to create people with negative well-being, but not good to create people with positive well-being, all else equal.**

While many find this principle intuitive,[49] it's notoriously difficult to provide a principled basis for it.[50] The procreative asymmetry also has several deeply problematic implications stemming from its failure to consider positive lives to be a good thing.

The simplest such view holds that positive lives make *no difference in value* to the outcome. But this falsely implies that creating lives with low positive welfare is just as good as creating an equal number of lives at a high welfare level. For example, consider the choice between creating either of two worlds inhabited by different sets of future people. In world A_1, everyone has a

---

48. Jeff McMahan, "Causing People to Exist and Saving People's Lives," *The Journal of Ethics* 17 (June 2013): 5–35, https://doi.org/10.1007/s10892-012-9139-1; McMahan, "Asymmetries in the Morality of Causing People to Exist," in *Harming Future Persons*, ed. Melinda A. Roberts and David T. Wasserman, vol. 35, *International Library of Ethics, Law, and the New Medicine* (Dordrecht: Springer, 2009).

49. Though one of the coauthors of this chapter has argued elsewhere that "it is thought to be 'intuitive' primarily because it has been implicitly confused with other, more plausible theses." See Richard Y. Chappell, "Rethinking the Asymmetry," in "Ethics and Future Generations," ed. Rahul Kumar, special edition, *Canadian Journal of Philosophy* 47, no. 2–3 (2017): 167–77, https://doi.org/10.1080/00455091.2016.1250203.

50. McMahan, "Asymmetries in the Morality of Causing People to Exist."

wonderful life. In world A_2, all people have lives that are much worse than in A_1 yet still positive.

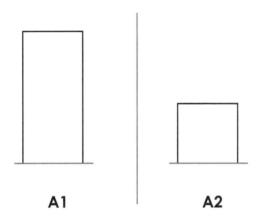

A1 | **A2**

Clearly, we should prefer world A_1 over A_2. However, the simplest version of the procreative asymmetry implies that both worlds are equally good—because they are not good at all.

In cases involving comparisons to empty worlds, the simple procreative asymmetry sometimes yields verdicts that seem even more misguided. Consider the following choice between world A and world B:[51]

> **In world A, all but a few people have excellent lives. But some people suffer from an extremely rare disease that makes life not worth living. In world B, no people exist.**

---

51. Case description adapted from Nicholas Beckstead, "On the Overwhelming Importance of Shaping the Far-Future" (PhD diss., Rutgers University, 2013), https://drive.google.com/file/d/0B8P94pg6WYCIc0lXSUVYS1BnMkE/view?resourcekey=0-nk6wM1QIPl0q WVh2z9FG4Q.

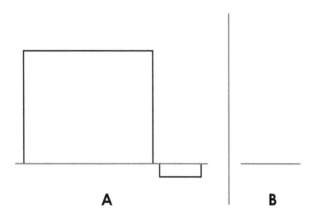

Person-affecting views and the asymmetry

Most people would prefer world A over an empty world B. But the simple procreative asymmetry would seem, perversely, to favor the empty world B since it counts the many good lives in world A for nothing while the few bad lives dominate the decision. On this view, there are no worthwhile trade-offs between good and bad lives. It would be better, supposedly, to have no lives at all.

To help address these problems, we may consider a more complex person-affecting view—one analogous to the critical range theory discussed above, but with infinite value blur, yielding the result that *all* (positive) lives are meh.[52] On such a view, it's better to create a flourishing life than a mediocre one (so A_1 is indeed better than A_2, at least if they contain the exact same number of people). However, *either* choice is merely on a par with creating neither.

But this brings us to a deeper problem with the procreative asymmetry, which is that it has trouble accounting for the idea that *we should be positively glad that the world (with all its worthwhile lives) exists.*[53] Granted, the immense incomparability introduced by all the putatively meh lives in A at least blocks the perverse conclusion that we must outright prefer the empty world B. Even so, holding the two worlds to be incomparable or "on a par" also seems wrong.

We should recognize that A is better. But to do that, we must reject the strict procreative asymmetry and hold that there is an upper limit to the "critical range"

---

52. A major challenge for such a view would be to explain how to render this value blur compatible with the asymmetry, so that miserable lives are appropriately recognized as bad (not merely meh).

53. At least on the assumption that good lives predominate over miserable ones, e.g., a person in world A should be glad that that world exists.

of lives that are merely meh. And this is independently plausible. After all, when thinking about what makes some possible universe *good*, the most obvious answer is that it contains a predominance of awesome, flourishing lives. How could that *not* be better than a barren rock? Any view that denies this verdict is arguably too nihilistic and divorced from humanistic values to be worth taking seriously.

We may also raise more theoretical objections to such a view. Person-affecting views typically fall afoul of one or more of the following problems:[54]

1. having moral rankings change when "irrelevant alternatives" are introduced (such as preferring A to B when they are the only choices, but then B over A when an inferior option C is also available);

2. having cyclical orderings of value (saying that A is better than B, B is better than C, and C is better than A); and

3. saying that all outcomes that differ even slightly in how many people exist are incomparable.

For all these reasons, utilitarians are largely united in rejecting person-affecting views, even as they continue to debate which impersonal theory provides the best way forward.[55]

Practical Implications of Population Ethical Theories

Population ethics is a field of great importance for real-world decision-making. In particular, which population ethical view we adopt shapes the importance we should assign to preserving and improving the long-term future of humanity. If human civilization persists and perhaps one day spreads to the stars, there could be an inconceivably large number of future people with good lives. Their existence

---

54. Arrhenius, "Future Generations," chap. 8; Ord, *Precipice*, esp. appendices, n25.

55. Another possibility would be some form of *hybrid* view combining an impersonal theory with additional person-affecting reasons to prioritize the interests of existing individuals. This would help to block "replaceability" worries—i.e., that impersonal views make it too easy to justify (killing and) replacing existing lives with "better" ones—without the extreme implications of pure person-affecting views. For a fascinating discussion of some of the complexities of adjudicating trade-offs between ordinary harms and benefits and the non-comparative good of bringing someone into (happy) existence, see McMahan, "Causing People to Exist and Saving People's Lives," 5–35.

and well-being depend in part on the choices we make today, especially how many resources we, the current generation, invest in preventing existential risks that threaten the continued survival and long-term flourishing of humankind.[56]

The total well-being enjoyed by all future people is potentially enormous. Consequently, on the total view, the disvalue of losing our future is immense, and the mitigation of existential risks becomes correspondingly important. The same conclusion also holds for critical level (or range) theories, assuming that the average well-being of future generations exceeds the critical level (or range).[57]

Even on the average view, there is reason to expect the long-term future to make a big difference to the overall value of the world. Human welfare has improved dramatically in recent centuries due to technological, social, and moral progress. Consequently, our generation is driving up the average of human well-being to date.[58] Further scientific and medical breakthroughs will likely continue to improve the average quality of life in the future. Therefore, even on the average view, it should be a priority to avoid existential risks by virtue of the large future gains in average well-being. The same is true for variable value theories, as they tend to approximate the average view for large populations.[59]

---

56. In addition to existential risk reduction, another promising strategy to improve the long-term future is "moral circle expansion": increasing the moral concern for members of some outlying groups to include, ideally, all sentient beings. Jacy Reese Anthis and Eze Paez, "Moral Circle Expansion: A Promising Strategy to Impact the Far Future," *Futures* 130 (June 2021), https://doi.org/10.1016/j.futures.2021.102756.

57. This assumption is plausible: with continued technological, social, and moral progress, the average quality of life in the future will likely increase further, as it has for hundreds of years. Only an implausibly high critical level—on which even the value of the average life in the present generation is negative—may render invalid the conclusion that existential risk reduction should be a priority.

58. Although the suffering on factory farms might mean that our generation is driving *down* the average well-being among sentient creatures, once you consider all the suffering-filled animal lives we have created. But technological improvements, particularly the development of cultivated meat and other animal product alternatives, could render factory farming a temporary phenomenon. See "The Science of Cultivated Meat," Good Food Institute, accessed May 23, 2024, https://gfi.org/science/the-science-of-cultivated-meat/.

59. If what counts as a "large" population is much greater than the current population, this further increases the importance assigned by variable values theories to avoiding existential risks since they approximate the total view for small populations.

Proponents of standard person-affecting views (with a strict procreative asymmetry) are skeptical of the claim that reducing existential risk is of enormous importance. They would still think that reducing these risks has some value because this reduces the risk of death for those alive today. But they would not regard the absence of future generations as an intrinsic moral loss. However, while these strict asymmetric views may not be concerned about the prospect of human extinction, they may seriously worry about the possibility of a dystopian future containing many miserable lives. Averting such a negative future would be critically important on these views.[60] Others might be drawn to a weaker (and correspondingly more plausible) version of the asymmetry, according to which we do have some reason to create flourishing lives but *stronger* reason to help existing people or to avoid lives of negative well-being. On these moderate views, ensuring that the future goes well would still be very important since so many lives are at stake.

Finally, there is an argument from moral uncertainty: given the difficult terrain of population ethics, we may not be entirely confident of any particular view. Therefore, we should figure out what degree of belief we ought to have in each theory and then take the action that is the best compromise between those theories. As we've seen, many plausible theories agree that improving the long-term future is of great moral importance. Therefore, unless one can be extremely confident in standard person-affecting views, it would seem prudent to pay heed to this conclusion and take significant steps to safeguard our future.[61]

---

60. For instance, David Althaus and Lukas Gloor argue that reducing risks of astronomical future suffering should be an ethical priority. Althaus and Gloor, "Reducing Risks of Astronomical Suffering: A Neglected Priority," Center on Long-Term Risk, last updated August 2019, https://longtermrisk.org/reducing-risks-of-astronomical-suffering-a-neglected-priority/.

61. Hilary Greaves and Toby Ord argue that (given a plausible approach for dealing with moral uncertainty) as the expected number of future lives grows, this "systematically pushes one toward choosing the option preferred by the Total View and critical-level views, even if one's credence in those theories is low." Greaves and Ord, "Moral Uncertainty about Population Axiology," *Journal of Ethics and Social Philosophy* 12, no. 2 (2017): https://doi.org/10.26556/jesp.v12i2.223. See also William MacAskill, Krister Bykvist, and Toby Ord, "Practical Ethics Given Moral Uncertainty," chap. 8 in *Moral Uncertainty* (Oxford: Oxford University Press, 2020); Ord, "Population Ethics and Existential Risk" appendix B to *Precipice*.

Conclusion

Our actions affect the quality, quantity, and identity of future lives. Population ethics deals with the thorny moral issues arising from such effects on future generations.

According to the total view of population ethics, an outcome's goodness depends only on the total well-being, which may be increased by either improving existing people's lives or creating more happy people. In contrast, the average view considers only average well-being and so only regards above-average lives as contributing (positive) value to the world. Variable value theories seek to better reflect commonly held intuitions about population ethics by approximating the total view for small populations and the average view for large populations. Critical level (or range) theories hold that adding an individual makes an outcome better to the extent that their well-being exceeds some critical level (or range). Finally, person-affecting views deny that additional lives ever make the outcome (non-instrumentally) better.

All of these views are subject to serious objections. The total view entails the repugnant conclusion, according to which, for any world A (however idyllic), there is a better world Z in which no one has a life that is more than barely worth living. The average view, variable value theories, and critical level theories all entail versions of the sadistic conclusion; that it can sometimes be better to create (few) lives with negative well-being than to create (more) lives with positive well-being. Person-affecting views rely on an unsupported asymmetry and struggle to explain the value of existence (even in the most idyllic cases). Critical range theories may do better, but even they cannot support the anti-repugnance intuition that an idyllic world A is strictly better than a repugnant world Z. The ubiquity of these problems is no coincidence: impossibility theorems prove that no population ethical theory can satisfy all the intuitive principles or axioms that we might have hoped for.

The most important practical implications of population ethics concern how much value we should assign to preserving and improving humanity's long-term future and hence how important it is to reduce existential risks.

The next chapter discusses the most important implications of utilitarianism for how we should think about leading an ethical life.

For additional resources and study aids, see https://utilitarianism.net/

6

Utilitarianism and Practical Ethics

Are we to extend our concern to all the beings capable of pleasure and pain whose feelings are affected by our conduct? or are we to confine our view to human happiness? The former view is the one adopted by . . . the Utilitarian school . . . it seems arbitrary and unreasonable to exclude from the end, as so conceived, any pleasure of any sentient being.

—Henry Sidgwick[1]

Introduction

Utilitarianism has important implications for how we should think about leading an ethical life. In this chapter, we focus on five of its theoretical implications. First, unlike many other ethical theories, utilitarianism does not regard actions and omissions as morally different. Second, it is unusually demanding: it asks us to sacrifice more than many other ethical theories do. Third, it implies that we should be *cause-impartial*: that we should apply our altruistic efforts wherever we can have the most positive impact. Fourth, it urges us to consider the well-being of individuals regardless of what country they live in, what species they belong to, and at what point in time they exist. Fifth, despite differing radically from commonsense morality as an approach to ethics, utilitarianism generally does endorse commonsense moral prohibitions.

We discuss how utilitarians should conduct their lives in Chapter 7 (Acting on Utilitarianism). In brief, most utilitarians should donate a significant portion of

---

1. Sidgwick, *The Methods of Ethics*, 7th ed. (Indianapolis, IN: Hackett Publishing, 1981), book IV, 414.

their income to address the world's most pressing problems, devote their careers to doing good, and aspire to high degrees of cooperativeness, personal integrity, and honesty.

Is There a Difference between Doing and Allowing Harm?

> *A person may cause evil to others not only by his actions but by his inaction,*
> *and in either case he is justly accountable to them for the injury.*
>
> —John Stuart Mill, *On Liberty*

Many non-consequentialists believe there is a morally relevant difference between *doing harm and allowing harm,* even if the consequences of an action or inaction are the same. This position is known as the Doctrine of Doing and Allowing, according to which harms caused by actions—by things we actively do—are worse than harms of omission. Those who subscribe to this doctrine may, for instance, claim that it's worse to harm a child, all else being equal, than it is to fail to prevent the same child from being harmed in an accident.

Of course, all else is typically not equal. From the perspective of consequentialists and non-consequentialists alike, a societal norm allowing people to harm children would be worse than one allowing people to neglect preventing children from being harmed accidentally. This is because actively harming children could set a precedent encouraging others to harm children more, which would have worse overall consequences. Doing harm may well be *instrumentally* worse than allowing harm, even if the *Doctrine of Doing and Allowing* is false.

However, while consequentialists—including utilitarians—accept that doing harm is typically instrumentally worse than allowing harm, they deny that doing harm is intrinsically worse than allowing harm. For utilitarians, only the outcomes matter. To the harmed child, the result is the same—whether you do the harming or someone else does and you fail to prevent it. When considered from the child's perspective, the action-omission distinction is irrelevant: whether their suffering results from your deliberate action or your neglect, they suffer the same either way.

It matters a great deal whether or not there is an intrinsic moral difference between doing and allowing harm. As pointed out above, the *Doctrine of Doing and Allowing* is at the heart of the disagreement between many consequentialists and non-consequentialists. Furthermore, it matters for real-world decision-making. For instance, the ethics guidelines of many medical associations never allow doctors to actively and intentionally cause the death of a patient. However, it's acceptable for doctors to intentionally let a patient die under certain circumstances, such as if the patient is in great pain and wants to end their life. This distinction—between a doctor letting a terminally ill patient die and a doctor actively assisting a patient who wants to end their life—is regarded as less relevant from a utilitarian perspective. If we allow doctors to let a terminally ill patient (who wishes to end their suffering) die, a utilitarian would argue that doctors should also be permitted to actively assist a patient to bring about their death with their consent.

Demandingness

Utilitarianism is typically understood to be a very demanding ethical theory: it maintains that any time you can do more to help other people than you can to help yourself, you should do so.[2] For example, if you could sacrifice your life to save the lives of several other people then, other things being equal, according to utilitarianism, you ought to do so.

Though occasions where sacrificing your own life is the best thing to do are rare, utilitarianism may realistically recommend many other significant sacrifices. For example, by donating to a highly effective global health charity, you can save a child's life for just a few thousand dollars.[3] As long as the benefits others receive from such donations exceeds what you would gain from keeping the money for yourself—as they almost certainly do, if you are a typical citizen of an affluent country—you should give it away. Indeed, you should probably donate

---

2. Though, as flagged in Chapter 13 (The Demandingness Objection), this may not actually be so demanding if the "should" claim merely indicates what is morally *ideal*, rather than what is *required to avoid deserving moral blame or criticism*. For a discussion of demandingness in the context of global poverty alleviation, see Peter Singer, *The Life You Can Save: Acting Now to End World Poverty*, 2nd ed. (Bainbridge Island, WA: The Life You Can Save, 2019), available free at http://www.thelifeyoucansave.org/the-book/.

3. "Your Dollar Goes Further Overseas," GiveWell, accessed May 23, 2024, https://www.givewell.org/giving101/Your-dollar-goes-further-overseas.

the majority of your lifetime income. According to utilitarianism, it's only truly justifiable to spend money on yourself—such as by going out to the movies or buying nice clothes—if you think that this expenditure would do more good than any possible donation (for example, by helping you work harder so that you will subsequently give away even more). This is a very high bar.

As well as recommending very significant donations, utilitarianism claims that you ought to choose whatever career will most benefit others. This might involve non-profit work, conducting important research, or going into politics or advocacy.

Cause Impartiality

The prevailing view on helping others is that whom we should help and how we should help them is a matter of personal preference. On this common view, one may choose whether to focus on education, the arts, endangered species, or some other cause on the basis of one's personal passions.[4]

However, utilitarians argue that we should not choose our focus based primarily on personal attachment to a social cause; instead, we should apply our focus wherever we can have the most positive impact on others. Utilitarianism entails what we may call *cause impartiality*.[5]

> **Cause impartiality is the view that one's choice of social cause to focus on should just depend on the expected amount of good that one would do by focusing on that cause.**

To illustrate this idea, suppose that you could donate to one of two different charities. One provides bednets to protect children from malaria, and the other treats cancer patients. Suppose that you will save twice as many lives by donating to the bednet charity than by donating to the cancer charity; however, a family

4. Johnathan Z. Berman et al., "Impediments to Effective Altruism: The Role of Subjective Preferences in Charitable Giving," *Psychological Science* 29, no. 5 (2018): 834–44, https://doi .org/10.1177/0956797617747648.

5. The case for cause neutrality is made in "The Benefits of Cause-Neutrality," *Effective Altruism Foundation* (blog), April 11, 2017, https://ea-foundation.org/blog/the-benefits-of-cause -neutrality-2/.

member died of cancer, so you have a personal attachment to that cause. Should you, therefore, give to the cancer charity?

The utilitarian would argue not. On the utilitarian view, the importance of saving twice as many lives outweighs the personal attachment that might bring the donor to prioritize the cancer sufferers. From the viewpoint of utilitarianism, we should be completely impartial in deciding which social cause to support and instead let this decision be driven only by the question of where we can do the most good.

Importantly, we know that some ways of benefiting individuals do much more good than others. For example, within the cause of global health and development, some interventions are over 100 times as effective as others.[6] Furthermore, many researchers believe that the difference in expected impact among *causes* is as great as the differences among *interventions within a particular cause*. If so, focusing on the very best causes is vastly more impactful than focusing on average ones.

The Expanding Moral Circle

A crucial question in deciding which cause to dedicate our efforts to regards which individuals we should include in our moral deliberations.

We now recognize that characteristics like race, gender, and sexual orientation do not justify discriminating against individuals or disregarding their suffering. Over time, our society has gradually expanded our moral concern to ever more groups, a trend of moral progress often called the *expanding moral circle*.[7] But what are the limits of this trend? Should the moral circle include all humans but stop there? Should it be expanded to include non-human animals as well? Or should it ultimately extend even to plants and the natural environment?

Utilitarianism provides a clear response to this question: we should extend our moral concern to all *sentient beings*, meaning every individual capable of experiencing positive or negative conscious states. This includes humans and many

---

6. Toby Ord, "The Moral Imperative towards Cost-Effectiveness in Global Health," *Center for Global Development*, March 2013, https://pdfs.semanticscholar.org/1016/bb6788716e7b 489c08853ce64f0063870a4b.pdf.

7. Cf. Peter Singer, *The Expanding Circle: Ethics, Evolution, and Moral Progress* (Princeton, NJ: Princeton University Press, 2011).

non-human animals, but presumably not plants or other non-sentient entities. This view is sometimes called *sentiocentrism*, as it regards sentience as the characteristic that entitles individuals to moral concern. Justifying this perspective, Peter Singer writes:

> The capacity for suffering and enjoying things is a prerequisite for having interests at all, a condition that must be satisfied before we can speak of interests in any meaningful way. It would be nonsense to say that it was not in the interests of a stone to be kicked along the road by a child. A stone does not have interests because it cannot suffer. Nothing that we can do to it could possibly make any difference to its welfare. A mouse, on the other hand, does have an interest in not being tormented, because mice will suffer if they are treated in this way. . . .
>
> *If a being suffers, there can be no moral justification for refusing to take that suffering into consideration.* No matter what the nature of the being, the principle of equality requires that the suffering be counted equally with the like suffering—in so far as rough comparisons can be made—of any other being. If a being is not capable of suffering, or of experiencing enjoyment or happiness, there is nothing to be taken into account. This is why the limit of sentience . . . is the only defensible boundary of concern for the interests of others.[8]

On this basis, a priority for utilitarians may be to help society to continue to widen its moral circle of concern. For instance, we may want to persuade people that they should help not just those in their own country but also those on the other side of the world; not just those of their own species but all sentient creatures; and not just people currently alive but any people whose lives they can affect, including those in generations to come.

---

8. Peter Singer, *Practical Ethics*, 3rd ed. (Cambridge: Cambridge University Press, 2011), 50.

Cosmopolitanism: Expanding the Moral Circle across Geography

According to utilitarianism, geographical distance and national membership are not intrinsically morally relevant. This means that, by the lights of utilitarianism, we have no grounds for discriminating against someone because of where they live, where they come from, or their nationality. This makes utilitarianism an example of *moral cosmopolitanism*. Proponents of moral cosmopolitanism believe that if you have the means to save a life in a faraway country, doing so matters just as much as saving a life close by in your own country; all lives deserve equal moral consideration, wherever they are.

Of course, the geographical distance between oneself and one's beneficiary may matter instrumentally—it's often easier to help people close by than far away. However, in an increasingly globalized world, it has become much easier to benefit even those who live on the other side of the world. And because of extreme global economic inequalities, an additional unit of resources benefits people in the least-developed countries much more than people in affluent countries like the United States or the United Kingdom—potentially 100 to 1,000 times more.[9]

Anti-Speciesism: Expanding the Moral Circle across Species

Utilitarianism cares not only about the well-being of humans but also about the well-being of non-human animals. Consequently, utilitarianism rejects *speciesism*: the practice of giving some individuals less moral consideration than others or treating them worse based on their species membership. To give individuals moral consideration is simply to consider how one's behavior will affect them, whether by action or omission. As Peter Singer describes it:

> Racists violate the principle of equality by giving greater weight to the interests of members of their own race when there is a clash between their interests and the interests of those of another race. Sexists violate the

---

9. Cf. William MacAskill, *Doing Good Better: Effective Altruism and How You Can Make a Difference* (New York: Penguin Random House, 2015), chap. 1.

principle of equality by favoring the interests of their own sex. Similarly, speciesists allow the interests of their own species to override the greater interests of members of other species. The pattern is identical in each case.[10]

There is a growing scientific consensus that many non-human animals are sentient,[11] though not necessarily to the same degree. This includes most vertebrates, such as mammals, birds, and fish, and potentially some invertebrates, such as octopodes or even insects. These animals can feel pleasure and pain, and these experiences are morally relevant from a utilitarian perspective.

Rejecting speciesism entails giving *equal moral consideration* to the well-being of all individuals but does not entail treating all species equally. Species membership is not morally relevant *in itself*, but individuals belonging to different species may differ in other ways that do matter morally. In particular, it's likely that individuals from different species do not have the same capacity for conscious experience—for instance, because of the differing numbers of neurons in their brains. Since utilitarians believe that only sentience matters morally in itself, the utilitarian concern for individuals is proportional to their capacity for conscious experience. It's perfectly consistent with a rejection of speciesism to say we should equally consider the well-being of a fish and a chimpanzee without implying that they have the capacity to suffer to the same degree.

From the utilitarian perspective, what matters *intrinsically* is the well-being of individual sentient beings, not the survival of the species or the integrity of the ecosystem or of nature. Individuals can suffer, while a "species," an "ecosystem," or "nature" cannot. Of course, the survival of species and the integrity of ecosystems

---

10. Peter Singer, *Animal Liberation Now: The Definitive Classic Renewed* (New York: Harper-Collins), 8. Indeed, there is psychological evidence suggesting that speciesism goes hand in hand with other discriminatory attitudes like racism, sexism, and homophobia. Cf. Lucius Caviola, Jim A. C. Everett, and Nadira S. Faber, "The Moral Standing of Animals: Towards a Psychology of Speciesism," *Journal of Personality and Social Psychology* 116, no. 6 (2017), 1011–29, https://doi.org/10.1037/pspp0000182.

11. For instance, see the "Cambridge Declaration on Consciousness," from Phillip Low et al. (2012). See Wikipedia, s.v. "Animal Consciousness," last modified April 24, 2024, 20:05, https://en.wikipedia.org/wiki/Animal_consciousness#Cambridge_Declaration_on_Consciousness.

and of nature may well be important instrumentally, to the extent that they contribute to the well-being of individuals.

Speciesism underlies the current exploitation of billions of non-human animals by humans. Animals are widely seen as resources: raised and slaughtered for food, used for clothing, or exploited for their work. These practices often result in the animals experiencing extreme suffering.

However, not all animal suffering is caused by humans. There are many more wild animals living in nature than there are domesticated animals.[12] In contrast to the widespread romanticized view of nature, wild animals generally live short lives in harsh environments. They experience suffering from many sources, including predation, disease, parasites, exposure to extreme heat or cold, hunger, thirst, and malnutrition. Against this background, it would be wrong to consider only the well-being of domesticated animals, which humans actively harm, while ignoring the well-being of wild animals, which humans merely allow to be harmed.[13] As noted earlier, for the utilitarian, the distinction between doing and allowing harm is irrelevant. Therefore, from the utilitarian viewpoint, we should care equally about the welfare of domestic and wild animals. That said, we currently know little about how to systematically improve the lives of wild animals. By contrast, reducing society's consumption of factory-farmed meat or improving conditions on factory farms would yield clear and enormous benefits for animals.[14]

---

12. Brian Tomasik, "How Many Wild Animals Are There?," updated August 7, 2019, https://reducing-suffering.org/how-many-wild-animals-are-there/.

13. There is an ongoing academic debate about the moral importance of wild animal welfare. For example, see Yew-Kwang Ng, "Towards Welfare Biology: Evolutionary Economics of Animal Consciousness and Suffering," *Biology and Philosophy* 10, no. 3 (July 2019): 255–85, https://doi.org/10.1007/BF00852469; Jeff McMahan, "The Moral Problem of Predation," in *Philosophy Comes to Dinner: Arguments on the Ethics of Eating*, ed. Andrew Chignell, Terence Cuneo, and Matthew C. Halteman (London: Routledge, 2013); Ole Martin Moen, "The Ethics of Wild Animal Suffering," *Etikk I Praksis - Nordic Journal of Applied Ethics* 10, no. 1 (2016): 1–14, https://doi.org/10.5324/eip.v10i1.1972.

14. For a further discussion of this topic we recommend this interview with researcher Persis Eskander: Robert Wiblin and Keiran Harris, "Animals in the Wild Often Suffer a Great Deal. We Ask Persis Eskander—What, If Anything—Should We Do about That?," *80,000 Hours Podcast with Rob Wiblin*, April 15, 2019, 02:57:57, https://80000hours.org/podcast/episodes/persis-eskander-wild-animal-welfare/.

Longtermism: Expanding the Moral Circle across Time

From the utilitarian perspective, people on the other side of the planet matter no less than people closer to us geographically. In the same way, utilitarianism regards the well-being of future generations as no less important, simply because they are far away in time, than the well-being of those alive today.

A striking fact about the history of civilization is just how early in it we appear to be. There are 5,000 years of recorded history behind us, but how many years are potentially still to come? If we merely last as long as the typical mammalian species, we still have 200,000 years to go. But humans are not typical mammals, and if we can preserve our species, there could be a further one billion years until the earth is no longer habitable,[15] and other planets and solar systems will be around for trillions of years. Even on the most conservative of these timelines, we've progressed through a tiny fraction of recorded history. If humanity's saga were a novel, we would still be on the first page.

There could be astronomically more people in the future than in the present generation. This strongly suggests that, to help people in general, your key concern should not be to merely help the present generation, but to ensure that the long-term future goes as well as possible.[16] This idea is known as *strong longtermism*:

> **Strong longtermism is the view that the most important determinant of the value of our actions today is how those actions affect the very long-run future.**

Strong longtermism is implied by most plausible forms of utilitarianism[17] if we assume that some of our actions can meaningfully affect the long-term future and that we can

---

15. Fred C. Adams, "Long-Term Astrophysical Processes," in *Global Catastrophic Risks*, ed. Nick Bostrom and Milan Ćirković (Oxford: Oxford University Press, 2008).

16. For a discussion of this idea and its underlying assumptions, see Nicholas Beckstead, "On the Overwhelming Importance of Shaping the Far-Future" (PhD diss., Rutgers University, 2013), https://drive.google.com/file/d/0B8P94pg6WYCIc0lXSUVYS1BnMkE/view?resourcekey=0-nk6wM1QIPl0qWVh2z9FG4Q.

17. Cf. Hilary Greaves and William MacAskill, "The Case for Strong Longtermism" (GPI Working Paper 5-2021, Global Priorities Institute, 2019), Section 4.1, https://globalpriorities institute.org/hilary-greaves-william-macaskill-the-case-for-strong-longtermism/.

estimate which effects are positive and which are negative. For example, there are risks to the continued survival of the human race, including from nuclear war, extreme climate change, man-made pathogens, and artificial general intelligence.[18] If we believe that the continued survival of the human race is positive in value, then reducing the risk of human extinction is a way of positively influencing the very long-run future.[19] A discussion of longtermism would go beyond the scope of this chapter, but to learn more, we recommend reading "The Case for Strong Longtermism."[20]

Respecting Commonsense Moral Norms

Sometimes, people mistake utilitarianism as claiming that *one ought always to explicitly calculate the expected value of each possible action and do whatever act scores highest.* Utilitarianism does *not* in fact recommend adopting this "naive utilitarian" decision procedure.[21]

Instead, as a multi-level theory, utilitarianism specifies moral goals—criteria for objectively judging the moral merits of an action, given all the relevant factual details[22]—but leaves open the question of what kind of *decision procedure* we should try to follow in practice. After all, it's an open empirical question how best to actually achieve the specified moral goals.

Utilitarianism implies that we should use whatever decision procedure would best help us to promote overall well-being (in expectation). While we cannot be certain what decision procedure satisfies this criterion, we can offer some

---

18. For a detailed discussion of existential risks and the moral importance of humanity's long-run future, see Toby Ord, *The Precipice: Existential Risk and the Future of Humanity* (London: Bloomsbury Publishing, 2020).

19. For a classic paper on the importance of reducing existential risk, see Nick Bostrom, "Existential Risk Prevention as Global Priority," *Global Policy* 4, no 1 (February 2013): 15–31, http://www.existential-risk.org/concept.pdf.

20. Greaves and MacAskill, "Case for Strong Longtermism."

21. As Chapter 2 explains: "To our knowledge, no one has ever defended single-level utilitarianism [i.e., using the utilitarian criterion as a universal decision procedure], including the classical utilitarians. Deliberately calculating the expected consequences of our actions is error-prone and risks falling into decision paralysis."

22. Such details might simply be stipulated in a hypothetical example. In real-life cases, our uncertainty about relevant factual details should generally carry over to make us similarly uncertain about our moral verdicts and evaluations.

educated guesses. As psychologists Stefan Schubert and Lucius Caviola argue in "Virtues for Real-World Utilitarians,"[23] we may best promote overall well-being by ambitiously pursuing robustly good actions that effectively help others while minimizing downside risks by means of commonsense virtues and constraints.

It's widely recognized that humans are unreliable at calculating utilities,[24] especially when they conflict with generally reliable rules and heuristics (such as those prohibiting harm to others). As a result, we cannot take rule-violating expected value calculations at face value. Even if you've calculated that it would somehow serve the greater good to murder your rival, you should be very skeptical that this is true. After all, if you don't really believe that it would overall be best for others (similarly situated) to do likewise, then you must believe that most calculations favoring murder have actually gone awry. So, if you've no special (symmetry-breaking) evidence establishing that you, in particular, are the rare exception to this rule, then you must conclude that your own murderous calculations have most likely gone awry.[25] Thus, absent special evidence, you should conclude that your rule-breaking actually has lower expected value, despite your initial calculation to the contrary.

We can be most confident that our actions have positive expected value when we instead seek to help others in ways that are supported by good evidence and minimize downside risk.[26] Over the long run, we should expect honest,

---

23. Schubert and Caviola, "Virtues for Real-World Utilitarians," accessed May 23, 2024, https://www.utilitarianism.net/guest-essays/virtues-for-real-world-utilitarians/.

24. See, e.g., J. L. Mackie, "Rights, Utility, and Universalization," in *Utility and Rights*, ed. R. G. Frey (Oxford: Basil Blackwell, 1985).

25. In particular, you can't take at face value your inclination to think that there are special reasons in your case if you believe that most people in subjectively similar situations are mistaken in taking themselves to have such special reasons. Symmetry-breaking evidence is evidence that *distinctively* establishes your reliability in comparison to others with similar (but, in their case, misguided) beliefs. Note that such symmetry-breaking evidence is very hard to come by!

26. That's not to say that we should strictly optimize for *confidence* in positive expected value (EV): Something that's *certainly barely good* in expectation may be less worth pursuing than something that is *almost* certainly high EV even if there's a slight risk that you've overlooked something that would mean the action is actually mildly negative in expectation. Such uncertainty could still result in higher "all things considered" expected value, in principle. The point is just that grounds for doubting a positive verdict from our initial EV calculations should rationally lead us to assign lower (and, in some cases, even *negative*) EV to that option, all things considered. And in practice, it seems that we should often have strong priors that

cooperative altruism to do more good than ruthless scheming for the "greater good" because (i) historically, ruthless schemers often do more harm than good; (ii) people rightly don't trust ruthless schemers; and (iii) in a complex world, it's difficult to get much done without others' trust and cooperation. If that's right, honest cooperative altruism systematically has *higher expected value* than ruthless scheming and should be preferred by utilitarians.

In summary, utilitarianism does *not* tell us to constantly calculate utilities and blindly follow whatever our calculations recommend. That would be predictably counterproductive, contrary to the pragmatic spirit of the theory. Instead, utilitarianism recommends decision procedures based on their expected value. When we are uncertain, we should be guided by whatever decision procedure can most reasonably (in light of everything we know about human biases and cognitive limitations) be expected to yield better outcomes. This means following *heuristics* or generally reliable rules of thumb.

As a very rough first pass, a plausible utilitarian decision procedure might direct us to:[27]

1. pursue any "low-hanging fruit" for effectively helping others while avoiding harm;
2. inculcate virtues for real-world utilitarians (including respect for commonsense moral norms); and
3. in a calm moment, reflect on how we could better prioritize and allocate our moral efforts, including by seeking out expert cost-benefit analyses and other evidence to better inform our overall judgments of expected value.[28]

---

rights-violating actions are net-negative, which a rough and broadly unreliable calculation should not suffice to overturn.

27. These claims are not, strictly speaking, built into utilitarianism as a fundamental moral theory. Rather, we are speculating about the further question of *what decision procedure has the highest expected value in typical circumstances*. (Note that, in principle, the answer may differ for individuals in different circumstances. Nothing in utilitarianism requires uniformity if that would not be for the best.)

28. This might (but need not) include performing some "back of the envelope" calculations of expected value. To truly maximize expected value, these naive calculations must be tempered by constraints against ruthless scheming, given our prior judgment that the latter is most likely counterproductive. That is, if we calculate a slightly higher explicit "expected value" for one act than another, but the former involves egregious norm-breaking, we should probably conclude that the latter (safer) option is *actually* better in expectation.

Conclusion

Utilitarianism has important implications for how we should think about leading an ethical life.

The theory rejects an intrinsic moral difference between doing and allowing harm. This position contributes to the demandingness of utilitarianism since it implies that whenever we decide not to help another person, we are complicit in their misery.

By the lights of utilitarianism, we should choose carefully which moral problems to work on and by what means, based on where we can do the most good. We should extend our moral concern to all sentient beings, meaning every individual capable of experiencing happiness or suffering. Utilitarianism urges us to consider the well-being of all individuals regardless of what species they belong to, what country they live in, and at what point in time they exist.

Though utilitarians should try to use their lives to do the most good they can, in practice they should do so while respecting commonsense moral virtues like honesty, integrity, fairness, and law-abidingness. There are reasons we do not see utilitarians robbing banks to donate the proceeds: these commonsense moral prohibitions help society to function smoothly, and any naive calculation that violating such a prohibition would promote the greater good is almost always mistaken.

7

Acting on Utilitarianism

Create all the happiness you are able to create; remove all the misery you are able to remove. Every day will allow you, will invite you to add something to the pleasure of others, or to diminish something of their pains.

—Jeremy Bentham[1]

Introduction

So far we've looked at utilitarianism from a theoretical viewpoint. But what does utilitarianism actually imply about *how we should live our lives*? What concrete actions does it say we should take? This chapter explains what it means to live an ethical life from the perspective of utilitarianism.

There are many problems in the world today, some of which are extremely large in scale. According to utilitarianism, each person ought to work on these problems and to try to improve the world by as much as possible, giving equal weight to the well-being of everyone. Unfortunately, our resources are scarce, so as individuals and even as a global society, we cannot solve all the world's problems at once. This means we must make decisions about how to prioritize the resources we have. Since not all ways of helping others are equally effective, utilitarianism implies that we should carefully choose which problems to work on and by what means.

To do the most good they can, in practice, many utilitarians donate a significant portion of their income to address the world's most pressing problems, devote their careers to doing good, and aspire to high degrees of cooperativeness, personal integrity, and honesty.

---

1. Bentham's advice to a young girl in 1830. Bentham, *Deontology Together with a Table of the Springs of Action and Article on Utilitarianism*, ed. Amnon Goldworth (Oxford: Clarendon Press, 1983), xix.

Throughout this chapter, we use expressions like "doing good" and "having an impact" as shorthand for increasing the well-being of others, in particular by promoting their happiness and preventing their suffering.

Opportunities to Help Others

Wealth and income are distributed extremely unequally across the globe. Middle-class members of rich countries like the United States and United Kingdom earn fifty times as much as the poorest 750 million people in the world, putting them in the richest 5 percent of the world's population.[2] This disparity in wealth means that well-off citizens of affluent nations are presented with outstanding opportunities to benefit others.

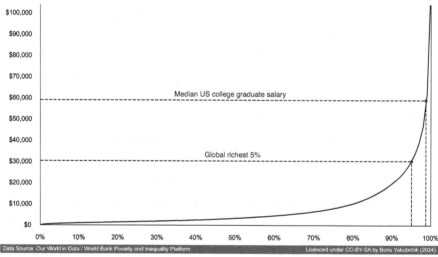

Global Income Distribution 2023
Percentile of world population vs income per household member
Incomes are adjusted and expressed in international dollars (PPP - Purchasing Power Parity)

Data Source: Our World in Data / World Bank Poverty and Inequality Platform   Licenced under CC-BY-SA by Boris Yakubchik (2024)

World income distribution. Earning above $30,000 per year puts you in the richest 5 percent of the world population.[3]

---

2. The World Bank estimated that 735 million people lived in extreme poverty in 2015, meaning they earned less than $1.90 per day (in 2011 prices). Thus, an annual income of $35,000 corresponds to fifty times the annual income of a person living just below the extreme poverty line. The World Bank, accessed Jan. 25, 2019, https://web.archive.org/web/20190125210957/ http://iresearch.worldbank.org/PovcalNet/povDuplicateWB.aspx.

3. Cf. "How Rich Am I?," Giving What We Can, accessed May 23, 2024, https://www.giving whatwecan.org/how-rich-am-i?income=30330&countryCode=USA&numAdults= 1&numChildren=0.

Wealth and income exhibit what economists call *diminishing marginal utility*.[4] The idea is simple: How much an individual's well-being is increased by receiving a higher income depends on their current income. While richer people report being more satisfied with their lives overall, the richer you become, the less well-being you get from additional money. An additional dollar benefits a poor farmer in Kenya much more than it benefits a middle-class member of a rich country.

The diminishing marginal utility of money implies that we can generally increase overall well-being by redistributing from the rich to the poor. The well-being affluent citizens forego by donating $100 is small compared to the benefit this money will give someone living in extreme poverty. Instead of buying new sneakers, your donation could give someone the equivalent of a year or more of healthy life.[5]

Given the diminishing marginal utility of money, the scourge of extreme global inequality implies that we can do an astonishing amount of good by donating to the global poor or other disadvantaged groups. For just a few dollars—the price of a coffee—we could pay for an insecticide-treated bednet that would protect two children in a developing country from malaria for two years.[6] And this money may go even further when spent on effective programs within other cause areas.

Utilitarianism implies that we should make helping others a central part of our lives. Further, utilitarianism urges us to use our resources not just to do some good but to do the most good we can. If we fail to produce the best outcome we can, more people will die than needed to die, or more people will suffer harms larger than they needed to suffer. If we think that the grave harms that others in this world suffer are urgent enough that we have a duty to use some of our resources

---

4. Cf. Moritz Drupp et al., "Discounting Disentangled," *American Economic Journal: Economic Policy* 10, no. 4 (2018): 109–34, http://www.lse.ac.uk/GranthamInstitute/wp-content/uploads/2015/06/Working-Paper-172-Drupp-et-al.pdf.

5. GiveWell estimates that their top charities have saved children's lives at an average cost of between $3,000 and $5,500, suggesting at least a year gained per $100. See "How Much Does It Cost to Save a Life," GiveWell, accessed May 23, 2024, https://www.givewell.org/how-much-does-it-cost-to-save-a-life.

6. "Mass Distribution of Insecticide-Treated Nets (ITNs)," GiveWell, accessed May 23, 2024, https://www.givewell.org/international/technical/programs/insecticide-treated-nets.

to fight those harms, that same duty requires us to use those resources in ways that help as much as possible.

How much should we sacrifice for the benefit of others? For well-off citizens of affluent countries, utilitarianism will say they should give a substantial portion of their resources to help others. However, utilitarians recognize that in deciding how much to give, it's important that we not let the best be the enemy of the good. It would be a mistake for us to give so much in the short run that we make ourselves miserable and burn out later on. In practice, most utilitarians try to figure out a level of sacrifice that is sustainable for them in the long run; for utilitarians focused on donations, this is typically between 10 percent and 50 percent of their income.

Effective Altruism

Many utilitarians undertake very significant personal sacrifices because of their belief in utilitarianism. But recently, some have argued that *what* one tries to do is even more important than *how much* sacrifice one undertakes. This is a key insight of the philosophy and social movement of *effective altruism*, which is endorsed by many utilitarians, such as Peter Singer.[7]

Those in the effective altruism movement try to figure out, of all the different uses of our resources, which ones will do the most good, impartially considered, and act on that basis. So defined, effective altruism is both a research project—to figure out how to do the most good—and a practical project to implement the best guesses we have about how to do the most good.[8]

---

7. In 2013, Peter Singer gave a TED talk on effective altruism: "The Why and How of Effective Altruism," filmed March 2013, TED video, 17:02, https://www.ted.com/talks/peter_singer_the_why_and_how_of_effective_altruism. For a more detailed and recent introduction to effective altruism, see William MacAskill, "Effective Altruism," forthcoming in *The Norton Introduction to Ethics*, ed. Elizabeth Harman and Alex Guerrero, https://www.williammacaskill.com/s/MacAskill_Effective_Altruism-1.pdf.

8. For a detailed philosophical discussion of effective altruism, see the sixteen articles in Hilary Greaves and Theron Pummer, eds., *Effective Altruism: Philosophical Issues* (Oxford: Oxford University Press, 2019).

While utilitarianism and effective altruism share certain similarities,[9] they are distinct and differ in important ways.[10] Unlike utilitarianism, effective altruism does not require that we sacrifice our own interests whenever doing so brings about a greater benefit to others. Unlike utilitarianism, effective altruism does not claim that we should always seek to maximize well-being, whatever the means. Finally, unlike utilitarianism, effective altruism does not equate the good with the total sum of well-being.[11] For these and other reasons, many members of the effective altruism community are not utilitarians; instead, they often give some weight to a range of different ethical theories.

Despite these differences, utilitarians are usually enthusiastic about effective altruism. The main reason is that, out of all communities, the effective altruism movement comes closest to applying core utilitarian ideas and values to the real world.

In addition, joining a community of people with shared aims like effective altruism can be one of the best ways for its members to increase their impact. Such a community allows a group of people to mutually support each other and to coordinate more effectively, thus achieving more than they could as individuals.

Members of the effective altruism movement often decompose the problem of how to do the most good into two parts: First, which problems ("causes") should I focus on? Second, what means should I take to address those problems? We will discuss these two questions in the remainder of this chapter.

Cause Prioritization

To figure out the most effective actions, we first need to know which causes to focus on. Utilitarians are *cause impartial*, meaning they aim to contribute to the causes where they expect to do the most good. Which causes would most

---

9. "It is true that effective altruism has some similarities with utilitarianism: it is maximising, it is primarily focused on improving wellbeing, many members of the community make significant sacrifices in order to do more good, and many members of the community self-describe as utilitarians." William MacAskill, "The Definition of Effective Altruism," in *Effective Altruism*.
10. See MacAskill, "The Definition of Effective Altruism."
11. Effective altruism "is compatible with egalitarianism, prioritarianism, and, because it does not claim that wellbeing is the only thing of value, with views on which non-welfarist goods are of value." MacAskill, "The Definition of Effective Altruism."

effectively promote well-being if they were further addressed? Finding the answer to that question is called *cause prioritization*.

Since some moral problems may be far more important than others, choosing what cause to focus on may be the greatest factor in how much good an individual will do. However, the world is complex, and we face high uncertainty about how best to improve the world. This uncertainty leads to reasonable disagreement about what causes to prioritize. But the effective altruism community has made some progress outlining three social causes that appear particularly pressing: (i) global health and development, (ii) farm animal welfare, and (iii) existential risk reduction.

Global Health and Development

One thing that greatly matters is the failure of we rich people to prevent, as we so easily could, much of the suffering and many of the early deaths of the poorest people in the world.

—Derek Parfit[12]

As explained in the previous chapter, utilitarians endorse cosmopolitanism, according to which the geographical distance between an actor and someone they can help is not morally relevant in itself. Cosmopolitanism implies that we should look for effective interventions to help others, regardless of their nationality, where they live, or where they come from.

On this basis, global health and development may be considered a particularly high-priority cause for utilitarians.[13] Efforts in this area have a great track record of improving lives, making this cause appear especially tractable. For most of human history, it was the norm that around two out of every five

---

12. Parfit, *On What Matters*, vol. 3 (Oxford: Oxford University Press, 2017), 436–37.
13. For instance, Peter Singer's book *The Life You Can Save* makes the case for the ethical importance of improving global health and international development. *The Life You Can Save: Acting Now to End World Poverty*, 2nd ed. (Bainbridge Island, WA: The Life You Can Save, 2019); the updated tenth anniversary edition is available for free download at https://www.thelifeyoucansave.org/the-book/.

children died before their fifth birthday, largely due to preventable causes. With improved sanitation and access to medical care, we've since made tremendous progress against child mortality, with global rates dropping as low as 4 percent by 2020.[14]

Global child mortality
The estimated share of newborns who die or survive the first five years of life.

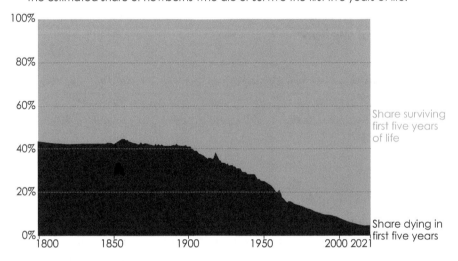

Data source: United Nations Inter-agency Group for Child Mortality Estimation (2023); Gapminder based on UN IGME & UN WPP (2020).
OurWorldInData.org/child-mortality | CC BY

However, this progress is no reason to rest on our laurels since we still have much further to go: around 16,000 children under fifteen still die worldwide every day.[15] Fortunately, we can help decrease this number even further. The best interventions in global health and development are incredibly cost-effective: GiveWell, a leading organization that conducts in-depth charity evaluations, estimates that

---

14. Saloni Dattani et al., "Child and Infant Mortality," OurWorldinData.org, accessed May 23, 2024, https://ourworldindata.org/child-mortality.

15. Saloni Dattani et al., "Child and Infant Mortality," OurWorldinData.org, accessed May 23, 2024, https://ourworldindata.org/child-mortality.

top-rated charities can prevent the death of a child from malaria for under $5,000 by providing preventive drugs.[16]

Other evidence-backed and cost-effective ways to help the very poor include distributing anti-malarial nets, offering vitamin A fortification, and simply transferring money.[17] All of these interventions present amazing opportunities to improve the well-being of others at very low cost to ourselves.

Farm Animal Welfare

The question is not, Can they reason? nor, Can they talk? but, Can they suffer? Why should the law refuse its protection to any sensitive being? . . . The time will come when humanity will extend its mantle over everything which breathes.

—Jeremy Bentham[18]

Improving the welfare of farmed animals should be a high moral priority for utilitarians. The argument for this conclusion is simple: first, animals matter morally; second, humans cause a huge amount of unnecessary suffering to animals in factory farms; and third, there are easy ways to reduce the number of farmed animals and the severity of their suffering. We will go over these premises one by one.

First, as explained in the previous chapter, utilitarians reject speciesism: discrimination against those who do not belong to a certain species. By the lights of utilitarianism, we should give equal moral consideration to the well-being of all individuals, regardless of what species they belong to.[19]

---

16. "Your Dollar Goes Further Overseas," GiveWell, accessed May 23, 2024, https://www.givewell.org/giving101/Your-dollar-goes-further-overseas.

17. "Our Top Charities," GiveWell, accessed May 23, 2024, https://www.givewell.org/charities/top-charities. See also GiveDirectly, https://www.givedirectly.org/.

18. Bentham, *An Introduction to the Principles of Morals and Legislation*, ed. Jonathan Bennett (London, 1789; Early Modern Texts, 2017), 143–44, https://www.earlymoderntexts.com/assets/pdfs/bentham1780.pdf.

19. As explained in the previous chapter, giving equal moral consideration to all animals does not necessarily imply that we should treat them all equally.

Second, we find ourselves in a historically unprecedented situation, where every year, humans kill around seventy billion land animals for food.[20] The vast majority of these spend their lives in factory farms in horrendous conditions,[21] crammed together with little space, without natural light or stimuli, and at constant risk of developing ailments such as weakened or broken bones, infections, and organ failure. Most have their lives ended prematurely when they are slaughtered for food. These suffering animals are probably among the worst-off creatures on this planet.

Third, we can significantly improve the lives of farmed animals for just pennies per animal. In recent years, activists have campaigned for numerous large retailers and fast-food chains to cut caged eggs from their supply chains. Research suggests these corporate animal welfare campaigns have significantly improved the lives of somewhere between 9 and 120 hens per dollar spent by sparing them a year of cage confinement.[22]

Because of the sheer numbers of sentient beings involved, making progress on improving farm animal welfare could avert a huge amount of suffering. Yet despite the size of the problem, farm animal welfare is highly neglected.

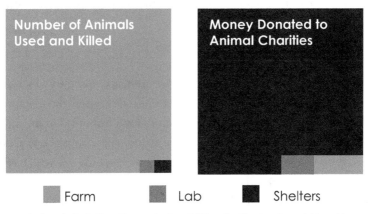

Animal statistics (From Animal Charity Evaluators: https://animalcharityevaluators.org/donation-advice/why-farmed-animals/)

---

20. Bas Sanders, "Global Animal Slaughter Statistics and Charts," Faunalytics, October 10, 2018, https://faunalytics.org/global-animal-slaughter-statistics-and-charts/.

21. Kelly Anthis and Jacy Reese Anthis, "Global Farmed and Factory Farmed Animals Estimates," Sentience Institute, updated February 21, 2019, https://www.sentienceinstitute.org/global-animal-farming-estimates.

22. Saulius Šimčikas, "Corporate Campaigns Affect 9 to 120 Years of Chicken Life per Dollar Spent," Effective Altruism Forum, July 8, 2019, https://forum.effectivealtruism.org/posts/L5EZjjXKdNgcm253H/corporate-campaigns-affect-9-to-120-years-of-chicken-life.

In the United States, only a few tens of millions of philanthropic dollars are donated yearly to organizations that focus on improving the lives of farmed animals. The amount spent is tiny compared to other animal causes. According to research nonprofit Animal Charity Evaluators: "Of domesticated and captive animals killed by humans in the U.S., about 99.987% are farmed animals, 0.007% are euthanized in companion animal shelters, and 0.006% are animals used in laboratories. However, about 95% of donations to animal charities in the U.S. go to companion animal organizations, 2% go to laboratory animal organizations, and 3% go specifically to farmed animal organizations."[23]

Existential Risk Reduction

> *Classical Utilitarians . . . would claim, as Sidgwick did, that the destruction of mankind would be by far the greatest of all conceivable crimes. The badness of this crime would lie in the vast reduction of the possible sum of happiness.*
>
> —Derek Parfit[24]

The previous chapter introduced *strong longtermism*, according to which the most important determinant of the value of our actions today is how those actions affect the very long-run future. Strong longtermism follows from utilitarianism—and a wide range of other moral viewpoints—if we assume that some of our actions can meaningfully affect the long-run future and that we can estimate which effects are positive and which negative.[25]

According to longtermism, the most important moral problems are the ones where we have the greatest leverage to positively affect future generations. In particular, we should be highly concerned with *existential risks*—such as all-out

---

23. Cf. "Why Farmed Animals?," Animal Charity Evaluators, updated January 2024, https://animalcharityevaluators.org/donation-advice/why-farmed-animals/.

24. Derek Parfit, *Reasons and Persons* (Oxford: Clarendon Press, 1984), 454.

25. For a discussion of longtermism and its underlying assumptions, see Hilary Greaves and William MacAskill, "The Case for Strong Longtermism" (GPI Working Paper 5-2021, Global Priorities Institute, 2019), https://globalprioritiesinstitute.org/hilary-greaves-william-macaskill-the-case-for-strong-longtermism/.

nuclear war, extreme climate change, or an engineered global pandemic—which are defined as follows:

> **An existential risk is a risk that threatens the destruction of humanity's long-term potential.**[26]

Besides the deaths of all eight billion people on this planet, an existential catastrophe would also entail the loss of all of humanity's future potential. In short, if an existential catastrophe occurred, the loss of value would be astronomical.[27]

If we avoid existential catastrophe, human civilization could survive for around a billion years before the earth is no longer habitable. And if someday we settled on other planets, civilization could continue for billions or trillions more.[28] We may also expect the quality of life to continue to improve. We've seen dramatic advancements in human welfare over the past few centuries, driven by technological development and moral progress. These trends have allowed more of us to lead longer, more fulfilling lives.[29] Fortunately, we should expect that further scientific and medical breakthroughs will continue to improve lives in the future.

Therefore, the extinction of humankind would irreversibly deprive humanity of a potentially grand future and preclude trillions of lives to come. The realization of an existential risk would be uniquely bad; much worse than non-existential catastrophes. Since the stakes involved with existential risks are so large, their mitigation may be one of the most important moral issues we face.[30]

---

26. Toby Ord, *The Precipice: Existential Risk and the Future of Humanity* (London: Bloomsbury Publishing, 2020), 37.

27. Cf. Nick Bostrom, "Astronomical Waste: The Opportunity Cost of Delayed Technological Development," *Utilitas* 15, vol. 3: 308–14, https://doi.org/10.1017/S0953820800004076.

28. Cf. Nicholas Beckstead, "On the Overwhelming Importance of Shaping the Far-Future" (PhD diss., Rutgers University, 2013), section 3, https://drive.google.com/file/d/0B8P94pg6WYCI c0lXSUVYS1BnMkE/view?resourcekey=0-nk6wM1QIPl0qWVh2z9FG4Q.

29. Max Roser, "The Short History of Global Living Conditions and Why It Matters That We Know It," Our World in Data, updated February 2024, https://ourworldindata.org/a -history-of-global-living-conditions-in-5-charts.

30. Cf. Nick Bostrom, "Existential Risks as a Global Priority," *Global Policy* 4, no. 1 (2013): 15–31, https://www.existential-risk.org/concept.html.

Work to ensure that humanity's long-run future goes well is not only very important but also very neglected. Future individuals do not get to influence the decisions we make today in our economic and political systems; they do not participate in markets today and do not have a vote. In essence, future individuals are voiceless. Against this background, it's unsurprising that our generation systematically neglects the interests and well-being of the many individuals that will exist in the future.

For a detailed discussion of existential risks and the moral importance of the long-run future of humanity, we recommend *The Precipice: Existential Risk and the Future of Humanity*, by Toby Ord.

Paths to Impact

How can we best address the most important causes? In general, there are three courses of action that are most impactful. First, we can donate money to charity. Second, we can work in a career that helps others. Last but not least, we can encourage other people to also engage in these actions.

As pointed out in the previous chapter, while utilitarians accept an obligation to try to do the most good they can, in practice they should almost always avoid violating commonsense moral prohibitions such as those against lying or killing. A good utilitarian would, therefore, generally do better by acting in accordance with commonsense moral virtues like integrity, trustworthiness, law-abidingness, and fairness and not trying to assess each action on utilitarian terms, case by case.

Charitable Giving

In slogan form, the utilitarian recommendation for using your money to help others is to "give more and give better." Giving more is self-explanatory. Giving better means finding and donating to the organizations that make the best use of your donation.

We've already seen that citizens of affluent countries are in the richest few percent of the world's population. By making small sacrifices, those in the affluent world have the power to improve the lives of others dramatically. Due to the extreme inequalities in wealth and income, one can do a lot more good by giving money to those most in need than by spending it on oneself.[31] Fortunately, an

---

31. Cf. William MacAskill, *Doing Good Better: Effective Altruism and How You Can Make a Difference* (New York: Penguin Random House), chap. 1.

increasing number of affluent people recognize the unique position they are in, and they have decided to give more of their resources to benefit others. For instance, Giving What We Can is a growing community of people who have pledged to give at least 10 percent of their income for the rest of their lives to wherever they believe the money will do the most good.[32] Over 9,000 people have taken the pledge, collectively promising to donate billions of dollars over their lifetimes.

Just giving more achieves little good, however, if the money is not spent wisely. Some ways of making a difference do vastly more good than others. Most people think that the best charities differ from the average in their effectiveness by only about a factor of 1.5 or so.[33] However, counterintuitively, the most cost-effective charities are tens or even hundreds of times more effective than typical charities.[34] Because of these vast differences between charities, the decision of where to donate is of great consequence; doing the most good requires us to make this decision very carefully.

To give better, one can follow the recommendations from organizations such as GiveWell, which conducts exceptionally in-depth charity evaluations. GiveWell's best-guess estimate is that the most cost-effective charities working in global health can save a child's life for under $5,000.[35] By donating 10 percent of their income each year, an affluent person will save a child's life every year—dozens of lives over their lifetime. And if that person focused on more important causes, it's plausible that they could do far more good again.

Perhaps surprisingly, a significant personal commitment to helping others involves sacrificing far less than one might initially have thought. Studies suggest that although there is a positive correlation between income and happiness, it's not as strong as one might think. In the United States, for example, a 10

---

32. Note that William MacAskill, coauthor of this textbook, is a cofounder of Giving What We Can.

33. Lucius Caviola et al., "Donors Vastly Underestimate Differences in Charities' Effectiveness," *Judgment and Decision Making* 15, no. 4 (2020): 509–16, https://ore.exeter.ac.uk/repository/bitstream/handle/10871/122268/Caviola et al._2020_JDM.pdf.

34. "Your Dollar Goes Further When You Fund the Right Program," GiveWell, updated November 2020, https://www.givewell.org/giving101/Funding-the-Right-Program; Toby Ord, "The Moral Imperative toward Cost-Effectiveness in Global Health," Center for Global Development, March 2013, https://pdfs.semanticscholar.org/1016/bb6788716e7b489c08853ce64f0063870a4b.pdf.

35. "Your Dollar Goes Further Overseas," GiveWell, accessed May 23, 2024, https://www.givewell.org/giving101/Your-dollar-goes-further-overseas.

percent reduction in income is associated with only a 1 percent drop on a scale measuring life satisfaction.[36] Moreover, it's not at all clear that we should think of donating 10 percent as equivalent to a 10 percent loss of income. There is some (conflicting) evidence to suggest that spending money on others can often improve our well-being by as much as or more than spending it on ourselves.[37] So, it's not even clear that donating 10 percent of one's income would be a personal sacrifice at all.[38]

Career Choice

A second way to help solve the world's most important problems is choosing the right career path: most of us will spend around 80,000 hours during our lives on our professional careers, and some careers achieve much more good than others. Your choice of career is, therefore, one of the most important moral choices of your life. By using this time to address the most pressing problems, we can do an enormous amount of good. Yet, it's far from obvious which careers will allow you to do the most good from a utilitarian perspective.

Fortunately, there is research available to help us make more informed choices. The organization 80,000 Hours[39] aims to help people use their careers to solve the world's most pressing problems. To do this, they research how individuals can maximize the social impact of their careers, create online advice, and support readers who might be able to enter priority areas.

As with donations, choosing an impactful career need not involve much of a personal sacrifice: We can enjoy a much broader variety of jobs than we might

---

36. Betsey Stevenson and Justin Wolfers, "Subjective Well-Being and Income: Is There Any Evidence of Satiation?" *American Economic Review, American Economic Association* 103, no. 3 (2013): 598–604, https://www.nber.org/papers/w18992.

37. Elizabeth Dunn, Daniel T. Gilbert, and Timothy D. Wilson, "If Money Doesn't Make You Happy, Then You Probably Aren't Spending It Right," *Journal of Consumer Psychology* 21, no. 2 (2011): 115–25, https://psycnet.apa.org/record/2011-17293-002.

38. For more detail, see William MacAskill, Andreas Mogensen, and Toby Ord, "Giving Isn't Demanding," in *The Ethics of Giving: Philosophers' Perspectives on Philanthropy*, ed. Paul Woodruff (New York: Oxford University Press), 178–203.

39. Note that William MacAskill, coauthor of this textbook, is a cofounder of 80,000 Hours.

think before we've tried them.[40] Also, you are unlikely to thrive in a job you do not enjoy. It would be unsustainable to pursue a career doing something that you hate. Relatedly, maintaining your physical health and emotional well-being are crucial to ensure you do not burn out and keep doing good over the long run. Therefore, choosing a career that maximizes your social impact does not involve giving up on a career that is satisfying, challenging, and enjoyable.[41]

Outreach

Third, by utilitarian lights, an effective way of doing good is by inspiring others to try to do more good. Thus, the best option for many people may be to develop and promote the ideas and values associated with utilitarianism or effective altruism and be a positive role model in their behavior. By raising awareness of these ideas, it's plausible that you could inspire several people to follow the recommendations of these philosophies. In this way, you will achieve a *multiplier effect* on your social impact—the people you inspire will do several times as much good as you would have achieved by working directly to solve the most important moral problems. Because utilitarianism and effective altruism are still little known and little understood, there may be a lot of value in promoting these ideas.

Some may also recommend political activism and volunteer work as ways to do good with one's time and efforts. Surprisingly little attention has been given to carefully assessing the marginal impact of different political activities. This paucity of information makes it especially hard to know which efforts in this sphere seem like good bets. But the high stakes suggest that the best-targeted efforts here could do immense good (though, as always, a dedicated career in the area may have even greater potential).[42]

---

40. Cf. Benjamin Todd, "We Reviewed Over 60 Studies about What Makes for a Dream Job: Here's What We Found," 80,000 Hours, updated May 2023, https://80000hours.org/career-guide/job-satisfaction/.

41. Though for an alternative perspective that puts much more weight on pursuing "excited curiosity," see Paul Graham, "How to Do Great Work," PaulGraham.com, July 2023, https://paulgraham.com/greatwork.html.

42. But note also the high risk of political efforts proving to be counterproductive. Consider, for example, environmental regulations that make it more difficult to build new solar, wind, and nuclear power plants to replace harmful coal power.

Conclusion

Utilitarians are committed to making *helping others* a very significant part of their lives. Also, they believe that when helping others, they should use their resources to do the most good, impartially considered, that they can.

The areas currently among the top priorities for utilitarians predominantly benefit groups that cannot defend their own interests. This includes people in extreme poverty, non-human animals, and future individuals. We've looked at three corresponding causes: improving the conditions of those in extreme poverty, reducing the suffering of factory-farmed animals, and protecting future generations by reducing existential risks.

To do the most good they can, utilitarians often donate money to effective charities, work on helping others with their career, and do outreach to encourage others to join in. We face many severe moral problems, which present opportunities to do an enormous amount of good. To benefit others as much as possible, utilitarians carefully prioritize their options, focusing their efforts wherever they believe they can make the biggest positive contribution to overall well-being.

The next chapter discusses important rival theories that may overlap significantly with utilitarianism in practice.

8

Near-Utilitarian Alternatives

Introduction

There are several different ways that one might end up departing from utilitarianism. How much of a practical difference do such departures make?

Utilitarianism is a particular form of aggregative consequentialism, one that is *welfarist* and *impartial*: taking well-being to be the only intrinsic value and giving equal weight to everyone's well-being. Other consequentialist views may weigh different people's interests differently or count additional things (beyond just well-being) as intrinsically good or worth promoting. Despite these theoretical differences, such views may be considered close cousins of utilitarianism. They tend to be motivated by similar arguments, are subject to similar objections, and have broadly similar practical implications.

This chapter surveys a range of these related consequentialist views with an eye to assessing (i) why some might prefer them over simple utilitarianism, and (ii) the extent to which their real-world practical implications coincide with those of utilitarianism. We close by considering whether even some non-consequentialist theories could closely match utilitarianism in practice. We find that adding deontic constraints makes little practical difference. However, significant departures from utilitarian recommendations are likely from theories that reject moral *aggregation*.

Beyond Welfarism

Most would agree that well-being is an important value. Suffering is bad, whereas happiness and human flourishing are good. But is well-being, as utilitarianism claims, the *only* intrinsic value? This seems more questionable. There is room for reasonable people to judge that other things matter in addition to just well-being. This section explores three possible examples of other candidate goods: *environmental value*, *aesthetic value*, and *distributive justice*.

Environmental Value

There is an active debate in environmental ethics over whether non-sentient nature—for instance, plants, species, and whole ecosystems—has intrinsic or merely instrumental value. This is difficult to resolve, as our intuitions pull us in different directions.

On the one hand, many find welfarist principles intuitive in their own right. For example, consider the claim that how good an outcome is depends entirely on the well-being of the individuals that exist in that outcome. Or that nothing can be good or bad if there is nobody who exists to care about it or to experience it.

On the other hand, we may be drawn toward certain judgments that seem to attribute intrinsic value to nature. For example, imagine that some disaster wiped out all sentient beings (including all animals) except for a single person. As this last person is on their deathbed, they look over a glorious landscape and face the choice of whether to set off a doomsday device that would cause the planet to explode, destroying all the remaining (non-sentient) plant life.[1] Even if we stipulate that there was somehow no chance of sentient life ever evolving again on earth, we may still judge it wrong to wipe out the remaining (non-sentient) plant life for no good reason. But it has (by stipulation) no further instrumental value for sentient beings, so any remaining value it possesses must be intrinsic.

Utilitarians might adapt their standard response to counterexamples (explained in Chapter 9) by showing how they can accommodate a closely related intuition. They must insist that in this weird scenario (with all its stipulations), it would technically be harmless, and hence permissible, to blow up the planet. But they may endorse our judgment that there would be something wrong with the character of an agent who wanted to blow up the world in this way. The agent would seem disturbingly callous and may be the kind of person who, *in more ordinary circumstances*, would risk significant harm by being insufficiently respectful of (immensely instrumentally valuable) natural ecosystems. Anyone unsatisfied by this response may prefer to instead add environmental intrinsic value to their moral theory, yielding a pluralist (rather than welfarist) form of consequentialism.

---

1. This is a variation of Richard Routley's famous Last Man thought experiment. See Richard Routley, "Is There a Need for a New, an Environmental, Ethic?," *Proceedings of the XVth World Congress of Philosophy* 1 (1973): 205–10, https://doi.org/10.5840/wcp151973136.

Some radical environmentalists may take environmental values to outweigh the well-being of all sentient lives, human and non-human alike.[2] But most would find this position too extreme and instead give more weight to well-being. This more moderate form of pluralism would then largely overlap with utilitarianism's practical recommendations, except in claiming that small well-being losses can be compensated for by large gains in environmental values. For example, while woodlands may be valuable, the moderate pluralist would agree that in the event of a wildfire, one must always save people before trees.[3]

Aesthetic Value

Welfarism may be challenged in a different way by considering our attitudes toward objects of beauty. Consider the awe you feel at observing a magnificent waterfall or pondering the immensity of the universe. It seems *fitting*, or genuinely appropriate, to directly appreciate these things and other objects of beauty—great art, music, natural wonders, etc. "Direct appreciation" here is a form of non-instrumental valuing, recognizably distinct from merely regarding something as instrumentally *useful*. But such non-instrumental valuing can only be truly warranted by objects that are non-instrumentally valuable.

Welfarists thus seem to face a dilemma: either deny that such eminently appropriate-seeming responses are *in fact* appropriate or grant that things besides welfare have intrinsic value.

One tempting welfarist response would be to insist that it's really our *appreciative aesthetic experience* that is valuable, rather than an object such as a waterfall

---

2. Some claim that humanity is overall harmful for the world, such that we should wish for human extinction. But it's important to note that this does not actually follow: even if humanity has *to date* imposed immense costs on the natural environment, it may well be that *future* generations of humanity are the best hope for undoing that damage. The near-term extinction of humanity might then be the worst possible outcome: all our past damage is done, but none of our future potential for remedy could then be realized. If that is right, then even radical environmentalists should care (at least instrumentally) about preventing human extinction.

3. Pluralists face interesting puzzles about how to make trade-offs involving *vastly more* of the typically less important value. Could a million trees outweigh a human life? Or outweigh a sufficiently tiny *risk* of death to one person? We will not attempt to solve this problem here, but note it as an important challenge for any pluralist view.

itself. In support of this view, it seems right that the value would be missing from a universe with no conscious observers to appreciate the waterfalls contained therein. But on the other hand, it seems that the appropriate *object* of our valuing attitudes (that is, what it is that we are in awe of and appropriately regard *as valuable*) is the waterfall *itself* rather than just our *experience* of it.[4]

Can these two verdicts be reconciled? One possibility—for those who accept an objective list theory of well-being—would be to hold that the waterfall itself is valuable, but only when it's perceived and appreciated, as it may then constitute a welfare good for the subject perceiving it. This is a way to accommodate aesthetic value without abandoning welfarism. A non-welfarist might instead claim that the waterfall has value *independently of its contribution to anyone's well-being* while nonetheless insisting that this value is only realized when it's perceived and appreciated by a conscious being.

It's ultimately unclear whether aesthetic value requires us to abandon welfarism. Either way, while these details may be of theoretical interest, they seem unlikely to yield significant divergences from utilitarianism in practice (unless one gives implausibly extreme weight to aesthetic value compared to welfarist priorities like relieving suffering and saving lives).

Egalitarianism and Distributive Justice

Egalitarianism is the view that inequality is bad *in itself*, over and above any instrumental effects it may have on people's well-being.

Utilitarians tend to favor equality entirely for instrumental reasons—because more equal outcomes tend to better promote overall well-being. Due to the diminishing marginal value of money, for example, an extra dollar makes a much bigger difference to a homeless person than to a billionaire.

Egalitarians feel this merely instrumental appreciation of equality does not go far enough. For example, they may prefer a world in which everyone gets fifty years of happy life over an alternative in which an average of sixty years of happy

---

4. Note that a subjectively indistinguishable hallucinatory experience (perhaps generated by an experience machine) does not seem quite so impressive. Of course, if the person does not realize they are hallucinating, they will feel just as impressed. But we may judge their valuing attitude to be objectively less warranted in such a case than in the non-hallucinatory case.

life is achieved by 75 percent of the population living happily to age seventy while 25 percent die early at age thirty. While this unequal outcome contains (we may suppose) more overall well-being, egalitarians may nonetheless regard it as worse due to the disvalue of inequality.

Note that there are two ways to remedy inequality: one may improve the lot of the worse off, or one may *worsen* the lot of the better off, to bring everyone down to the same level. The former route is obviously better on well-being grounds. But either route could equally reduce inequality and hence qualify as an "improvement" by egalitarian lights. According to the *Leveling-Down Objection* to egalitarianism, it counts against the view that it implies there is *something* good about harming the better off while helping no one.[5] Welfarists instead believe that such one-sided harms are *entirely* bad.[6]

Chapter 16 (The Equality Objection) further explores the intuition that equality of distribution matters intrinsically and how utilitarians may respond. For now, we may note that substantial practical agreement should be expected between utilitarian and egalitarian views (assuming that the latter appropriately care not merely about local but also global inequality, as well as interspecies inequality and intertemporal inequality).

Beyond the Equal Consideration of Interests

One might accept welfarism while nonetheless rejecting utilitarianism due to giving more weight to the interests or well-being of some individuals than others. This section explores four such views: *prioritarianism, desert-adjusted views, egoism,* and *partialism.*

---

5. Derek Parfit, "Equality and Priority," *Ratio* 10, no. 3 (December 1997): 202–21, https://doi .org/10.1111/1467-9329.00041. Cf. Kurt Vonnegut's short-story satire, "Harrison Bergeron." Wikipedia, s.v. "Harrison Bergeron," last modified March 20, 2024, 02:54, https://en.wikipedia .org/wiki/Harrison_Bergeron.

6. This is a subtle disagreement with limited practical implications, so long as the egalitarian sensibly agrees that the well-being losses from leveling down make it *overall* bad.

Prioritarianism

According to *prioritarianism*, "benefiting people matters more the worse off these people are."[7] Like egalitarianism, prioritarianism implies that it's better to give a fixed-size benefit—for instance, an extra boost of happiness—to the worse off than to the better off. But whereas egalitarianism implies that there is *something* good about "leveling down," or reducing inequality purely by harming the better off, prioritarianism (like utilitarianism) avoids claiming that there is anything good about harming people in the absence of compensating benefits to others.

This is a subtle but important theoretical difference. Egalitarians value *equality* per se, which could be promoted by *reducing* well-being. Prioritarians maintain welfarism, valuing only *well-being*, while departing from utilitarianism by instead giving *extra weight* to the interests of the worse off.

Prioritarianism may thus seem like a nice compromise between egalitarian intuitions and welfarist theoretical principles. But it raises theoretical puzzles of its own.[8] To bring this out, recall how utilitarians accommodate our egalitarian intuitions by appealing to the *diminishing marginal value* of resources: the more you have, the less of a difference one more unit tends to make.

Strangely, prioritarianism treats well-being itself as having diminishing marginal value. Suppose that Jane has the choice to either provide herself a small benefit at a time when she is poorly off or a greater benefit at a time when she is better off. By stipulation, the latter option benefits her more. But prioritarianism implies that the former may be "more important." That is, *considering only this person's well-being, it might be better to do what is worse for her.* Could that really be right?

This objection assumes, for simplicity, that prioritarianism applies to momentary rather than lifetime well-being. To address lifetime prioritarianism, we must tweak the objection to invoke counterfactual rather than temporal comparisons. Suppose that Shane will be happier if a flipped coin lands heads and can further grant himself either of two conditional benefits: a greater benefit if the coin lands heads or a small benefit if tails. If benefits matter more to the worse off, and

---

7. Parfit, "Equality and Priority," 213.

8. The following paragraphs directly draw from Richard Y. Chappell, *Parfit's Ethics* (Cambridge: Cambridge University Press, 2021).

he is worse off if it lands tails, then the 50 percent chance of a smaller benefit (conditional on tails) may be recommended by prioritarianism as better than the 50 percent chance of a greater benefit. But that would not be the prudent choice.[9]

Utilitarians may agree that many of our intuitions support prioritarianism but then seek to give a debunking explanation of these intuitions rather than accepting them at face value. Experimental evidence suggests that our intuitive appreciation of the diminishing marginal value of resources overgeneralizes when applied to abstract "units of well-being" with which we lack intuitive familiarity.[10] As Joshua Greene explains it: "When we imagine possible distributions of [well-being] . . . it's very hard not to think of distributions of stuff, rather than distributions of experiential quality."[11] Utilitarians agree that stuff often has diminishing marginal value. If prioritarian intuitions reflect a confused overgeneralization of this point, we may do best to stick with utilitarianism.

Alternatively, some people might be drawn to the view that various basic goods—such as happiness—that directly contribute to well-being have diminishing marginal value, then confuse this with the prioritarian claim. To ensure theoretical clarity, we must take care to distinguish the prioritarian idea that the well-being of the worse off simply *matters* more from the utilitarian-compatible idea that basic goods like happiness would constitute *a greater benefit* for the worse off, by making a greater difference to their (inherently equally important) well-being. We might call this new view *diminishing basic goods utilitarianism*,[12] in contrast with the traditional utilitarian view that basic goods like happiness have constant, non-diminishing value. For diminishing basic goods utilitarians, an extra minute of happiness might be intrinsically *more beneficial* to someone

---

9. This assumes that prioritarianism takes an ex post form. For objections to ex ante prioritarianism, see Johan E. Gustafsson, "Ex-Ante Prioritarianism Violates Sequential Ex-Ante Pareto," *Utilitas* 34, no. 2 (2022): 167–77, https://doi.org/10.1017/S0953820821000303.

10. Joshua Greene and Jonathan Baron, "Intuitions about Declining Marginal Utility," *Journal of Behavioral Decision Making* 14 (June 2000): 243–55, https://dx.doi.org/10.2139/ssrn.231183.

11. Cf. Greene, *Moral Tribes: Emotion, Reason, and the Gap between Us and Them* (New York: Penguin Books, 2013), chap. 10.

12. Again, note that this directly draws from Chappell, *Parfit's Ethics*.

who was previously suffering than to someone who was already fairly happy.[13] This view seems to yield the same practical verdicts as prioritarianism but without some of the theoretical costs.

In any case, as with egalitarianism, the differences between *prioritarianism*, *diminishing basic goods utilitarianism*, and *traditional utilitarianism* are subtle. These differences will be most pronounced in cases where we may benefit the extremely well-off at a relatively smaller cost to the least well-off. However, such cases are rare (since diminishing returns mean that it's usually much easier to increase the well-being of the have-nots than of the haves). Consequently, all of these views can be expected to share broadly similar practical implications.[14]

Desert-Adjusted Views

Utilitarianism counts everyone's interests equally. An alternative form of consequentialism might involve counting only *innocent* interests equally while discounting the interests of those who are, in some relevant sense, less deserving.[15] For example, it would seem unfair to harm one person to save another from harms that were gratuitously self-inflicted and entirely avoidable.

Many people have *retributivist* intuitions, endorsing punishment of the guilty even independently of any instrumental benefits this might have for deterrence or

---

13. Note that this is not the empirical claim that happiness would have greater downstream (instrumental) benefits for the worse-off person, say by shifting them into a more positive frame of mind. That may or may not be true, but if it is, then it would be taken into account even by traditional utilitarians. No, diminishing basic goods utilitarians make the more radical normative claim that the same amount of pleasure inherently *constitutes* a greater *intrinsic* benefit to the worse-off person. The pleasure *in itself* makes a bigger difference to their well-being, in the sense that we have prudential reason to more strongly prefer a fixed-size boost to our pleasure or happiness when we are worse off.

14. A possible exception might be that if you assigned *extreme* priority to the worse off, this could lead to inefficiently pouring resources into hard-to-reach or difficult-to-help populations for minor gains, when utilitarians would instead recommend using those resources to get greater benefits for larger numbers of (possibly slightly better-off) people.

15. Fred Feldman, "Adjusting Utility for Justice: A Consequentialist Reply to the Objection from Justice," *Philosophy and Phenomenological Research* 55, no. 3 (September 1995): 567–85, https://doi.org/10.2307/2108439; Peter A. Graham, "Avoidable Harm," *Philosophy and Phenomenological Research* 101, no. 1 (July 2020): 175–99, https://doi.org/10.1111/phpr.12586.

reduced recidivism. Even more would at least think that serious wrongdoers have *less claim* on receiving benefits from others in society. For example, if you could choose to give an extra happy day to either Gandhi or Hitler, you probably do not feel that you need to flip a coin to decide between them. (You might even prefer for Hitler to positively suffer.)[16] Desert-adjusted views accommodate such intuitions by making the degree to which one's interests count morally proportionate to the extent to which one *deserves* to benefit (or, perhaps, to suffer).

Is it possible for some people to be more deserving of happiness than others? Intuitively, it certainly seems so. But skeptics about free will and moral responsibility argue that this is an illusion, which would preclude any such desert-adjustments. While it's beyond the scope of this chapter to try to adjudicate that debate here, we'll briefly flag two points. First, *if* there is such a thing as genuine desert, then consequentialists can take this into account—though doing so would be a departure from utilitarianism. And second, even if we end up adopting a desert-adjusted consequentialist view, it will still share the most important practical implications of utilitarianism. After all, there is no serious question about the innocence of those groups we can help the most, such as future generations, factory-farmed animals,[17] and (the vast majority of) the global poor.

---

16. Jeremy Bentham, by contrast, assigned no less *intrinsic* value even "to the most abominable pleasure which the vilest of malefactors ever reaped from his crime." Bentham, "Principles Opposing the Principle of Utility," chap. 2 in *An Introduction to the Principles of Morals and Legislation*, ed. Jonathan Bennett (London, 1789; Early Modern Texts, 2017), https://www.earlymoderntexts.com/assets/pdfs/bentham1780.pdf.

17. An alternative view that would allow some discounting of non-human animals would be to weigh interests in proportion to the moral status of the individual (and further hold that non-human animals have lesser moral status). While utilitarians already allow that some animals may have a greater capacity for conscious experiences than others, this alternative view would instead claim that even equal pains matter less if experienced by a "lesser" animal. But even with moderate discounting, the severe harms of factory farming are unlikely to prove justifiable. We surely should not discount animals so much that it would become permissible to torture them for fun.

Egoism and Partialism

Egoists claim that only their *own* well-being matters, and consequently, they should do whatever is best for themselves. While some people initially claim to find this "rational," few philosophers regard it as a defensible view on reflection.[18] Most of us care deeply about at least *some* other people, such as our close friends and family, and would regard it as neither ethical nor rational to benefit ourselves at greater cost to our loved ones.

For example, suppose an evil demon made you the following offer: murder your friends and family, and they will wipe your memory of the past (including the horrendous deed) and set you up in a *new* life (with new friends and family) in which you are guaranteed to be very slightly happier, more fulfilled, or have marginally more of whatever else you believe contributes to your well-being. Would it necessarily be *irrational* to decline? Worse, are you even *required* to commit these murders? That seems an absurdly strong and implausible claim. Surely you could reasonably care more about the well-being of your friends and family than about marginally improving your own well-being. Selfishly murdering your loved ones for a piddling benefit seems like the epitome of moral error.

So let us put aside egoism. A more plausible view, which we might call *partialism*, lies somewhere between the two extremes of egoism and impartial utilitarianism. According to partialism, while we must take everyone's interests into account to some extent, we may give *extra* weight to our nearest and dearest (including ourselves).[19]

One important challenge for partialism is that it's unclear *how much* extra weight partiality allows or how there could even be a precise fact of the matter. Any particular answer would seem arbitrary, and there's no consensus among partialists as to how much extra weight is justified here.[20] We can make theoretical sense of how everyone might have equal moral weight. But if some degree of

---

18. For a classic discussion, see Derek Parfit, "Rationality and Time," part 2 in *Reasons and Persons* (Oxford: Clarendon Press, 1984).

19. Philosophers call this an *option* or *agent-centered prerogative*. See Samuel Scheffler, *The Rejection of Consequentialism: A Philosophical Investigation of the Considerations Underlying Rival Moral Conceptions*, rev. ed. (Oxford: Clarendon Press, 1994).

20. One option would be to accept a vague range of permissible weightings, but this can begin to look mysterious.

partiality is intrinsically (and not just instrumentally) warranted, how could we determine what degree is warranted?

In any case, it at least seems clear that there must be limits to how much extra weight partiality allows. On any plausibly moderate weighting, the standard utilitarian prescriptions for improving the world at large will still apply, given that well-targeted donations can often do *hundreds* of times more good for distant others than for ourselves and those close to us.[21]

Beyond Consequentialism

Some non-consequentialist views—particularly anti-aggregative views on which "the numbers do not count"[22]—are radically at odds with utilitarianism. Anti-aggregative views license deliberately doing less good than one easily could, at least when the benefits are so widely distributed that no one individual has an especially strong "claim" on your acting optimally. This makes a big practical difference since many real-world moral problems pit the concentrated interests of a few against the distributed interests of many. Aggregative and anti-aggregative views will have sharply divergent verdicts about what should be done in such cases. But at least some other non-consequentialist views, while disagreeing deeply about the theoretical role of moral options and/or constraints, may nonetheless still largely overlap with utilitarianism in practice.

Two features distinguish many non-consequentialist views from utilitarianism: *options* to favor oneself and loved ones, and *constraints*, such as against violating rights. The conflict between these forms of non-consequentialism and utilitarianism is often overstated. Regarding moral options, the section on partialism above highlighted that any plausibly moderate degree of partiality would not be enough to outweigh the immense good we can do for others in high-stakes decisions. Utilitarianism may also endorse some partial practices, such as parenting, as conducive

---

21. Mogensen further argues that long-term considerations will swamp pretty much *any* finitely weighted personal prerogative, even ones that initially seem extremely immoderate (such as giving a *million* times more weight to the interests of those to whom you are partial). Andreas Mogensen, "Moral Demands and the Far Future," *Philosophy and Phenomenological Research* 103, no. 3 (November 2021): 567–85, https://doi.org/10.1111/phpr.12729.

22. E.g., John M. Taurek, "Should the Numbers Count?," *Philosophy and Public Affairs* 6, no. 4 (Summer 1977): 293–316, https://www.jstor.org/stable/2264945.

to the general good. As for moral constraints, utilitarians wholeheartedly embrace respecting rights in practice, viewing them as instrumentally justified by their tendency to promote better societal outcomes.

Any plausible view must allow that reducing suffering and promoting well-being are important moral goals. It would be extremely implausible to deny this entirely.[23] But this means that—on *any* plausible view—we will have strong moral reasons to reduce suffering and promote well-being whenever we can do so without conflicting with other important goals or requirements (such as to respect others' rights).

In practice, the most effective ways to improve the world do not require violating others' rights. So it seems that almost any reasonable view that endorses aggregation should end up largely agreeing with utilitarianism about what matters in practice: namely, pursuing effective ways to vastly improve the world[24] while behaving in a trustworthy fashion, advancing social coordination, and respecting important moral constraints.

Conclusion

There are several ways to reject aspects of utilitarianism while remaining on board with the general thrust of the theory (at least in practice). First, one could add other values into the mix, so long as they are not taken to such extremes as to completely swamp the importance of well-being. Second, one could reject the equal consideration of interests, giving extra weight to the worse off, the more deserving, or those to whom one is partial. But again, as long as such weightings are not taken to implausible extremes (such as strict egoism), the moral imperative to seek effective improvements to the world will remain in force. Finally, one might even reject consequentialism and accept fundamental moral constraints on

---

23. Even John Rawls, the father of contractualist ethics and a prominent critic of utilitarianism, remained committed to the core aspect of consequentialism, writing that "All ethical doctrines worth our attention take consequences into account in judging rightness. One which did not would simply be irrational, crazy." John Rawls, *A Theory of Justice*, rev. ed. (Cambridge, MA: Harvard University Press, 1999), 26.

24. One important proviso: non-consequentialists may be more drawn to person-affecting views of population ethics, which could result in their giving much less weight to the interests of future generations.

one's pursuit of the good. But many such non-consequentialists may still allow that the good remains worthy of pursuit nonetheless (as long as that pursuit does not require violating important moral constraints), and many utilitarians will likely approve of their proposed constraints in practice.

Of course, there are ways to reject utilitarianism wholesale. One might embrace egoism and deny that others matter at all. Or one might reject aggregation and insist that helping millions is no more intrinsically important than helping one. (Or that helping millions, each a little, is worse than helping one person a lot.) Anyone drawn to these views is unlikely to sympathize with utilitarianism or its practical recommendations.

But those are a fairly narrow range of views. By contrast, it's noteworthy—and to many readers, possibly quite surprising—that a broad range of theoretical approaches may happily form an overlapping consensus about the practical importance of efficiently promoting the good in the ways discussed in the previous chapter. At least when it comes to practical ethics, we may be climbing the same mountain from different sides.[25]

---

25. We borrow this metaphor from Derek Parfit, *On What Matters* (Oxford: Oxford University Press, 2011). Parfit used the mountain-climbing metaphor to support the more ambitious claim that different moral traditions (consequentialist, Kantian, and contractualist) may end up converging on the same moral *theory*. We make no such claim.

For additional resources
and study aids, see
https://utilitarianism.net/

Part II: Objections and Responses

Objections to Utilitarianism and Responses

Bernard Williams . . . concluded a lengthy attack on utilitarianism by remarking: "The day cannot be too far off in which we hear no more of it." It is now more than forty years since Williams made that comment, but we continue to hear plenty about utilitarianism.

—Katarzyna de Lazari-Radek and Peter Singer[1]

Introduction

Utilitarianism is a very controversial moral theory. Critics have raised many objections against it, and its defenders have responded with attempts to defuse them.

While our presentation focuses on utilitarianism, it's worth noting that many of the objections below could also be taken to challenge other forms of consequentialism (just as many of the arguments for utilitarianism also apply to these related views). Part II of this textbook explores objections to utilitarianism and closely related views in contrast to non-consequentialist approaches to ethics.

General Ways of Responding to Objections to Utilitarianism

Many objections rest on the idea that utilitarianism has counterintuitive implications. We can see these implications by considering concrete examples or *thought*

---

1. Katarzyna de Lazari-Radek and Peter Singer, preface to *Utilitarianism: A Very Short Introduction* (Oxford: Oxford University Press, 2017).

experiments. For instance, in Chapter 10 (The Rights Objection), we consider the Transplant case:

> **Transplant:** Imagine a hypothetical scenario in which there are five patients, each of whom will soon die unless they receive an appropriate transplanted organ—a heart, two kidneys, a liver, and lungs. A healthy patient, Chuck, comes into the hospital for a routine check-up, and the doctor finds that Chuck is a perfect match as a donor for all five patients. Should the doctor kill Chuck and use his organs to save the five others?

At first glance, it seems that utilitarianism has to answer the question affirmatively. It's better that five people survive than that just one person does. But killing Chuck seems morally monstrous to many. This apparent implication of utilitarianism is taken as an argument against its being the correct moral theory.

Utilitarians can respond to such objections in four general ways. If we think of an objection or counterintuitive implication as akin to a shot fired at a theory, a defender of the theory might try to (i) dodge the bullet, (ii) disarm or expose it as illusory, (iii) show that rivals are equally caught in the blast, or (iv) absorb the impact by "biting the bullet." To explain each strategy in turn:

To *dodge the bullet*, defenders of utilitarianism may seek to *accommodate the intuition* underlying the objection by arguing that a sophisticated application of utilitarian principles avoids the counterintuitive implication. To more reliably promote good outcomes, sophisticated utilitarians recognize their cognitive limitations and act according to commonsense norms and heuristics other than in exceptional circumstances. If a critic merely claims that we should embrace or oppose certain norms *in practice*, utilitarians can often straightforwardly agree. (If the critic instead invokes outlandish hypotheticals, a different response may be needed.)

Second, to *disarm* or expose the threat as illusory (like the "shot" of a toy cap gun), one may instead attempt to *debunk the moral intuition* invoked in a particular case. For example, one might try to show that the intuition resulted from an unreliable process.[2] If a debunking argument succeeds, the targeted moral intuition should not be given much weight in our moral reasoning.

---

2. For a discussion of evolutionary debunking arguments, see Robin Hanson, "Why Health Is Not Special: Errors in Evolved Bioethics Intuitions," *Social Philosophy and Policy* 19, no. 2

Third, to *expand the blast radius*, one might try to show that rival views—such as deontological or virtue ethical theories—*fare no better* and have implications no less counterintuitive, in the relevant area, than those of utilitarianism. An objection can't give you overall reason to prefer a rival view if that rival view is equally undermined by careful consideration of the issue at hand.

Finally, one might simply *bite the bullet* and accept a counterintuitive implication. To weaken the force of the blow, one might emphasize that the costs of accepting a counterintuitive implication may be outweighed by the force of the arguments in favor of utilitarianism and the greater problems faced by other views (in other areas). Our moral intuitions may pull us in multiple conflicting directions, making it impossible to find consistent and plausible principles without giving up on *some* of our initial moral assumptions. We must carefully reflect on which intuitions and theoretical commitments we regard as non-negotiable, and which we should be willing to compromise on in pursuit of "reflective equilibrium," or the most plausible and coherent overall combination of moral verdicts and principles.

The Utilitarian's Toolkit

There are further ideas that utilitarians may appeal to in developing the above general strategies.

- *Keep hypotheticals at a distance.*[3] The distinction between utilitarianism's *criterion of rightness* and its *recommended decision procedure* is crucial to utilitarian attempts to *accommodate* common intuitions. Given that utilitarianism is fundamentally scalar, we needn't be committed to taking utilitarian verdicts as corresponding to the ordinary concept of "rightness." Common intuitions about "right" and "wrong" may be best understood as addressing the question of what norms we (as

---

(2002): 153–79, http://mason.gmu.edu/~rhanson/bioerr.pdf. See also the related discussion in Chapter 3 (Arguments for Utilitarianism).

3. Public health experts recommend maintaining a social distance of six feet or more from silly hypothetical cases at all times, lest they infect your understanding of what utilitarianism actually calls for in practice. If closer contact is required, protect yourself and others by first reading up on the utilitarian case for respecting commonsense norms, explained in Chapter 6.

fallible agents) should endorse in practice, rather than what ideally ought to be done (by an omniscient being) in principle. If justified, this interpretive move can drastically reduce the apparent conflict between utilitarianism and commonsense moral intuitions.

- *Accommodate nearby intuitions.* More generally, utilitarians may seek to reduce their apparent conflict with common sense by identifying *nearby* intuitions they *can* accommodate. For example, if critics claim that a specific welfare-maximizing action is intuitively *wrong*, utilitarians may argue that our intuition here is better thought of tracking one of the following features:

  - that it would be good to *inculcate practical norms* against actions of that type;

  - that a person willing to perform such an action would likely have *bad character* and be likely to cause greater harms on other occasions; and

  - that the action is *reckless* or plausibly wrong *in expectation*, even if it happens to turn out (objectively) for the best.[4]

- *Gobble up competing values.* Critics sometimes allege that utilitarians don't value obviously good things like rights, freedom, virtue, equality, and the natural environment. But while these things may be obviously good, it's less obvious that they are all *non-instrumentally* good. And utilitarians can certainly value them instrumentally. Moreover, utilitarians who accept an objective list theory of well-being may even be able to give non-instrumental consideration to goods (like freedom

---

4. As further explained in Chapter 10 (The Rights Objection), standard "counterexamples" to utilitarianism invite us to imagine that a typically disastrous class of action (such as killing an innocent person) just so happens, in this special case, to produce the best outcome. But the agent in the imagined case generally has no good basis for discounting the typical risk of disaster. So it would be unacceptably risky for them to perform the typically disastrous act. We maximize expected value by avoiding such risks. For all practical purposes, utilitarianism recommends that we refrain from rights-violating behaviors. This constitutes a generalizable defense of utilitarianism against a wide range of alleged counterexamples.

and beauty) that could plausibly be counted as welfare goods when part of a person's life.

- *Stuff people into suitcases.* Rival moral theories may be undermined by appeal to the "Veil of Ignorance," and the related idea of *ex ante Pareto*—or what it would be in *everyone's* best interests to agree to in advance (before learning about their particular position in life). Our intuitive reluctance to stick with the overall best policy can start to seem biased. To make the point vivid, when faced with difficult trade-offs between conflicting interests, just imagine putting each affected person in a separate suitcase and shuffling their positions.[5] All would then rationally endorse the utilitarian-recommended action. Resistance to utilitarian verdicts in suitcase-free scenarios thus looks like unjustified "special pleading" on behalf of those privileged by the status quo.

- *Look for neglected interests.* Putative counterexamples to utilitarianism ask us to *negatively judge* an action that *does the most good.* Isn't that odd? It's worth considering what psychological mechanisms could explain such a judgment. Such cases commonly involve *unequal vividness*: we are implicitly led to focus our attention on a salient "victim" and pay much less attention to the greater harms to others that would result under the status quo.[6] Reflecting on this potential source of psychological distortion, and making a special effort to *attend equally* to each individual in a scenario, may help to undermine the biasing effect. You may then find that you are less inclined to negatively judge the action that actually helps people the most.[7]

---

5. Caspar Hare, "Should We Wish Well to All?," *Philosophical Review* 125, no. 4 (2016): 454–55, https://doi.org/10.1215/00318108-3624764. See also the discussion in our Chapter 3 (Arguments for Utilitarianism).

6. Neil Sinhababu, "Unequal Vividness and Double Effect," *Utilitas* 25, no. 3 (2013): 291–315, https://doi.org/10.1017/s0953820812000362. See also Richard Y. Chappell, and Helen Yetter-Chappell, "Virtue and Salience," *Australasian Journal of Philosophy* 94, no. 3 (2016): 449–63, https://doi.org/10.1080/00048402.2015.1115530.

7. At the very least, you should avoid the common mistake of thinking that utilitarian verdicts are unpopular "because they are contrary to most people's interests" (as is sometimes claimed in online debates). This mistake presumably stems from imagining oneself in the position of a possible

- *The Pluralist's Dilemma* (between extremism and arbitrariness). If you hold that there are non-utilitarian moral reasons (e.g., deontic constraints) that sometimes outweigh utilitarian reasons, this raises tricky questions about how the two kinds of reasons compare. If the non-utilitarian reason always trumps—no matter how great the cost to overall well-being—then this seems implausibly extreme. But the "moderate" pluralist alternative risks arbitrariness, due to lacking a clear account of where to draw the line, or precisely how much weight to give to non-utilitarian reasons relative to utilitarian ones.[8]

- *Bang the drums of war.* We live in a *morally unusual world.* During high-stakes emergencies like fighting a just war, many activities that would otherwise seem above and beyond the call of duty, or even wrong, may instead be morally required—including risking your life, imposing burdens on your loved ones or leaving them for years, and killing enemy combatants. But in fact, our "ordinary circumstances" involve horrific amounts of preventable suffering, with stakes as high as any war. Utilitarian verdicts may thus be bolstered by noting that much sentient life is (metaphorically) under siege, and some moral heroism may accordingly be required to set things right.[9]

"victim" of utilitarian sacrifice, where one is killed to save five, *without* also imagining oneself in the position of any of the possible beneficiaries. You should realize that a policy of killing one to save five is *five times more likely to save your life* than to end it. If the way you imagine the scenario doesn't reflect this fact, then you're imagining it wrong. Look for the neglected interests.

8. By contrast, utilitarianism offers a clear and principled account of (e.g.) when constraints can reasonably be violated—namely, just when doing so would truly best serve overall well-being. This answer similarly explains when it is worth damaging the natural environment, how to weigh small harms to many against grave harms to a few, and so on. That's not to say that it will always be easy to *tell* what utilitarianism recommends in real-life situations since it can be difficult to predict future outcomes. But it is at least clear *in principle* how different considerations weigh against each other, whereas other theories often do not offer even this much clarity. (Though utilitarians who accept an *objective list theory* of well-being, as discussed in Chapter 4, may face "pluralist's dilemmas" of their own.)

9. Of course, that's not to suggest that the same particular actions are called for. Adopting a "war-like" stance outside of war might be expected to prove counterproductive. The point is just that the stakes are high enough that we shouldn't necessarily expect truly moral advice in our circumstances to be *comfortable.*

- *Make winning distinctions.* Different versions of utilitarianism may be more or less vulnerable to different objections. For example, a version of the view that combines scalar, expectational, and hybrid elements may be better equipped to mitigate concerns about demandingness, cluelessness, and praiseworthy motivations. Objections to specifically hedonistic utilitarianism (such as the Experience Machine and Evil Pleasures objections) do not apply to utilitarians who accept a different theory of well-being.

Despite the silly labels, these are serious philosophical moves. We employ each, where appropriate, to respond to the specific objections listed below. (Students are encouraged, when reading an objection, to anticipate how to apply the utilitarian's toolkit to address the objection at hand.)

Road Map: Specific Objections to Utilitarianism

In the remaining chapters, we discuss the following critiques of utilitarianism:

1. **The Rights Objection:** Many find it objectionable that utilitarianism seemingly licenses outrageous rights violations in certain hypothetical scenarios, killing innocent people for the greater good. Chapter 10 explores how utilitarians might best respond.
2. **The Mere Means Objection:** Critics often allege that utilitarianism objectionably instrumentalizes people—treating us as mere means to the greater good rather than properly valuing individuals as ends in themselves. In Chapter 11, we assess whether this is a fair objection.
3. **The Separateness of Persons Objection:** The idea that utilitarianism neglects the "separateness of persons" has proven to be a widely influential objection. But it is one that is difficult to pin down. Chapter 12 explores three candidate interpretations of the objection and how utilitarians can respond to each.
4. **The Demandingness Objection:** In directing us to choose the impartially best outcome, even at significant cost to ourselves, utilitarianism can seem an incredibly demanding theory. Chapter 13 explores whether this feature of utilitarianism is objectionable, and if so, how defenders of the view might best respond.

5. **The Alienation Objection:** Abstract moral theories threaten to alienate us from much that we hold dear. Chapter 14 explores two possible defenses of utilitarianism against this charge. One recommends adopting motivations other than explicitly utilitarian ones. The second argues that suitably concrete concerns can be subsumed within broader utilitarian motivations.

6. **The Special Obligations Objection:** Relationships like parenthood or guardianship seemingly give rise to special obligations to protect those who fall under our care (where these obligations are more stringent than our general duties of beneficence toward strangers). Chapter 15 explores the extent to which impartial utilitarianism can accommodate intuitions and normative practices of partiality.

7. **The Equality Objection:** Utilitarianism is concerned with the overall well-being of individuals in the population, but many object that justice requires an additional concern for how this well-being is distributed across individuals. Chapter 16 examines this objection, and how utilitarians might best respond.

8. **The Cluelessness Objection:** Is utilitarianism undermined by our inability to predict the long-term consequences of our actions? Chapter 17 explores whether utilitarians can still be guided by near-term expected value even when this is small in comparison to the potential value or disvalue of the unknown long-term consequences.

9. **The Abusability Objection:** Some argue that utilitarianism is self-effacing, or recommends against its own acceptance, due to the risk that mistaken appeals to the "greater good" may actually result in horrifically harmful actions being done. Chapter 18 explores how best to guard against such risks, and questions whether it is an objection to a theory if it turns out to be self-effacing in this way.

10

The Rights Objection

Introduction

According to commonsense morality and many non-utilitarian theories, there are certain *moral constraints* you should never violate. These constraints are expressed in moral rules like "do not lie!" and "do not kill!" These rules are intuitively very plausible and they present a problem for utilitarianism. The reason for this is that utilitarianism not only specifies which outcomes are best—those having the highest overall level of well-being—but also directs us to realize these outcomes.

Sometimes, securing the best outcome may require violating moral constraints against harming others—that is, violating their rights. There is no guarantee that commonsense moral rules will always coincide with the best ways to act according to utilitarianism; we could imagine commonsense morality and good outcomes conflicting. As previously mentioned, critics offer the Transplant thought experiment as an example of such a conflict:[1]

> **Transplant:** Imagine a hypothetical scenario in which there are five patients, each of whom will soon die unless they receive an appropriate transplanted organ—a heart, two kidneys, a liver, and lungs. A healthy patient, Chuck, comes into the hospital for a routine check-up, and the doctor finds that Chuck is a perfect match as a donor for all five patients. Should the doctor kill Chuck and use his organs to save the five others?

At first glance, it seems that utilitarianism has to answer the question with "Yes, the doctor should kill Chuck." It's better that five people survive than only one

---

1. Adapted from Judith Jarvis Thomson, "Killing, Letting Die, and the Trolley Problem," *The Monist* 59, no. 2 (April 1976): 206, https://doi.org/10.5840/monist197659224.

(all else equal). But on commonsense morality and virtually every other moral theory, the answer is "No, do not kill Chuck." Killing Chuck would be widely regarded as morally monstrous. Utilitarianism seems to be the rare exception that claims otherwise. This apparent implication is often taken to show that utilitarianism must be wrong.

Proponents of utilitarianism might respond to this objection in four ways. We will go through them in turn.

Accommodating the Intuition

A first utilitarian response to the thought experiment might be to *accommodate the intuition* against killing Chuck by showing that utilitarianism does not *actually* imply that doctors should kill their patients. Critics of utilitarianism *assume* that, in Transplant, the doctor killing Chuck will cause better consequences. But this assumption is itself highly counterintuitive. If the hospital authorities and the general public learned about this incident, a major scandal would result. People would be terrified to go to the doctor. As a consequence, many more people could die or suffer serious health problems due to not being diagnosed or treated by their doctors. Since killing Chuck would not clearly result in the best outcome and may even result in a terrible outcome, utilitarianism does not necessarily imply that the doctor should kill him.

Even if we *stipulate* that the scenario is an unusual one in which killing Chuck *really would* lead to the best outcome (with no further unintended consequences), it's hard to imagine how the *doctor* could be so certain of this. Given how incredibly bad it would be to undermine public trust in our medical institutions (not to mention the reputation harm of undermining utilitarian ethics in the broader society),[2] it would seem unacceptably *reckless*, according to expectational utilitarianism, for the doctor to risk such population-wide harm to save just a small

---

2. This reputational harm is far from trivial. Each individual committed to (competently) acting on utilitarianism could be expected to save *many* lives. So, doing things that risk deterring *many* others in society (at a population-wide level) from following utilitarian ethics risks *immense* harm. On the reputational costs of instrumental harm, see Jim A. C. Everett et al., "The Costs of Being Consequentialist: Social Inference from Instrumental Harm and Impartial Beneficence," *Journal of Experimental Social Psychology* 79 (November 2018): 200–16, https:// doi.org/10.1016/j.jesp.2018.07.004.

handful of lives. Utilitarianism can certainly condemn such recklessness, even while allowing that there are rare cases in which, by unpredictable fluke, such reckless behavior could turn out to be for the best.

This is a generalizable defense of utilitarianism against a wide range of alleged counterexamples. Such "counterexamples" invite us to imagine that a typically disastrous class of action (such as killing an innocent person) just so happens, in this special case, to produce the best outcome. But the agent in the imagined case generally has no good basis for discounting the typical risk of disaster. So it would be unacceptably risky for them to perform the typically disastrous act.[3] We maximize expected value by avoiding such risks.[4] For all practical purposes (as explained in Chapter 6), utilitarianism recommends that we should refrain from rights-violating behaviors, just as moral intuition suggests.

Debunking the Intuition

A second strategy to deal with the Transplant case (once fleshed out with all necessary stipulations) is to *debunk the intuition* against killing Chuck by showing that the intuition is unreliable. It's *almost* always wrong to commit murder, and we might not be reliable at identifying the exceptions. As noted above, utilitarians tend to hold that we should cultivate strong character dispositions and social norms against murder precisely because we are so unreliable at identifying the rare exceptions: stricter norms and dispositions will presumably lead to overall better consequences than maintaining an open attitude toward murder. But this means that our intuition against killing Chuck may just result from our having— correctly, by utilitarian lights—embraced a *useful but imperfect* moral norm against

---

3. Eduardo Rivera-López, "The Moral Murderer: A (More) Effective Counterexample to Consequentialism," *Ratio* 25, no. 3 (August 2012): 307–25, https://doi.org/10.1111/j.1467 -9329.2012.00544.x. For critical informal discussion, see Richard Y. Chappell, "Counterexamples to Consequentialism," Philosophy, et cetera (blog), August 23, 2012, https://www .philosophyetc.net/2012/08/counterexamples-to-consequentialism.html.

4. Even if we can somehow stipulate that the agent's first-order evidence supports believing that murder is net-positive in their case, we also need to take into account the *higher-order evidence* that most people who make such judgments are mistaken. Given the risk of miscalculation and the far greater harms that could result from violating widely accepted social norms, utilitarianism may well recommend that doctors adopt a *strictly* anti-murder disposition, rather than being open to committing murder whenever it *seems* to them to be for the best.

murder. While this norm is correct in the vast majority of cases, it can fail under those very exceptional circumstances in which killing someone would actually bring about the best consequences.

We may also worry that the intuition reflects an objectionable form of status quo bias. However terrible it is for Chuck to die prematurely, is it not—upon reflection—equally terrible for any *one* of the five potential beneficiaries to die prematurely? Why do we find it so much easier to ignore their interests in this situation, and what could possibly justify such neglect? There are practical reasons why instituting rights *against being killed* may typically do more good than rights *to have one's life be saved*, and the utilitarian's recommended "public code" of morality may reflect this. But when we consider a specific case, there's no obvious reason why one right should be more important (let alone five times more important) than the other, as a matter of principle. So attending more to the neglected moral claims of the five who will otherwise die may serve to weaken our initial intuition that what matters most here is just that Chuck not be killed.

Rivals Fare No Better

A third response to the Transplant case is to argue that *rival views fare no better*.

As noted above, the charge of status quo bias seems especially pressing in this context. If you asked all six people from behind the veil of ignorance whether you should kill one of them to save the other five, they'd all agree that you should. A five-in-six chance of survival is far better than one-in-six, after all. And it's morally arbitrary that the one happens to have healthy organs while the other five do not. There's no moral reason to privilege this antecedent state of affairs just because it's the status quo. Yet that's just *what it is* to grant the one a right not to be killed while refusing the five any rights to be saved. It is to arbitrarily uphold the status quo distribution of health and well-being as morally privileged, no matter that we could improve upon it (as established by the impartial mechanism of the veil of ignorance). That seems pretty bad.

Another challenge may be presented by increasing the stakes in our thought experiment:

> **Revised Transplant:** Suppose that scientists can grow human organs in the lab, but only by performing an invasive procedure that kills the

original donor. This procedure can create up to one million new organs. Like before, our doctor can kill Chuck, but this time, she can use his body to save one million people. Should she do this?

Consider how two non-utilitarians would react to Revised Transplant. The *Moderate non-utilitarian* says that, unlike in the original case, the doctor should kill Chuck because the constraint against harming others is outweighed since enough is at stake. The *Absolutist non-utilitarian*, on the other hand, says that the doctor still should not kill Chuck since no amount of benefit can outweigh the injustice of killing him.

One objection to the Moderate is that their position seems *incoherent*. The rationale underlying the prohibition against killing Chuck in Transplant should also forbid killing him in Revised Transplant. In both cases, an innocent person is sacrificed for the greater good. Another objection to the Moderate is that their position is *arbitrary*. The Moderate must draw a line past which constraint violations become permissible, for example, when the benefit is for at least one million people. But why draw the line precisely at that point rather than higher or lower? What is so special about this particular number, 1,000,000? Yet the same question can be asked for any specific number of lives saved. The only non-arbitrary positions are that of the Absolutist, for whom there is no number of lives saved that can justify killing Chuck, and that of the utilitarian, who says that killing Chuck is justified whenever the overall benefits outweigh the costs.

Absolutism seems even more counterintuitive than utilitarianism. If we continue to increase the number of lives we could save by killing Chuck—say, from one million to one billion, and so on—it soon becomes absurd to claim that doing so is impermissible. This position appears even more absurd when we consider cases involving uncertainty. For instance, it seems the Absolutist is committed to saying it's impermissible to perform the medical procedure on Chuck, even if it had only a very small chance of killing him and is guaranteed to save millions of lives.

Biting the Bullet

The final response is to *bite the bullet* and simply accept that we should—in this bizarre hypothetical situation—kill Chuck despite the intuition that killing Chuck is wrong. It's regrettable that the only way to save the five other people involves Chuck's death. Yet the right action may be to kill him since it allows the five others to continue living, any one of whom matters just as much as Chuck does. Chuck's death, while unfortunate, is *stipulated* by the thought experiment to be required to create a world where there is as much well-being as possible.

All of the standard arguments against deontic constraints become relevant at this point. For example, the hope objection flags that a benevolent observer should prefer that the five be saved, and it's hard to see how deontic moral rules could matter more than what we—or any impartial benevolent observer—should hope is done.

Of course, it's important to stress that real-life outcomes can't be stipulated in advance, so in real-life cases, utilitarians overwhelmingly opt to "accommodate the intuition" and reject the critic's assumption that killing innocent people leads to better outcomes.

For additional resources and study aids, see https://utilitarianism.net/

11

The Mere Means Objection

Introduction

Critics often allege that utilitarianism objectionably *instrumentalizes* people—treating us as "mere means" to the greater good rather than properly valuing individuals as "ends in themselves."[1] This chapter assesses whether this is a fair objection.

There is something very appealing about the Kantian *Formula of Humanity* that one should "act in such a way as to treat humanity, whether in your own person or in that of anyone else, always as an end and never merely as a means."[2] If utilitarianism were truly incompatible with the plain meaning of this formula, then that would constitute a serious objection to the theory. For it would then be shown to be incompatible with the basic point that people have intrinsic value as ends in themselves.

Why think that utilitarianism treats anyone merely as a means? Three possibilities seem worth exploring. The first involves mistakenly leaving out the crucial word "merely," though this radically changes the meaning of the Formula of Humanity in a way that undermines its plausibility. The second hinges on the utilitarian preference for saving lives that are themselves more instrumentally useful for indirectly helping others. And the third involves a distinctly Kantian interpretation of what is essential to treating someone as an end in themselves. But as we will see, none of these three moves validates the conclusion that utilitarianism

---

1. Strictly speaking, this objection applies to all (aggregative) consequentialist theories. The responses we offer on behalf of utilitarianism in this discussion would equally apply in defense of other consequentialist theories.

2. Immanuel Kant, *Groundwork of the Metaphysics of Morals*, trans. Jonathan Bennett (n.p., 1785; Early Modern Texts, 2017), https://www.earlymoderntexts.com/assets/pdfs/kant1785.pdf.

violates the plain meaning of the Formula of Humanity, or literally treats anyone as a "mere means."

Using as a Means

Utilitarianism allows people to be used as a means to bring about better outcomes. For example, in stylized thought experiments, it implies that one person should be killed to save five. More generally, it allows harm to be imposed on some in order to secure greater overall benefits for others. But many ways of using others are morally innocuous. As Kantians will agree: if you ask a stranger for directions, you are using them as a means, but not *objectionably*. Asking someone for directions is compatible with still regarding them as intrinsically valuable or an end in themselves. Is utilitarian sacrifice different in a way that makes it incompatible with such moral regard?

There are important differences between the two cases. Most obviously, utilitarian sacrifice involves *harming* (sometimes even killing) the targeted individual. So it's not as innocuous as asking for directions: there is a significant moral cost here, which could only be justified by sufficiently great compensating moral gains. Even so, on the crucial question of whether utilitarians still regard the sacrificed individual as an intrinsically valuable end in themselves, the answer is a clear *YES*. After all, the utilitarian agent would be willing to sacrifice other goods of significant value[3]—including their own interests—to spare the sacrificed individual of their burden. But one obviously would not be willing to sacrifice in such a way for any entity that one regarded as a *mere* means, entirely lacking in moral importance.[4] So we see that the utilitarian regards the sacrificed individual as morally important (emphatically *not* a *mere* means), albeit not *as* important as five other people combined.

Utilitarianism counts the well-being of *everyone* fully and equally, neglecting none. So, while it (like other theories) permits some forms of using people as a means, it never loses sight of the fact that all individuals have intrinsic value. That is precisely why the theory directs us to do whatever will best help all those

---

3. Specifically, they would be willing to sacrifice goods that added up to an equal or lesser loss of well-being value in order to relieve this burden.

4. Cf. Derek Parfit, "Merely as a Means," chap. 9 in *On What Matters*, vol. 1 (Oxford: Oxford University Press, 2011).

individuals. This may lead to outcomes where some particular individuals are disadvantaged. However, it's important not to conflate *ending up worse off* with *counting for less* in the process of determining what would be best overall (counting everyone's interests equally).

For example, suppose a group of friends draw lots to determine who should perform some unpleasant chore. The person who draws the short straw will not be *mistreated* in any way: the bad (for him) outcome would result from a fair process that treats him the same as everyone else in the group. In a similar way, utilitarianism counts everyone's interests equally, even when it yields results that are better for some than for others. Since everyone is counted fully as ends in themselves, it's not accurate to claim that utilitarianism treats anyone as a "mere means."

By contrast, utilitarianism *does* treat non-sentient things, like the environment, as having merely instrumental value. Environmental protection is immensely important, not for its own sake, but for the sake of people and other sentient beings. There is a big difference between how utilitarianism values the environment and how it values people, which is another way to see that the theory does not value people merely instrumentally.

Instrumental Favoritism

Suppose that you are faced with a medical emergency but only have enough medicine to save either one adult or two children. Two children and an adult pharmacist are on the brink of death, and three other children are severely ill and would die before anyone else is able to come to their assistance. If you save the pharmacist, she will be able to manufacture more medicine in time to save the remaining three severely ill children (though not in time to save the two that are already on the brink). If you save the two children, all the others will die. What should you do?

By utilitarian lights, the answer is straightforward: you should save the pharmacist and thereby save *four* individuals (including three children), rather than only saving two children. It does not matter whether you save an individual *directly* (by giving them medicine yourself) or *indirectly* (by enabling the pharmacist to give them medicine); all that matters is that they are saved.

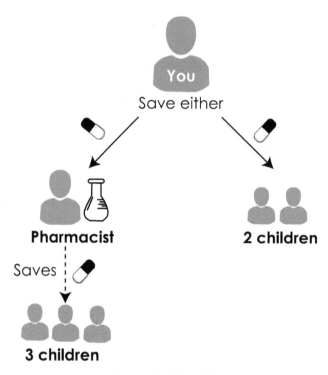

Instrumental favoritism

But some critics object to this. Frances Kamm, for example, claims:

> To favor the person who can produce [extra utility] is to treat people "merely as means" since it decides against the person who cannot produce the extra utility on the grounds that he is not a means. It does not give people equal status as "ends in themselves" and, therefore, treats them unfairly.[5]

In our example, the two children on the brink miss out on the medicine because—unlike the pharmacist—they are unable to save additional lives. While the two children together have greater intrinsic value than the pharmacist alone, the pharmacist has vastly greater *instrumental* value in this context, as only by saving her are we thereby able to (indirectly) save the three other children. And

---

5. F. M. Kamm, "Are There Irrelevant Utilities?" chap. 8 in *Morality, Mortality*, vol. 1, *Death and Whom to Save From It* (New York: Oxford University Press, 1993), 147.

when the intrinsic values of saving these four lives are combined, it outweighs the intrinsic value of saving just two children.

Kamm charges that, in deciding against the two children on these grounds, we would fail to give them "equal status as ends in themselves." But why think this? As the above reasoning makes clear, the utilitarian does not ascribe any extra intrinsic value to the pharmacist. The pharmacist is thus *not* regarded as any more important *as an end in herself*. Intrinsically, or in herself, she may be regarded equally to any other individual.[6] We prioritize saving her over the two children simply because we can thereby save the three other children in addition. The utilitarian's disagreement with Kamm stems not from the utilitarian unfairly giving extra weight to the pharmacist but from Kamm's failure to give equal weight to the three children we could save by means of saving the pharmacist.

To emphasize this point, consider a variation of the case in which the pharmacist is replaced with a duplicator machine.[7] Suppose you could either save the two children on the brink of death immediately or place the medicine in a duplicator that will (after some time) produce enough medicine to save the other three severely ill children. In simply opting to save the larger number, the utilitarian is clearly not treating anyone as a "mere means." But how could it possibly be morally worse to save the pharmacist *in addition to* those three children?

That said, there are many cases in which instrumental favoritism would seem less appropriate. We do not want emergency room doctors to pass judgment on the social value of their patients before deciding who to save, for example. And there are good utilitarian reasons for this: such judgments are apt to be unreliable, distorted by all sorts of biases regarding privilege and social status, and institutionalizing them could send a harmful, stigmatizing message that undermines social solidarity. Realistically, it seems unlikely that the minor instrumental benefits to be gained from such a policy would outweigh these significant harms. So utilitarians may endorse standard rules of medical ethics that disallow medical providers from considering social value in triage or when making medical allocation decisions. But this practical point is very different from claiming that, as a

---

6. Strictly speaking, her interests are given equal weight, but if she has lower remaining life expectancy than the children (and hence correspondingly less future well-being at stake), then the intrinsic value of her future life may be *lower* than that of those with longer yet to live.

7. Thanks to Toby Ord for suggesting this variant.

matter of principle, utilitarianism's instrumental favoritism treats others as mere means. There seems to be no good basis for that stronger claim.

Kantian Interpretations

Kantians and utilitarians disagree about how to respond to the intrinsic value of each person. Utilitarians believe that the correct way to appreciate the intrinsic value of all individuals is to count their interests equally in the utilitarian calculus. Kantians offer a different account, typically appealing to considerations of possible or actual consent.[8] Advocates of the "mere means" objection may further claim that, in failing to follow the Kantian standard for how to appreciate the intrinsic value of persons, utilitarians fail to regard people as intrinsically valuable at all. But that is uncharitable. Everyone agrees that people are ends in themselves; the disagreement is just about what follows from that morally.

Different moral theories, such as utilitarianism and Kantianism, offer different accounts of the morally correct way to respond to the intrinsic value of persons. We make no attempt to adjudicate that dispute here. Someone who is convinced by the arguments for Kantianism may certainly be expected to reject utilitarianism on that basis. But there is no *independent* basis for rejecting utilitarianism merely on the grounds that it violates *Kantian* standards for treating people as ends in themselves. We might just as well turn the objection around and charge Kantians with violating *utilitarian* standards for how to value people equally as ends in themselves. Either charge would seem equally question-begging and provides the target with no independent grounds for doubting their view.

Conclusion

We've seen that it's inaccurate to claim that utilitarians treat people as "mere means." All plausible moral theories sometimes allow people to be treated as a means (while *also* respecting them as ends in themselves). When utilitarianism allows such treatment, even in the most extreme cases of "utilitarian sacrifice," it does not thereby treat the affected individuals as *mere* means. Even those who end up worse off are not subject to procedural unfairness or disregard: their interests

---

8. For example, they may claim that you should not treat people in ways they either do not consent to or could not reasonably consent to.

are counted fully and equally to anyone else's, as befits their intrinsic value. And while Kantians disagree with utilitarians about the right way to *respond* to the intrinsic value of persons, everyone agrees that individual persons *are* intrinsically valuable and not mere means to some other goal.

But there may be other, closely related, objections that people sometimes have in mind when they accuse utilitarianism of treating people as mere means. Some may have in mind the "separateness of persons" objection—criticizing utilitarianism for treating trade-offs *between* lives the same way as trade-offs *within* a life—which we address in the next chapter. Others may be concerned about how utilitarianism (in theory) permits instrumental harm when the benefits outweigh the costs. The previous chapter addressed this concern in more detail. Note that in practice, utilitarians tend to be strongly supportive of respecting rights, as societies that respect individual rights tend to do a better job of promoting overall well-being.

For additional resources and study aids, see https://utilitarianism.net/

The Separateness of Persons Objection

Introduction

It's widely agreed that self-interest (or prudence) calls for aggregating harms and benefits across different moments *within* one's life to maximize one's overall well-being. For example, visiting the dentist is prudent despite the immediate unpleasantness because it helps to avert greater harm to one's future self. Aggregative consequentialist theories like utilitarianism go one step further: they aggregate harms and benefits *between* different people's lives to maximize overall societal well-being. It can be worth imposing harms on some individuals, utilitarians claim, if that prevents greater harms to others. This leads some critics to claim that utilitarianism neglects the moral significance of the boundaries between individuals.

This *separateness of persons* objection was stated most famously by John Rawls:

> [Utilitarianism] is the consequence of extending to society the principle of choice for one man, and then, to make this extension work, conflating all persons into one. . . . Utilitarianism does not take seriously the distinction between persons.[1]

Despite its influence, the reasoning behind this objection can be difficult to pin down. The idea that utilitarians must "conflat[e] all persons into one" seems to presume that they (i) *start* with "the principle of choice for one man," and then (ii) argue for their view *on the basis that* all of society can be treated (perhaps metaphorically) as just another individual. But in fact many utilitarian arguments, as

---

1. Rawls, *A Theory of Justice* (Cambridge, MA: Belknap Press, 1971), 27.

laid out in Chapter 3, do *not* take this form. So this interpretation of the objection seems too narrow. It might debunk one particular argument for utilitarianism, but utilitarianism itself may still be well-supported on other grounds.

On a broader interpretation, we may take the objection to assert that respecting the distinction between persons requires treating inter-personal trade-offs (those *between* lives) differently from intra-personal ones (those *within* one life). On this interpretation, it's the implications of utilitarianism, not what argument led to it, that are seen as objectionable. But what is the positive case for treating intra- and inter-personal trade-offs differently?[2] The remainder of this discussion explores three candidate arguments, based on (i) compensation, (ii) fungibility, and (iii) anti-aggregative intuitions.

Compensation

The standard interpretation of the separateness of persons understands it to be a matter of *compensation*.[3] The agent who gets harmed is *compensated* if they later receive a greater benefit as a result, whereas they receive no such compensation if the benefit goes to someone else. As Nozick put it: "To use a person [for another's benefit] . . . does not sufficiently respect and take account of the fact that he is a separate person, that his is the only life he has. *He* does not get some overbalancing good from his sacrifice."[4]

Utilitarians may respond that every person in need is an individual, equally deserving of moral concern and respect, living the only life *they* have.[5] To make the

---

2. As R. M. Hare presses the challenge: "To have concern for someone is to seek his good, or to seek to promote his interests; and to have equal concern for all people is to seek equally their good, or to give equal weight to their interests, which is exactly what utilitarianism requires. To do this is to treat others' interests in the same way as a prudent person treats his own interests, present and future. . . . To do this is not to fail to 'insist on the separateness of persons.'" See Hare, "Rights, Utility, and Universalization: Reply to J. L. Mackie," in *Utility and Rights*, ed. R. Frey (Oxford: Basil Blackwell, 1985), 107.

3. David O. Brink, "Consequentialism, the Separateness of Persons, and Aggregation," in *The Oxford Handbook of Consequentialism*, ed. Douglas W. Portmore (New York: Oxford University Press, 2020).

4. Robert Nozick, *Anarchy, State, and Utopia* (New York: Basic Books, 1974), 33.

5. An interestingly different line of response would be to appeal to a Veil of Ignorance argument. While the individual who gets harmed is not compensated for it *in the moment*, each

challenge vivid, we may imagine ourselves in the position of the one being used as a means. When utilitarianism demands that we bear a cost, it does not deny that the beneficiaries are distinct from us. It merely denies the egoistic assumption that their distinctness means that they should not matter to us; it denies that we could reasonably demand a *veto* over every trade-off in which our interests are negatively implicated.[6] And indeed, this is hardly unique to utilitarians. As Katarzyna de Lazari-Radek and Peter Singer write, "Anyone who supports taxing people on high incomes and using the revenue to provide benefits to others in need must agree that it is sometimes justifiable to impose a cost on one person to benefit another."[7]

Fungibility

A deeper concern is that utilitarianism might seem to treat individuals as entirely fungible or replaceable without regret. As Peter Singer characterizes the view: "It is as if sentient beings are receptacles of something valuable, and it does not matter if a receptacle gets broken so long as there is another receptacle to which its contents can be transferred without any getting spilt."[8]

To make the problem vivid, imagine that Connie the Consequentialist is faced with two poison victims, and just enough anti-venom to save one of them.[9] And suppose that, faced with their pleading faces, but realizing that it makes no

---

individual should be willing *in advance* (i.e., from behind the veil of ignorance) to agree to utilitarian trade-offs since this is the best way for them to maximize their own well-being, in expectation.

6. To expand on this point: If we reject egoism, we should also reject the assumption that compensation is essential for moral justification. For on any other view, we may be morally *required* to accept some costs for others' sake. Next, note that we need not be granted a veto power that it would not be morally legitimate for us to exercise. So, some *may* use us, for another's benefit, compatibly with full moral respect if the use is one that we are morally required to accept. Brink notes that Rawls's own egalitarian view often requires uncompensated sacrifices from the wealthy. Brink, "Consequentialism, the Separateness of Persons, and Aggregation," 387.

7. de Lazari-Radek and Singer, "Objections," chap. 4 in *Utilitarianism: A Very Short Introduction* (Oxford: Oxford University Press, 2017), 82.

8. Singer, *Practical Ethics*, 3rd ed. (Cambridge: Cambridge University Press, 2011), 106.

9. The following paragraphs draw directly from Richard Y. Chappell, "Value Receptacles," *Noûs* 49, no. 2 (June 2015): 322–32, https://doi.org/10.1111/nous.12023.

difference to the total amount of well-being which person she saves, Connie finds herself feeling completely *indifferent* about her choice. It's as if she had to choose between a twenty-dollar bill or two tens.

It seems that Connie is making a deep moral mistake here. She is treating the two people's interests as completely fungible, like money, and neglecting the fact that each person is of distinct intrinsic importance, in their own right, and not merely a fungible means to aggregate well-being. The correct moral theory, we feel, must attribute intrinsic value to particular individuals and not just to the sum total of their well-being.[10]

One of the authors (Chappell) has argued that there is no barrier to utilitarianism assigning intrinsic value to individuals in this way:

> There is not just one thing, the global happiness, that is good. Instead, there is my happiness, your happiness, Bob's, and Sally's, which are all equally weighty but nonetheless distinct intrinsic goods. What this means is that the morally fitting agent should have a corresponding plurality of non-instrumental desires: for my welfare, yours, Bob's, and Sally's. Tradeoffs between us may be made, but they are acknowledged as genuine tradeoffs: though a benefit to one may *outweigh* a smaller harm to another, this does not *cancel* it. The harm remains regrettable, for that person's sake, even if we ultimately have most reason to accept it for the sake of more greatly benefiting another.[11]

On this view, what it's appropriate for Connie to feel is not *indifference* but rather *ambivalence*—to be genuinely torn, as she is pulled (equally strongly) in different directions by the conflicting interests of the two individuals who need her help. In this way, the utilitarian can avoid treating individuals as fungible, and instead fully recognize and appreciate each individual's separate value.

This utilitarian response rejects the assumption that *commensurability* of value (that is, the ability to compare and make trade-offs between competing interests or

---

10. Cf. G. A. Cohen, "Rescuing Conservatism: A Defense of Existing Value," chap. 9 in *Reasons and Recognition: Essays on the Philosophy of T. M. Scanlon*, ed. R. Jay Wallace, Rahul Kumar, and Samuel Freeman (Oxford: Oxford University Press, 2011).
11. Chappell, "Value Receptacles," 328.

values) entails *fungibility* of value (or replaceability without regret). The assumption may be rejected since non-fungibility can be secured by having multiple genuinely *distinct* values, which may nonetheless be weighed against each other.[12]

This is perhaps clearest when considering other forms of (putative) value: an art-lover might intrinsically value each item in their art collection and yet still be willing to smother a fire with one painting if that would save five others. In valuing each painting separately, they will regret the loss of the unique painting that is thereby destroyed. But they may regard the sacrifice as worth it, even so. Nothing in their attitude here betrays an objectionably instrumental attitude toward their artworks. Just as this art consequentialist respects the separateness of paintings, so the utilitarian (or welfare consequentialist) respects the separateness of persons.

Anti-Aggregative Intuitions

Finally, critics might grant that utilitarianism really does separately value individual persons, but just *not in the right way*. On this view, there is something intuitively problematic about utilitarian aggregation. Instead of summing different people's interests, strictly anti-aggregative views might advocate for a *maximin* approach that simply seeks to improve the position of the worst-off. As Nagel writes:

> Where there is a conflict of interests, no result can be completely acceptable to everyone. But it is at least possible to assess each result from each point of view to find the result that is the least unacceptable to the person to whom it is most unacceptable. . . . A radically egalitarian policy of

---

12. "Value pluralism" is often used to refer to the idea of multiple distinct *types* or kinds of values. Instead, the relevant form of pluralism to secure non-fungibility is *token* pluralism. Bob's and Sally's interests may both be values of the same *kind* (namely, welfare value), but they are distinct individual (or "token") values in the sense that it is fitting to have a *separate* intrinsic desire for each. Contrast this with money, where distinct twenty-dollar bills are *not* distinctly valuable: it would be strange to desire each bill separately, rather than just having a single overarching desire for "more money" that any twenty-dollar bill could equally well satisfy.

giving absolute priority to the worst-off, regardless of numbers, would result from always choosing the least unacceptable alternative, in this sense.[13]

Maximin has severe problems as an alternative to utilitarian aggregation. Taking maximin literally, it would be preferable to give a lollipop to the most miserable person on earth rather than, say, to avert a global pandemic or nuclear war that would happen after the most miserable person's death (or that would somehow leave this individual unharmed).

Still, there are particular cases in which utilitarian aggregation seems (intuitively) to yield the wrong result. Consider Scanlon's famous Transmitter Room case:[14]

Jones has suffered an accident in the transmitter room of a television station. To save Jones from an hour of severe pain, we would have to cancel part of the broadcast of a football game, which is giving pleasure to very many people.[15]

Intuitively, it does not matter how many people are watching the football game; it's simply *more important* to save Jones from suffering severe pain during this time.[16]

Reinterpreting the Intuition

Why is it more important to save Jones? One answer would be that we cannot aggregate distinct interests, so all that is left to do is to satisfy whichever individual

---

13. Thomas Nagel, "Equality," in *Mortal Questions* (Cambridge: Cambridge University Press, 1979), 123.

14. T. M. Scanlon, *What We Owe to Each Other* (Cambridge, MA: Belknap Press, 1998).

15. This is a quote from Derek Parfit's concise summary of the thought experiment. Parfit, "Justifiability to Each Person," *Ratio* 16, no. 4 (December 2003): 375, https://doi.org/10.1046/j.1467-9329.2003.00229.x.

16. The following subsections draw directly from Richard Y. Chappell, *Parfit's Ethics* (Cambridge: Cambridge University Press, 2021), section 3.2.

moral claim is strongest, namely, Jones's. But Parfit suggests an alternative—prioritarian—explanation: perhaps we should help Jones because he is much worse off and thus has greater moral priority.[17]

(While utilitarians reject this prioritarian claim, they may nonetheless take comfort if it turns out that our intuitions are more closely aligned with prioritarianism than with anti-aggregationism. This is for two main reasons. First, they may regard prioritarian intuitions as easily debunkable. And second, they may regard prioritarianism as close enough to utilitarianism that they are not so concerned to press the dispute.)

Parfit argues that his prioritarian account is preferable to Scanlon's anti-aggregative approach in cases where the two diverge. We can see this by imagining cases in which the many smaller benefits would go to some of the worst-off individuals. For example, it would clearly be better to give an extra five years of life to each of a million child cancer victims than to give fifty more years of life to a single adult. In rejecting aggregation, we might have to prioritize a single large benefit to someone already well-off rather than (individually smaller but collectively immensely larger) benefits to a great many worse-off individuals. That seems clearly wrong. It would not, for example, be a good thing to take a dollar from each of a billion poor people in order to give a billion dollars to someone who was wealthy to begin with.

So, rather than refusing to aggregate smaller benefits, Parfit suggests that we should simply weigh harms and benefits in a way that prioritizes the worse-off. Two appealing implications of this view are that: (i) We generally should not allow huge harms to befall a single person, if that leaves them much worse off than the others with competing interests. (ii) But we should allow (sufficient) small benefits to the worse-off to (in sum) outweigh a single large benefit to someone better-off. Since we need aggregation in order to secure claim (ii), and we can secure claim (i) without having to reject aggregation, it looks like our intuitions are overall best served by accepting an aggregative moral theory.

---

17. Parfit, "Justifiability to Each Person," 368–90. What if the watchers are somehow even worse off? Then Parfit's explanation fails, but he could comfortably suggest that slightly improving the lot of billions of worse-off individuals really should be prioritized over offering great relief to a single individual who is already in a better state than these others.

Debunking the Intuition

Common intuitions suffer from *scope insensitivity*, reflecting our inability to truly grasp large numbers.[18] Our intuitions do not respond very differently to whether the number of competing interests is a million, a billion, or a googolplex. But the real difference in value between these numbers is immense. So, we should not trust our intuitions when they treat these vastly different numbers as morally alike. Utilitarians may thus feel comfortable rejecting anti-aggregative intuitions as especially untrustworthy.

Despite Parfit's arguments described above, even prioritarians may ultimately need to follow the utilitarian in accepting a debunking response. Consider: critics may insist that Parfit's prioritarian account cannot do full justice to our starting intuition about the Transmitter Room case. Granted, sufficient priority weighting may explain how Jones's suffering can outweigh the aggregate pleasure of a million, or even a billion, better-off football fans. But so long as the priority weighting is finite, there will be *some* (perhaps astronomically large) number of smaller pleasures that could, in theory, outweigh Jones's suffering. At this point, defenders of aggregation may simply accept this implication and suggest that any residual intuitive discomfort with this conclusion is best explained as a mistake resulting from scope neglect.

Rivals Fare No Better

Contrary to utilitarianism, one might be tempted to think that some benefits are so *trivial* that we should round them down to zero rather than allow vast numbers of them to sum to something morally significant. But Parfit proves that this way of thinking is a mistake. To see why, consider the following plausible-seeming claim:

> (P): We ought to give one person one more year of life rather than lengthening any number of other people's lives by only one minute.[19]

18. Stephan Dickert et al., "Scope Insensitivity: The Limits of Intuitive Valuation of Human Lives in Public Policy," *Journal of Applied Research in Memory and Cognition* 4, no. 3 (2015): 248–55, http://doi.org/10.1016/j.jarmac.2014.09.002.
19. Parfit, "Justifiability to Each Person," 385.

One year is about half a million minutes. So Parfit invites us to imagine a community of just over a million people and apply the choice described in (P) to each of them. Each person in the community would then gain one year of life. But consider the opportunity cost. If each time we had instead given one more minute of life to everyone else, the end result would be a gain of *two* years of life for each person. So the choice described in (P), when repeated in this way, results in everyone being worse off than they otherwise would have been.

This clearly shows that (P) is a bad principle *in iterative contexts* like that described above. Does it show that (P) is a bad principle, even in a one-off application? That is less immediately clear, but we may be able to show this with further argument.[20] Parfit himself appeals to a distinction between fundamental moral *principles* and mere *policies* (or rules of thumb), suggesting that only the latter should be contingent on context in this way. If he is right about that, this would suggest that our fundamental moral principles must allow for unrestricted aggregation, in contrast to claims like (P). Any rule that we take to apply only some of the time (e.g., in one-off applications but not iterated ones) must, for Parfit, be a mere rule of thumb rather than a fundamental moral principle.

We might supplement Parfit's argument by observing that the expected value of each choice described above is *independent* of the other choices being made. The value of giving everyone one more minute (just once) is the same as the value of giving everyone one more minute (for the millionth time).[21]

This is important for two reasons. First, independence implies that the expected value of the one-off choice is equal to the average value of the repeated choice. So, since repeatedly choosing *one minute for everyone* is more worthwhile than repeatedly choosing *one year for one person*, it follows (from independence) that

---

20. This text continues to draw directly from Chappell, *Parfit's Ethics*, section 3.2.

21. There are ways of imagining the case where this would not be so. For example, if we imagine giving the extra minutes of life to each person on their deathbed, the first several such minutes might be disproportionately lacking in value, compared to a more representative minute of life. To properly test principles of aggregation, we should imagine a setup where the independence assumption holds—for instance, by supposing that the extra minutes are given to people at some earlier point in their lives, before mortal illness strikes. This makes it clearer how a single minute might, in some cases, have significant value, by being just what the recipient needed to complete some important life project.

the former choice is also more worthwhile in the one-off case. This is a surprising and important result.

The second reason why the independence claim is important here is that it can help to shed light on why this initially surprising result makes sense, and is plausible upon reflection. Whatever valuable events an extra year of life would offer—all the moments of happiness, completed projects that would otherwise have been cut short, etc.—we should expect twice as many such events to be enabled by offering an extra minute of (representative) life to each of a million people.

Putting this all together, then, defenders of aggregationism can offer a two-pronged response to their critics. First, our initial anti-aggregative intuitions may be explained away. And second, further reflection shows that anti-aggregative principles would have implications that are arguably more objectionable than those of aggregationism.

Conclusion

We've seen that the separateness of persons objection to utilitarianism can take three forms, none of which is decisive. The compensation objection rests on implausibly egoistic assumptions. The fungibility objection involves a misconception: utilitarianism need not treat distinct individuals as fungible. Finally, while anti-aggregative intuitions have some force, we've also seen that there are ways for utilitarians to resist them, and that these anti-aggregative views face even worse difficulties.

For additional resources and study aids, see https://utilitarianism.net/

13

The Demandingness Objection

Utilitarianism doesn't ask us to be morally perfect. It asks us to face up to our moral limitations and do as much as we humanly can to overcome them.

—Joshua Greene[1]

The Demandingness Objection

Many critics argue that utilitarianism is too *demanding* because it requires us always to bring about the best outcome. The theory leaves no room for actions that are permissible yet do not bring about the best consequences. Philosophers label such actions that are morally good but not required as *supererogatory*; maximizing utilitarianism (like maximizing consequentialism more broadly) denies that any action can be supererogatory. As a result, some critics claim that utilitarianism is a morality only for saints.[2]

No one, including utilitarian philosophers, lives their life in perfect accordance with utilitarianism. For instance, consider that the money a person spends on dining out could pay for several bednets, each protecting two children in a low-income country from malaria for about two years.[3] From a utilitarian perspective, the benefit to the person from dining out is much smaller than the benefit to the children of being protected against malaria, so it would seem the person has acted wrongly in choosing to have a meal out. Analogous reasoning applies to how

---

1. Joshua Greene, *Moral Tribes: Emotion, Reason, and the Gap between Us and Them* (New York: Penguin Books, 2013), 284.

2. Cf. Wolf, "Moral Saints," *The Journal of Philosophy* 79, no. 8 (August 1982): 419–39, https://www.jstor.org/stable/2026228.

3. "Against Malaria Foundation," GiveWell, accessed May 23, 2024, https://www.givewell.org/charities/amf.

we use our time: the hours someone spends on social media should apparently be spent volunteering for a charity or working harder at one's job to earn more money to donate.

To many people, these extreme obligations of utilitarianism seem absurd at first glance. According to commonsense morality, we are permitted to spend most of our income on ourselves, our loved ones, and our personal projects. Charity, by commonsense lights, is good and praiseworthy, but not obligatory.

Proponents of utilitarianism might respond to this objection in four ways. We will go through them in turn.

Accommodating the Intuition

One way to soften the demands from utilitarianism is to argue that morality should consider human psychological limitations, such as our weakness of will. Utilitarianism recognizes that we cannot work all the time to help others without burning out, which would lead to us doing less overall good in the long run. Similarly, we need to spend money on ourselves to stay reasonably happy and healthy and sustain our long-term motivation to do good.

In addition, it's often justified for utilitarians to spend money or time to accommodate the expectations and needs of other people. If utilitarianism is associated with extreme self-sacrifice, others may not want to join utilitarian causes. Likewise, it may sometimes be justified on utilitarian grounds to buy expensive dinners if that allows one to have valuable meetings with non-utilitarians who would not want to self-sacrifice.

However, even if we accept that spending resources on ourselves can be of great instrumental importance for us to be able to benefit others, most of us must admit that we could be doing more. Utilitarianism remains a demanding ethical theory in practice, even when we account for the psychology of ourselves and others.

A more robust accommodation may be secured by rejecting the ordinary notion of moral "requirement." As explained in Chapter 2:

> Utilitarians agree that you *ideally* ought to choose whatever action would best promote overall well-being. That's what you have the *most* moral reason to do. But they do not recommend *blaming* you every time you fall short of this ideal. As a result, many utilitarians consider it misleading

to take their claims about what *ideally ought* to be done as providing an account of moral "rightness" or "obligation" in the ordinary sense.

According to utilitarianism, whether someone should be blamed for their actions is itself something to be decided by the consequences that blaming them would have. Blaming people whenever they fail to do the most good will likely have bad consequences because it discourages people from even trying. Instead, utilitarianism will generally recommend praising people who take steps in the right direction, even if they fall short of the utilitarian ideal. This shows how the utilitarian notion of "wrongness" comes apart from the commonsense understanding of "wrongness," which is much more tied to blameworthiness.

Indeed, on a scalar or satisficing version of utilitarianism, doing less than the best need not be considered "wrong" at all. It's simply less than would be ideal. Satisficing utilitarianism identifies some lower minimum threshold for what is "required" to avoid blameworthiness. In contrast, scalar consequentialism eschews such thresholds entirely, instead assessing the moral quality of actions on a continuous scale from better to worse. It's *better* for an affluent person to donate 10 percent of their income to charity than to donate only 1 percent, which itself is better than donating nothing at all.

Debunking the Intuition

The second line of response is to argue that ordinary demandingness intuitions *presuppose* (rather than independently *support*) non-consequentialism. By asking the comparatively wealthy to do a lot to help the less fortunate, utilitarianism imposes some non-trivial costs on the wealthy. But compare this to the harms endured by the less fortunate by the wealthy doing less (or nothing) to help them. These harms vastly exceed the costs that utilitarianism would impose on the wealthy. Utilitarians may thus argue that it's the *non-utilitarian* views that are "too demanding" since they impose greater overall costs and focus these costs on those who are least able to bear them.

David Sobel develops this argument in "The Impotence of the Demandingness Objection:"[4]

---

4. Sobel, "The Impotence of the Demandingness Objection," *Philosophers' Imprint* 7, no. 8 (September 2017): 3, http://hdl.handle.net/2027/spo.3521354.0007.008.

Consider the case of Joe and Sally. Joe has two healthy kidneys and can live a decent but reduced life with only one. Sally needs one of Joe's kidneys to live. Even though the transfer would result in a situation that is better overall, the Demandingness Objection's thought is that it's asking so much of Joe to give up a kidney that he is morally permitted to not give. The size of the cost to Joe makes the purported moral demand that Joe give the kidney unreasonable, or at least not genuinely morally obligatory on Joe. Consequentialism, our intuitions tell us, is too demanding on Joe when it requires that he sacrifice a kidney to Sally.

But consider things from Sally's point of view. Suppose she were to complain about the size of the cost that a non-Consequentialist moral theory permits to befall her. Suppose she were to say that such a moral theory, in permitting others to allow her to die when they could aid her, is excessively demanding on her. Clearly Sally has not yet fully understood how philosophers typically intend the Demandingness Objection. What has she failed to get about the Objection? Why is Consequentialism too demanding on the person who would suffer significant costs if he was to aid others as Consequentialism requires, but non-Consequentialist morality is not similarly too demanding on Sally, the person who would suffer more significant costs if she were not aided as the alternative to Consequentialism permits?[5]

---

5. Sobel continues: "What must the Objection's understanding of the demands of a moral theory be such that that would make sense? There is an obvious answer that has appealed even to prominent critics of the Objection—that the costs of what a moral theory requires are more demanding than the costs of what a moral theory permits to befall the unaided, size of cost held constant. The moral significance of the distinction between costs a moral theory requires and costs it permits must already be in place before the Objection gets a grip. But this is for the decisive break with Consequentialism to have already happened before we feel the pull of the Demandingness intuitions."

It seems, then, that there are no *neutral* grounds for considering utilitarianism to be "more demanding" than rival moral theories, at least in the sense of imposing excessively great costs on agents. One can only get this verdict by stacking the deck against utilitarianism by implicitly defining "demandingness" in such a way as to only take a certain subclass of costs fully into account.

We may cast further doubt on our demandingness intuitions by noting other apparent inconsistencies in their application. For instance, many philosophers—utilitarian and non-utilitarian alike—would readily accept that morality can be very demanding in wartime. Under the circumstances of war, they might think that people may have to make great sacrifices, including giving up their property or even their lives. Yet in peacetime today, hundreds of millions of people live in dire circumstances of extreme poverty, and billions of animals suffer in factory farms and are killed every year. At the same time, many affluent people enjoy a wide range of luxury goods and have access to effective channels through which they could assist the poor. From the utilitarian perspective, the world today is just as high-stakes as it is in wartime. For this reason, it's no more demanding—and arguably much less—to require the affluent to donate money to assist the poor in the present day than it is to require soldiers to sacrifice their lives in a war against, say, cruel authoritarianism.

Many assume that utilitarianism would not ask as much of us if most affluent individuals acted morally and shared more of their resources with those most in need. Utilitarianism only becomes so demanding, they suggest, because few affluent people do anything significant to address the major problems in the world. This may be true of our duties of beneficence toward the global poor. But once the long-term future is taken into account, it seems that utilitarianism could continue to recommend very significant sacrifices from everyone alive today, even if we *all* had already done significant good for others.[6]

Rivals Fare No Better

A third response is to argue that non-utilitarian moral views are often *insufficiently demanding*. We've already established that citizens of affluent countries can prevent a substantial amount of suffering and death in developing nations at a comparably low cost to themselves by donating to highly effective aid organizations. According to many non-utilitarian views, it is good but entirely *optional* to donate a significant portion of our income to charity. However, this is arguably not demanding enough since it entails that we are not required to save lives even when we can do so at a low cost to ourselves. These views violate Peter Singer's

---

6. Andreas L. Mogensen, "Moral Demands and the Far Future," *Philosophy and Phenomenological Research* 103, no. 3 (September 2020): 567–85, https://doi.org/10.1111/phpr.12729.

intuitively plausible assertion that "if it is in our power to prevent something bad from happening, without thereby sacrificing anything of comparable moral importance, we ought, morally, to do it."[7] As Singer explains, most people agree that it would be morally monstrous just to watch a child drown in a shallow pond when you could easily save them at the cost of ruining your expensive clothes.[8] Saving innocent lives is worth some moderate financial cost, and any reasonable moral theory needs to reflect that fact.

In addition, proponents of utilitarianism can note that non-utilitarian views are sometimes even more demanding. For example, recall Sobel's example involving Joe and Sally. Commonsense ethics prohibits Sally from stealing one of Joe's kidneys, even if that would be the only way to save her own life (and the harm to Joe would only be moderate). This shows that commonsense morality can be very demanding sometimes, even requiring you to give up your life on moral grounds. While utilitarianism makes *different* demands from other moral theories, the demands of utilitarianism are not obviously less reasonable. They always have a good principled basis, after all.

Biting the Bullet

Finally, proponents of utilitarianism may simply accept that morality is very demanding. They may point out that utilitarian demands are grounded in the compelling goal of creating a flourishing world with as much well-being as possible for everyone. Whenever utilitarianism requires us to give up something we value to benefit others, at least we know that this benefit is greater, often much greater, than the cost to us.

---

7. Singer, "Famine, Affluence, and Morality," *Philosophy and Public Affairs* 1, no. 3 (Spring 1972): 231, https://www.jstor.org/stable/2265052.
8. Singer, "Would You Save a Drowning Child," The Life You Can Save, posted April 12, 2021, YouTube video, 2:22, https://youtu.be/wMb26ryjDuU.

For additional resources
and study aids, see
https://utilitarianism.net/

The Alienation Objection

The Alienation Objection

Most of us have a wide range of concerns and motivations. We care about our friends and family. We strive for success in our studies, careers, and personal projects. We become absorbed in hobbies, social or political causes, or cheer on the local sports team. And perhaps we have some general desire that the world as a whole become a better place. All of these things matter to us.

But suppose utilitarianism insisted that, of all your many motivations, only the latter desire—for an impartially better world—is morally legitimate. Everything else you care about is an unhelpful distraction. On this picture, the vast majority of ordinary human concerns are dismissed as selfish impulses to be suppressed or otherwise "managed" in whatever way would best serve the one morally legitimate goal of promoting the impartial good.

Such a view would seem deeply *alienating*. Imagine trying to live your life in accordance with such a theory, forcing your unruly desires into conformity with its narrow conception of moral legitimacy. You visit your friend in hospital and when he expresses gratitude for your apparent concern, you coldly reply, "I'm not visiting out of personal concern. I simply calculated that I could do more good here trying to cheer you up since the soup kitchen is already fully staffed today."[1]

Such impersonal motivations threaten to starve our interpersonal relations of the human warmth that they need to flourish. By subordinating all other motivations to a single, overwhelming desire for the "greater good," critics allege

---

1. This example is adapted from Michael Stocker, "The Schizophrenia of Modern Ethical Theories," *Journal of Philosophy* 73, no. 14 (August 1976): 462, https://doi.org/10.2307/2025782. Of course, if you wanted to cheer up your friend, you would refrain from voicing such a callous thought aloud. But it seems bad enough to even be *thinking* that way.

that impersonal theories like utilitarianism demand "one thought too many"[2] of agents—alienating us from our loved ones, our personal projects, and any other goods that ordinarily seem to warrant *direct* concern.

We will consider two ways utilitarians might respond to this alienation objection. The *sophisticated utilitarian* strategy recommends adopting (or at least tolerating) motivations other than explicitly utilitarian ones. The *subsumption* strategy instead argues that direct concern for particular goods or individuals can be subsumed *within* straightforwardly utilitarian motivations.

Sophisticated Utilitarianism

Peter Railton introduced the *sophisticated consequentialist* as someone who is committed to an objectively consequentialist life but is not especially concerned about thinking like a consequentialist.[3] Instead, they may have many interests and personal concerns, including care for their loved ones, which they maintain as long as it is overall for the best. As Railton explains, "while [the sophisticated consequentialist] ordinarily does not do what he does simply for the sake of doing what's right, he would seek to lead a different sort of life if he did not think his were morally defensible."[4]

It's empirically hard to know which motivations would actually maximize well-being for any particular circumstances. It's unlikely that *all* our default dispositions would pass muster from the perspective of global utilitarian evaluation, so we cannot entirely dismiss calls for moral self-improvement. But it also seems unlikely that withdrawing from one's relationships with loved ones (or other sources of personal fulfillment) would have good effects on global well-being. Trying to do this would risk severe depression, which is hardly conducive to a morally successful, high-impact life. For this reason, if we step back and ask what sort of life one should lead, forming friendships and other special attachments seems likely to be endorsed by utilitarians because these help motivate us to achieve our

---

2. Bernard Williams, "Persons, Character and Morality," in *Moral Luck: Philosophical Papers, 1973–1980* (Cambridge: Cambridge University Press, 1981).

3. Railton, "Alienation, Consequentialism, and the Demands of Morality," *Philosophy and Public Affairs* 13, no. 2 (Spring 1984): 153, https://www.jstor.org/stable/2265273.

4. Railton, "Alienation, Consequentialism, and the Demands of Morality," 151.

other goals, including maximizing global well-being. (This response also applies to the special obligations objection to utilitarianism, discussed in the next chapter.)

These facts about human psychology provide utilitarians with strong reasons to resist pressure to alienate themselves from sources of personal meaning and value. If it would prove counterproductive to strive for pure impartiality, starving yourself of ordinary human affection, then utilitarianism certainly would not recommend any such detrimental course of action. Even if it was in some sense more "rational" or "objectively warranted," utilitarians do not intrinsically value rationality or warranted attitudes; they value *well-being*, and if overall well-being is better promoted by embracing some of our human foibles, then by utilitarian lights we should embrace those foibles.

Still, this response may seem unsatisfactory to some. Even if utilitarianism can endorse personal concerns for their *usefulness*, we may worry that this is the wrong kind of reason for such endorsement—or at least less than we might have hoped for. It's not just that visiting your friend in the hospital out of direct concern would be *more useful* than visiting in order to maximize the overall good. Direct concern also seems *intrinsically* more appropriate.

Another way to bring out this worry is to note that the sophisticated utilitarian seems to exhibit what Michael Stocker describes as "moral schizophrenia"[5]—that is, a troubling *disconnect* between the (utilitarian) normative reasons they accept in theory and the (personal) motivating reasons that they act upon in practice.[6] As a result, sophisticated utilitarianism might seem to condemn us to do the right thing for the wrong reasons, like someone who saves a child from drowning purely in hopes of getting their name in the newspaper. But of course visiting your friend out of direct concern does not seem *at all* like the "wrong reason." Quite the opposite: the alienation objection stems from the conviction that this seems a much *better* reason to visit than any considerations to do with maximizing overall

---

5. Stocker, "The Schizophrenia of Modern Ethical Theories," 73: 453–66.

6. This is related to, but subtly distinct from, the standard multi-level utilitarian distinction between one's *criterion of rightness* and one's *decision procedure*. Multi-level utilitarians note that heuristics (such as respecting rights) might help us to better achieve utilitarian goals, but this is a mere change in strategy, not a change in what they ultimately want. Sophisticated utilitarians go further, adopting non-utilitarian goals or intrinsic desires when this would have good results. This introduces a disconnect between theory and *motivation* that is not necessarily found in routine multi-level utilitarianism.

value. But if direct concern is really the right reason to act, then our moral theory should reflect this. Helping individuals, and not *just* "overall well-being," should be recognized as an intrinsic moral goal by our moral theory. Our next section explores how utilitarianism might accommodate this idea.

The Subsumption Strategy

Richard Yetter Chappell argues that utilitarians can accept many personal reasons (to help particular individuals) at face value, in theory as well as in practice, and thus avoid both alienation *and* moral schizophrenia.[7] The key idea here is that overall well-being only matters because *each particular individual* matters.[8] So while utilitarians may speak, in abbreviated fashion, of wanting to promote overall well-being, this is just a way of summarizing a vast array of specific desires for the well-being of *each* particular individual. And while we have the most reason to do what will best promote overall well-being, the particular reasons we have for so acting will instead stem from the particular individuals whose interests are thereby protected or advanced.

We may thus secure the desired result that the correct moral reason to visit your friend in the hospital is that doing so would cheer *him* up. If some alternative action would better promote overall well-being, then you would have stronger moral reasons to help those other individuals instead. But in either case, you may be properly motivated by direct concern for the affected individuals rather than being driven by anything so abstract as the "general good."

If successful, this solution promises to cut off the alienation objection at its root. According to this diagnosis, the alienation objection stems from a common misconception: the idea that utilitarianism must be fundamentally impersonal in its justifications—concerned with abstractions (like aggregate well-being) rather than concrete individuals. If concern for the overall good is instead *built up* out of concern for each individual, and these individuals have direct and foundational moral importance, then there is nothing in the theory that should lead us toward alienating ourselves from them. Direct concern for others is precisely

---

7. Richard Y. Chappell, "The Right Wrong-Makers," *Philosophy and Phenomenological Research* 103, no. 2 (2020): 426–40, https://doi.org/10.1111/phpr.12728.
8. Richard Y. Chappell, "Value Receptacles," *Noûs* 49, no. 2 (June 2015): 322–32, https://doi.org/10.1111/nous.12023.

what is rational and morally warranted on this view of utilitarianism. We need only resort to impersonal moral motivations when our psychological capacities for direct concern run out, and we cannot give to billions of strangers the kind of personalized concern that—according to this interpretation of utilitarianism—they truly warrant.

One might object that we care far more about those we know than we do about distant strangers. Does it follow that our level of direct concern is *excessive*? Assuming that greater impartiality is truly warranted, it's an interesting question whether we should "level down" by caring less about those we know or "level up" by caring more about strangers. People are often quick to assume that, by utilitarian lights, we care *too much* about those we know. But why think that? We are far more aware of those individuals. Strangers, by contrast, we tend to simply ignore. As a general rule, we should expect to more accurately appreciate the value of those we closely attend to than those we largely overlook. So, we should expect the amount of care that is truly universally warranted is closer to the amount that we currently give to those we know best.

So utilitarianism seems well able to vindicate direct concern for individuals.[9] But this approach has its limitations. Many other common interests (such as sports and hobbies) are most plausibly of only *instrumental* value. And it seems plausible that deliberate attention to this fact could risk alienating the hobbyist, the athlete, or the sports fan from their favored activity.

Is this a problem? It may be a practical problem, but that can be addressed through sophisticated utilitarianism (as described in the previous section): just as it does not pay for insomniacs to dwell on the importance of sleep as they lie in bed awake at night, so the happiness of a tennis player may be best served by "devot[ing] himself more to the game" than might seem strictly warranted from the point of view of the universe.[10] Utilitarians have long stressed that excessive

---

9. More generally, the subsumption strategy may extend to whatever welfare goods the utilitarian recognizes as having intrinsic value. Depending on their theory of well-being, this might include just happiness, just desire satisfaction, or any number of putative objective goods such as friendship, knowledge, etc.

10. Railton, "Alienation, Consequentialism, and the Demands of Morality," 144. Note that Railton uses the tennis player example in a different context (and with a different contrasting motivation) than our use here.

deliberation can be counterproductive[11] and instead recommend a more strategic, multi-level approach to agency and decision-making, as explained in Chapters 2 and 6.

So the practical problem is resolvable. And there is no theoretical problem or objection here, so long as we can agree, on reflection, that our attachments to sports and hobbies are *unlike* our attachments to other people. Specifically, there does not seem any deep moral error involved regarding hobbies as having merely instrumental value. Our hobbies do not really have intrinsic value themselves but are at most useful means to other—intrinsically valuable—ends such as happiness or social camaraderie.

Conclusion

It would be deeply alienating for a moral theory to invalidate the overwhelming majority of our ordinary motivations, including moral motivations that stem from direct concern for particular individuals. Utilitarians may seek to avoid this fate via sophisticated utilitarianism or the subsumption strategy. Each approach has its limitations. But by suitably combining the two—insisting upon the subsumption of genuine intrinsic goods, together with a sophisticated approach to merely instrumental goods—utilitarians may be able to offer a full response to the alienation objection.

Note that this chapter exclusively addresses the concern that utilitarianism might seem to *invalidate* our ordinary motivations. For the distinct worry that it too easily *overrides* our personal projects and interests, see Chapter 13 (The Demandingness Objection).

---

11. Philip Pettit and Geoffrey Brennan, "Restrictive Consequentialism," *Australasian Journal of Philosophy* 64, no. 4 (1986): 438–55, https://doi.org/10.1080/00048408612342631.

For additional resources
and study aids, see
https://utilitarianism.net/

15

The Special Obligations Objection

Introduction

Impartiality is clearly important within institutional contexts, where we want judges, policymakers, and other civic actors to make fair and unbiased decisions. But a striking feature of utilitarianism is that it does not restrict impartiality to just those special contexts. It holds that, fundamentally, all individuals are *always* deserving of receiving full and equal consideration. This starkly conflicts with much of our ordinary decision-making, as in everyday life, we would not usually think twice about prioritizing our friends and loved ones over total strangers. Indeed, many would think it outright *wrong* for a parent to fail to prioritize the needs of their own children. It's usually thought that certain relationships, like parenthood or guardianship, give rise to *special obligations* to protect those who fall under our care. If utilitarianism denied this, for example by recommending that parents neglect their own children in order to save a larger number of strangers, that could seem to count seriously against the theory. The following discussion explores this *special obligations objection* against utilitarianism.

Accommodating the Intuition

While utilitarianism *as a theory* is fundamentally impartial, it does not recommend that we attempt to naively implement impartiality in our own lives and decision-making if this would prove counterproductive in practice. This allows plenty of scope for utilitarians to accommodate various kinds of partiality on practical grounds. (Though it's a tricky empirical question, just *how* partial or impartial we ideally ought to be.)

For example, most people need intimate bonds of friendship, family, and romantic partners to stay emotionally healthy and motivated. To build and maintain these strong relationships requires us to invest a significant share of our time, attention, and resources in them. Utilitarianism may thus recommend investing significantly in such relationships, as this may better enable us, over the course of our whole lives, to *also* invest significant resources in doing as much good as possible. If we always tried to be purely impartial, by contrast, our personal capacities[1] might be so gravely impaired that we would risk having a greatly lessened lifetime impact (even just insofar as the impartial good itself is concerned).

This consideration may suffice to justify some degree of partiality given our actual emotional needs and dispositions. But what if these dispositions could be changed? Does utilitarianism imply that it would be *better* if we could (somehow) make ourselves capable of pure impartiality without falling into depression or other psychological impairments? While it's possible to imagine situations in which this would be true, even this more limited commitment to impartiality does not necessarily follow in real-life circumstances.

Besides the instrumental benefits to our agential capacities, caring relationships can be of vital importance to the recipients of our care, such as young children. As there are obviously good utilitarian reasons to want the next generation of people to grow up to be emotionally healthy and capable agents, there are thus good utilitarian reasons to endorse the social norms of parental care that help to promote this goal.

Robert Goodin suggests a utilitarian-friendly conception of special obligations as *distributed general duties*.[2] That is, the moral goal of providing care to children (generally) may be best pursued through the delegation of special obligations to individual parents and guardians rather than by having everyone attempt to meddle in everyone else's upbringing. While this model seems to make good sense of

---

1. "Personal capacities" here could include mental health, willpower, moral motivation, etc.—basically, anything that enables you to be effective in achieving your goals—in contrast to things like depression, burnout, etc., that could be expected to significantly reduce your ability to accomplish things.

2. Goodin, "What Is So Special about Our Fellow Countrymen?," *Ethics* 98, no. 4 (July 1988): 663–86, https://doi.org/10.1086/292998. See also Frank Jackson, "Decision-Theoretic Consequentialism and the Nearest and Dearest Objection," *Ethics* 101, no. 3 (April 1991): 461–82, https://doi.org/10.1086/293312.

special obligations, it strikingly does *not* justify wanton disregard for others. If it becomes clear that some children (for instance, orphans or refugees) are not being provided for or that others are being abused by their parents or guardians, the full weight of their moral status—as no less important, in principle, than our own children—compels us to seek a remedy for their situation. And that is, arguably, just as it should be.

Utilitarianism thus plausibly endorses special obligations *as a moral practice*, even while denying them any foundational role in the theory. Your children are not *really* more important than anyone else's, even if it may be useful for you to prioritize them more than is objectively morally warranted. This can lead to a curious tension between the actions and the attitudes that utilitarianism recommends.

Imagine you have to decide between either saving the life of your child or the lives of five other children. According to utilitarianism, the morally *right* choice is to save the five children (any one of whom matters just as much as your child). But the right *attitude* is to love your child and even feel a special obligation for their well-being. Having the best attitude here will naturally incline you toward performing the worse action—saving your own child. Derek Parfit describes such actions as *blameless wrongdoing* because they are wrong acts done from morally good motivations.[3] Overall, it's better for society when parents feel strongly protective of their own children and are willing to go to great lengths to prevent them from being harmed. So it's worth endorsing and encouraging such motivations, even if they lead to suboptimal actions being performed from time to time.[4]

While utilitarianism can thus endorse some partiality in practice, this is different from holding partiality to be *fundamentally* warranted. So critics may insist at this point that the utilitarian reply given so far is not *sufficiently* accommodating. They may insist that partiality is not *merely* useful but rather is *rationally*

---

3. Parfit, *Reasons and Persons* (Oxford: Clarendon Press, 1984).

4. Furthermore, there may be reputational costs to utilitarians failing to prioritize their family members, which could reverse the long-run expected value of so acting once the risk of social backlash is taken into account. Acting in ways that are widely regarded as wrong is socially risky, which gives utilitarians extra practical reasons to think twice before violating widely accepted norms of "special obligation." See Jim A. C. Everett et al., "The Costs of Being Consequentialist: Social Inference from Instrumental Harm and Impartial Beneficence," *Journal of Experimental Social Psychology* 79 (November 2018): 200–16, https://doi.org/10.1016/j .jesp.2018.07.004.

warranted, on the grounds that relationships generate genuine normative reasons and associated special obligations that have intrinsic (non-instrumental and non-derivative) moral force, quite independently of whether the associated social practices are overall beneficial.[5] For example, many people claim that we should prioritize local charities over global ones, even if they are less cost-effective. In the following sections, we will look at how utilitarians might address these stronger claims.

Debunking the Intuition

Many utilitarians are suspicious of gut intuitions favoring partiality, as there are obvious social and evolutionary pressures that could have distorted our judgments here.[6] Most of us intuitively favor our fellow citizens over distant strangers, humans over non-human animals, and present people over future generations. But on reflection, it can be hard to believe that these broader forms of partiality (toward loosely affiliated strangers) are truly objectively warranted; they seem arbitrary and biased. The moral reasoning in support of impartiality, by contrast, seems better supported. As a result, we might be justified in dismissing our pro-partiality intuitions as ill-founded.

Some pro-partiality intuitions may also stem from conflating moral theory and practice. That is, one might start from the view (shared by many utilitarians) that we should in practice endorse norms of special obligation, and mistakenly conclude from this that morality must be partial at the fundamental theoretical level. But the practical endorsement of partiality is, as we've seen, actually perfectly compatible with utilitarianism and so poses no essential threat here. (Though the precise contours of partiality justified by utilitarianism may differ significantly from those assumed by commonsense morality.)

---

5. This is closely related to the "moral schizophrenia" objection to sophisticated utilitarianism, discussed in the previous chapter. The current objection seems weaker however. The alienation objection concerned things that utilitarianism putatively failed to value *at all*. Whereas in this case, utilitarianism certainly values the well-being of your child; the question is just whether *even more* concern is warranted. Firm confidence on such matters of degree seems inherently more difficult to establish.

6. Katarzyna de Lazari-Radek and Peter Singer, "The Objectivity of Ethics and the Unity of Practical Reason," *Ethics* 123, no. 1 (October 2012): 9–31, https://doi.org/10.1086/667837.

Rivals Fare No Better

Critics of utilitarian impartiality might prefer a partialist form of welfarist consequentialism, which assigns extra weight to the interests of one's nearest and dearest instead of counting everyone equally. But this alternative view can seem troublingly unprincipled, as we may bring out in a few different ways.

First, consider that morality is often thought to be essentially about striving for a neutral, unbiased, or impartially justifiable perspective that can peacefully resolve conflicts between competing interests. But partialism does not fully resolve our interpersonal conflicts. It gives different aims to different people and no guidance—beyond the obviously amoral default outcome of "might makes right"—about how to balance these when they conflict.

As Parfit shows, these conflicting aims make partialism *directly collectively self-defeating*. Consider Parfit's Parent's Dilemma, modeled after the famous Prisoner's Dilemma. Suppose that you and I each have one child. We are each given a choice: (i) benefit our own child slightly, or (ii) enable the other to benefit their child more.[7] It would be nice if we could agree to both choose option (ii), so that both of our children receive the greater benefit. But suppose that we cannot communicate and must decide without seeing what the other has chosen. Whatever I choose, your child will do better if you choose option (i). Partialism thus directs you to make this choice. (And likewise for me, as my child does better by *my* choosing (i), whatever choice you make.) But if we both successfully follow this guidance, we will each have achieved our partialist aims *worse* than if we had both chosen the second option instead. (Each child ends up with a slight benefit, whereas if we had both opted for (ii), each child would have received the greater benefit.) That is a serious problem for partialism. As Parfit puts it: "If there is any assumption on which it is clearest that a moral theory should not be self-defeating, it is the assumption that it is universally successfully followed."[8]

---

7. Parfit, *Reasons and Persons*, rev. ed. (1984; Oxford: Clarendon Press, 1987), 97.

8. Derek Parfit, *Reasons and Persons*, rev. ed. (1984; Oxford: Clarendon Press, 1987), 103. As Parfit notes, a minimal revision would temporarily prohibit partiality in just these sorts of situations where greater cooperation is in *everyone's* interests (conditional on your expecting a sufficient number of others likewise to cooperate). This minimal revision may seem ad hoc if partiality is *fundamental* to ethics, but makes much more sense on utilitarian accounts which take partiality to be merely instrumentally justified in the first place.

Second, any appropriately *moderate* form of partialism will have to draw arbitrary lines. *Absolutist partialism* claims that you should always save the life of your own child, regardless of how many other lives are at stake. But this extreme view becomes untenable as the stakes increase: the Absolutist insists that you should save your own child, even if that meant that a billion other children had to die instead. Most partialists would instead accept the *Moderate* view that you can give *some* (finite) extra weight to the interests of your own child, but when the stakes are sufficiently high you may be required to save many others instead.

The Moderate must draw a line past which it becomes impermissible to save the life of your child. But why draw the line precisely at that point rather than higher or lower? What is so special about this particular number?[9] Yet the same question can be asked for any specific number of other lives at stake. The only non-arbitrary positions are that of the Absolutist, for whom there is no number of lives at which it becomes impermissible to save your child, and that of the utilitarian, who counts all lives equally.[10] Since absolutism is untenable, that leaves utilitarianism as the best view on offer here.

Finally, it's worth flagging that the history of partiality includes many examples of group discrimination, such as discrimination based on race, sex, or religion, that we now recognize as morally unacceptable. While this certainly does not prove that all forms of partiality are similarly problematic, it should at least give us pause, as we must consider the possibility that some of our presently favored forms of partiality (or discrimination on the basis of perceived similarity or closeness) could ultimately prove indefensible.

Conclusion

We've seen that utilitarianism supports many forms of partiality in practice, including social practices of parenting, friendship, and other close relationships that are vital to us as human beings. But it is a fundamentally impartial theory. It

---

9. Utilitarians who endorse partiality for instrumental reasons have a simple criterion for determining this answer: we should draw the line in whatever way would have the effect of maximizing overall well-being. But this answer is not available to those who take partiality to be intrinsically rather than instrumentally justified.

10. Assuming, for simplicity, that the lives are all relevantly similar in terms of their expected future well-being.

only supports these practices of partiality insofar as they serve to promote *overall* well-being in practice.

Against those who insist upon partiality at a fundamental theoretical level, utilitarians may respond that their intuitions are ill-founded and that their resulting view is troublingly unprincipled (and even self-defeating). If we start to think of (fundamental) impartiality as the moral default and partiality as something that stands in need of special justification, then utilitarianism may look to be on much firmer footing.

For additional resources
and study aids, see
https://utilitarianism.net/

16

The Equality Objection

Introduction

Some argue that utilitarianism conflicts with the ideal of equality. Suppose, for example, that you could choose between two possible distributions of well-being, Equality and Inequality: Equality has 1,000 people at well-being level 45, while Inequality has 500 people at 80 well-being and another 500 people at 20 well-being.

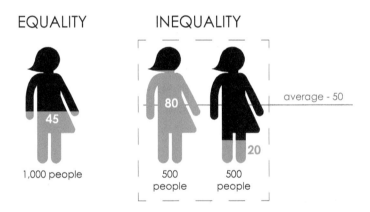

By the lights of utilitarianism, only the sum total of well-being determines the goodness of an outcome: it does not matter how that well-being is distributed across people. Since the sum total of well-being is greater in Inequality than in Equality, the unequal outcome is preferable according to utilitarianism.

Some philosophers object to the utilitarian view regarding this choice, claiming that the equal distribution of well-being in Equality provides a reason to choose this outcome. On this view, total well-being is not all that matters; equality of distribution also matters. Equality, it is claimed, is an important moral consideration that the utilitarian overlooks.

Proponents of utilitarianism might respond to this objection in four ways. We will go through these in turn.

Accommodating the Intuition

The first response to this objection is to point out that utilitarians accept that equality is an extremely important guiding concept in our everyday decision-making. The difference is merely that utilitarians value equality because of its instrumental benefits rather than because it is intrinsically important.

Utilitarians care deeply about equality largely because most goods exhibit *diminishing marginal utility*. This means that the more an individual already has of a particular good, such as money or nice clothes, the less they benefit from having even more of it. This provides a strong instrumental reason for utilitarians to care about equality in distributing goods. The diminishing marginal utility of goods implies that we can often increase overall well-being by redistributing from the haves to the have-nots. Also, excessive inequality between people may cause social conflict and harm society in the long run. This provides an additional reason to prefer equal distributions of wealth among people.

As a practical matter, many utilitarians use their time and money to improve the lives of the most disadvantaged, trying to create a more equitable world for all.

Debunking the Intuition

A second response to the objection is to argue that since equality is instrumentally good, perhaps we get confused into thinking it is good in and of itself. A utilitarian might argue that these moral concepts are so valuable for society that we should cultivate strong character dispositions and social norms to endorse, protect, and promote them. Therefore, our intuition against particular inequitable outcomes may just result from us having embraced a general moral norm in favor of equality. While our intuitions in favor of equitable outcomes generally increase well-being, they fail when the best achievable outcome is inequitable.

Furthermore, a utilitarian might argue that our intuitions in the choice between Equality and Inequality may be unreliable since we are not used to comparing outcomes directly in the well-being of the individuals involved in them. Moral psychologist Joshua Greene argues that people find it difficult to reason quantitatively about well-being since they confuse well-being with physical goods. Greene writes:

> We're used to quantifying stuff, things out in the world, or features of things in the world: How many apples? How much water? . . . How much money? But we don't ordinarily quantify the quality of our experiences. And thus, when we imagine possible distributions of [well-being] . . . it's very hard not to think of distributions of stuff, rather than distributions of experiential quality.[1]

This confusion that Greene describes may mislead our intuitions in the choice between Equality and Inequality because we are intuitively used to thinking about goods as having diminishing marginal utility. If the numbers in the hypothetical choice between Equality and Inequality represented levels of goods and not well-being, the utilitarian would choose the equal outcome. However, it would be a mistake to apply this thinking when comparing distributions of well-being since well-being does not exhibit diminishing marginal utility. By definition, a given unit of well-being is equally valuable to the person to whom it accrues, no matter how well-off they are already. So we must consider this in our intuitions.

If we specify the original example in money and use the standard economic measure of the rate of diminishing returns to money,[2] then we should represent the choice between Equality and Inequality as follows: In Equality, 1,000 people get $13,500, while in Inequality, 500 people get $10,000 and 500 people get $50,000.

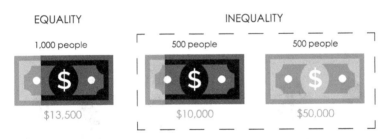

Put in these terms, we think it's no longer intuitively obvious that the utilitarian choice, favoring Inequality over Equality, is the wrong one. Everyone would agree that

1. Greene, *Moral Tribes: Emotion, Reason, and the Gap between Us and Them* (New York: Penguin Books, 2013), chap. 10.

2. Cf. Moritz Drupp et al., "Discounting Disentangled," *American Economic Journal: Economic Policy* 10, no. 4 (2018): 109–34, http://www.lse.ac.uk/GranthamInstitute/wp-content/uploads/2015/06/Working-Paper-172-Drupp-et-al.pdf.

some level of inequality can be justified by greater total well-being; how exactly to make this trade-off is tricky, and it's not obvious that utilitarianism gets the wrong answer.

Rivals Fare No Better

The third line of response is to show that rival views have even more counterintuitive implications here. For example, egalitarianism is subject to the *Leveling Down Objection* that it countenances harming the well-off (without benefiting anyone) since that has the effect of increasing equality.[3] If you don't think that there's anything good about such *leveling down*, then your judgment supports the utilitarian view that equality is only valuable instrumentally: valuable when and because it serves to promote overall well-being.[4]

We can also show that the alternatives to the utilitarian distribution of well-being violate a principle called *ex ante Pareto*: that, in a choice between two gambles, if everyone would rationally prefer gamble A to gamble B, then gamble A is better than gamble B.

To see this, suppose that you can choose between one of two options for distributions of well-being, Safe Bet and Risky Gamble: In Safe Bet, both Abel and Beth are guaranteed 45 well-being. In Risky Gamble, a fair coin is tossed. If it lands heads, Abel receives 80 well-being and Beth receives 20 well-being. If it lands tails, Beth receives 80 well-being and Abel receives 20 well-being.

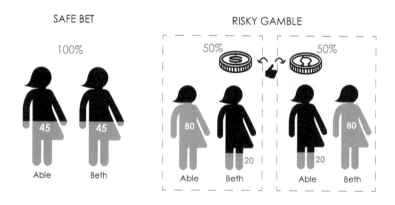

3. Derek Parfit, "Equality and Priority," *Ratio* 10, no. 3 (December 1997): 202–21, https:// doi.org/10.1111/1467-9329.00041.

4. Though this leaves open the choice between the utilitarian's equal consideration of interests and the prioritarian approach of giving extra weight to the interests of the worst off.

We can stipulate that both Abel and Beth would rationally prefer Risky Gamble over Safe Bet. They do so because their expected well-being in Risky Gamble is 50 (= (80 + 20) × 50%), which is higher than the expected well-being in Safe Bet of 45.[5] So, if we follow ex ante Pareto, then we should prefer Risky Gamble to Safe Bet. However, Risky Gamble results in an unequal outcome. Those who preferred Equality to Inequality must therefore also prefer Safe Bet to Risky Gamble. They must do so even though doing so is against the best interests of all parties concerned.

This argument has been developed formally by the economist John Harsanyi, who proved it in his utilitarian aggregation theorem.[6]

Biting the Bullet

Finally, proponents of utilitarianism may once again "bite the bullet" and simply accept that utilitarianism sometimes conflicts with our intuitions about equality. These conflicts occur because the outcomes favored by utilitarianism are those with the highest possible levels of overall well-being, which do not always coincide with the most egalitarian outcomes. Utilitarians will insist that it's better for people overall to be better off (even if these benefits are not distributed equally) than for them all to share equally in a lower level of well-being.

---

5. Indeed, the standard way of defining a magnitude of well-being is in terms of rational decisions in the face of uncertainty. On this account, what it means for an outcome to provide 100 well-being is that one, for example, ought to be indifferent between that outcome and a fifty-fifty chance of 200 well-being or 0 well-being.

6. Cf. Harsanyi, "Cardinal Welfare, Individualistic Ethics, and Interpersonal Comparisons of Utility," *The Journal of Political Economy* 63, no. 4 (August 1955): 309–21, https://www.jstor.org/stable/1827128.

For additional resources
and study aids, see
https://utilitarianism.net/

17

The Cluelessness Objection

Utilitarianism directs us to promote overall well-being. But we cannot be certain how to do this. Worse, there are powerful reasons to think we are completely *clueless* about the long-run consequences of our actions, including whether they will be positive or negative overall. Does this make utilitarianism unworkable? Is it a reason to think that utilitarianism is *false*?

The Epistemic Objection to Consequentialism

James Lenman's "Consequentialism and Cluelessness" presents an influential *epistemic objection* against consequentialism (and hence, by extension, utilitarianism).[1] We may reconstruct the argument roughly as follows:

> P1. We have no idea what the long-term effects of any of our actions will be.
>
> P2. But the long-term effects determine what we ought, according to consequentialism, to do. So, if consequentialism is true, we have no idea what we really ought to do—our reasons for action[2] lie beyond our epistemic grasp.
>
> P3. But an adequate ethical theory must be action-guiding—it cannot posit reasons beyond our epistemic grasp.
>
> Therefore,
>
> C. Consequentialism is not an adequate ethical theory.

Let us examine each of the three premises in turn.

---

1. Lenman, "Consequentialism and Cluelessness," *Philosophy and Public Affairs* 29, no. 4 (October 2000): 342–70, https://doi.org/10.1111/j.1088-4963.2000.00342.x.
2. That is, the considerations that count in favor of acting one way rather than another.

Premise 1: Long-Term Cluelessness

Imagine a doctor saving the life of a pregnant woman many centuries ago.[3] This seems like a clearly good act. Alas, it turns out that the woman was an ancestor of Hitler. So the seemingly good act turned out to have actually disastrous overall consequences.

This example illustrates how we might fail to grasp the long-term effects of our actions. But the point generalizes even to less dramatic actions, as small changes can ripple unpredictably into the future. For example, one's choice of whether or not to drive on a given day will "advance or delay the journeys of countless others, if only by a few seconds,"[4] and they in turn will slightly affect others. Eventually the causal chain will (however slightly) affect the timing of a couple conceiving a child. A different sperm will fertilize the egg than would otherwise have been the case, leading to an entirely different child being born. This different person will make different life choices, impacting the timing of other couples' conceptions, and the identity of the children they produce, snowballing into an ever more different future. As a result, we should expect our everyday actions to have momentous—yet unpredictable—long-term consequences. Some of these effects will surely be very bad, and others very good. (We may cause some genocidal dictators to come into existence thousands of years from now and prevent others.) And we've no idea how they will balance out.

Long-term consequences swamp short-term ones in total value. And because we generally can't predict the long-term consequences of our actions, it follows that we generally can't predict the *overall* consequences of our actions.

But there may be some exceptions. Proponents of longtermism believe that some actions—such as reducing existential risk—have robustly positive expected value in the long term. So, at a minimum, the sub-conclusion (premise 2) needs to be weakened to the claim that we've no idea what to do *other than work on reducing existential risks*. But even this weakened claim would remain surprising: it sure seems like we *also* have good reason to save lives in the here and now. The next section evaluates whether this is so.

---

3. Adapted from Lenman, "Consequentialism and Cluelessness," 344.
4. Hilary Greaves, "Cluelessness," *Proceedings of the Aristotelian Society* 116, no. 3 (October 2016): 314, https://doi.org/10.1093/arisoc/aow018.

Premise 2: Cluelessness and Expected Value

The natural response to cluelessness worries is to move to expectational consequentialism: promoting *expected* value rather than *actual* value. Further, as a multi-level theory, utilitarianism allows that we may best promote expected value by relying on heuristics rather than explicit calculation of the odds of literally every possible outcome. So if saving lives in the near term generally has positive expected value, that would suffice to defang the cluelessness objection.

Lenman distinguishes the "visible" (epistemically accessible) and "invisible" (entirely unknowable) consequences of an action.[5] Using this distinction, there is a very quick argument that saving lives has positive expected value. After all, if we've no idea what the long-term consequences of an action will be, then these "invisible" considerations are (given our evidence) simply *silent*—that is, speaking neither for nor against any particular option. So the visible reasons win out, unopposed. For example, saving a child's life has an expected value of "+1 life saved," which doesn't change when our long-term ignorance is pointed out.

Lenman is unimpressed with this response,[6] but the reasons he offers are all highly disputable. Here we'll focus on his two primary objections.[7]

First, he suggests that expectational consequentialists must rely on controversial probabilistic indifference principles (the idea that, by default, we should assume that every possibility is equally probable).

In response, Hilary Greaves argues that some restricted principle of indifference seems clearly warranted in simple cluelessness cases, whatever problems might

---

5. Lenman, "Consequentialism and Cluelessness," 363.

6. See Lenman, "Consequentialism and Cluelessness," 353–59.

7. He offers four objections in all. The fourth presupposes the second and so is addressed by our response to that. The third objects that we need to distinguish two very different reasons for judging an act to lack expected value: (i) we might *know* that it makes no difference, or (ii) we might be *clueless* about whether it's incredibly good or incredibly bad. Given that these two epistemic states are so different, Lenman reasons, it makes no sense to treat them the same way. It's true that this is a significant difference. But it's a mistake to assume that anything morally significant must change how we assess *acts* when often *attitudes* are better suited to reflect such significance. We should feel vastly more angst and ambivalence—and strongly wish that more information was available—in a high-stakes "total uncertainty" case than in a "known zero" case. That seems sufficient to capture the difference.

apply to a fully general such principle.[8] After all, it would seem entirely unwarranted to have asymmetric (rather than fifty-fifty) expectations about whether saving an arbitrary person's life now was more likely to randomly cause or to prevent genocides from occurring millennia hence. So, we can reasonably ignore such random causal factors.

However, as Greaves herself notes, this leaves open cases of "complex cluelessness" involving reasons to think that one option is *systematically better* than another for the long-term future, other reasons to judge the *opposite*, and it's unclear how to weigh the conflicting reasons against each other.[9] For example, if averting child deaths from malaria tends to result in a lasting larger global population, you might think there are some reasons to judge this positively, and other reasons to judge this to be overall bad (due to "overpopulation"[10]). If we're confident of a systematic effect but unsure of its direction, then it's less obvious that we can reasonably ignore it. At least, it doesn't seem like the principle of indifference appropriately applies here: it doesn't seem justified to assume that a larger population is equally likely to be good or bad.

But consequentialists may nonetheless repeat the earlier argument that "invisible" (unknowable) reasons can't guide our actions, so the only reasons left are the "visible" (knowable) ones, which speak in favor of saving lives and other seemingly good acts until proven otherwise. This response does not rely on any principle of indifference. Instead, it stresses that the burden is on the skeptic to show *how* we should revise our initial judgment that saving a child's life has an expected value of "+1 life saved." It hardly seems better to throw up our hands in despair in the face of complex cluelessness. So until we're presented with a better alternative, it seems most reasonable to stick with our initial judgment.[11]

---

8. Greaves, "Cluelessness," section IV.

9. Greaves, "Cluelessness," section V. See also Andreas Mogensen, "Maximal Cluelessness," *The Philosophical Quarterly* 71, no. 1 (January 2021): 141–62, https://doi.org/10.1093/pq/pqaa021.

10. For an exploration of whether the world is overpopulated or underpopulated, see Toby Ord, "Overpopulation or Underpopulation?" chap. 3 in *Is the Planet Full?* ed. Ian Goldin (Oxford: Oxford University Press, 2014).

11. For a related defense of the "procedural rationality" of relying on heuristics in the face of cluelessness, see David Thorstad and Andreas Mogensen, "Heuristics for Clueless Agents: How to Get Away with Ignoring What Matters Most in Ordinary Decision-Making" (GPI

Second, Lenman assumes that, given the sheer immensity of the "invisible" long-term stakes, the "visible" reason for consequentialists to save a life must be extremely weak—merely "a drop in the ocean."[12] But this is mistaken. In absolute terms, saving a life is incredibly important. The presence of *even greater* invisible stakes doesn't change the absolute weight of this reason.

You might assume that were consequentialism true, the strength of a reason for action must be proportionate to the action's likelihood of maximizing overall value. On this assumption, since the value of one life is vanishingly unlikely to tip the scales when comparing the long-term value of each option, saving one life must be an "extremely weak" reason to pick one option over another. But the earlier assumption is false. The strength of a consequentialist reason is given by its associated (expected) value in absolute terms: what matters is the size of the drop, not the size of the ocean.

Why Expected Value Matters

Specific objections aside, Lenman's larger worry is that it isn't clear *why* consequentialists should prefer prospects with greater expected value if we're clueless about the actual consequences.[13]

This is a subtle issue. The point of being guided by expected value is *not* to increase our chance of doing the objectively best thing, as some risky prospects that are unlikely to turn out well may nonetheless be worth the risk.[14] Roughly

---

Working Paper 2-2020, Global Priorities Institute, 2020), https://globalprioritiesinstitute.org/david-thorstad-and-andreas-mogensen-heuristics-for-clueless-agents-how-to-get-away-with-ignoring-what-matters-most-in-ordinary-decision-making/. Whether it's worth evaluating overpopulation concerns more deeply will depend on factors such as: (i) how many resources are at stake—more investigation is plausibly warranted for a grant-maker directing billions of dollars than for an individual donating a few hundred dollars; and (ii) how tractable the uncertainty seems, or what the expected value-of-information is of further investigation. For a small donor with little chance of swiftly resolving their uncertainty, it will often be most reasonable to ignore complex cluelessness.

12. Lenman, "Consequentialism and Cluelessness," 356.

13. Lenman, "Consequentialism and Cluelessness," 360.

14. For example, a 10 percent chance of saving a million lives is better in expectation than saving one life for certain, even though the latter option is 90 percent likely to yield a better

speaking, it's a way to *promote value as best we can* given the information available to us (balancing stakes and probabilities).[15] After all, if there were an identifiably better alternative, to follow *it* would then maximize expected value. So if Lenman's critique were accurate, it would imply not that maximizing expected value is unmotivated, but rather that (contrary to initial appearances) saving a life lacks positive expected value after all.

If the question is instead asked, "Why think that saving a life has positive expected value?" Then, one may simply reply: "Why not? It's visibly positive, and invisible considerations can hardly be shown to count against it!"

Granted, cluelessness in the face of massive invisible long-term stakes can be angst-inducing. It should make us strongly wish for more information and motivate us to pursue longtermist investigation if at all possible. But if no such investigations prove feasible, we should not mistake this residual feeling of angst for a reason to doubt that we can still be rationally guided by the smaller-scale considerations that we do see. To undermine the latter, it's not enough for the skeptic to gesture at the deep unknown. Unknowns, as such, are not epistemically undermining (greedily gobbling up all else that is known). To undermine an expected value verdict, you need to show that some alternative verdict is epistemically superior. Proponents of the epistemic objection, like radical skeptics in many other philosophical contexts, have not done this.[16]

Premise 3: The Possibility of Moral Cluelessness

The epistemic argument's final premise claims that *an adequate ethical theory must be action-guiding*: it cannot posit moral reasons beyond our epistemic grasp. But why think this? We may certainly *hope* for action-guidance. But if the world

---

outcome. The precise magnitudes and probabilities matter, not just whatever is "more likely" to be (however slightly) better.

15. One important feature of maximizing expected value is that we cannot expect any subjectively identifiable alternative to do better in the limit (that is, imagining like decisions being repeated a sufficient number of times, across different possible worlds if need be).

16. One interesting proposal is that we should instead have *imprecise credences* covering a wide range of reasonable-seeming credal points. One worry with such proposals is that they may end up implying that we've just as much reason to support the *For Malaria Foundation* as the *Against Malaria Foundation*, which may undermine the apparent reasonableness of the starting assumptions. Cf. Andreas Mogensen, "Maximal Cluelessness," 141–62.

doesn't cooperate—if we're deprived of access to the morally relevant facts—then it seems more appropriate to blame the world, not a moral theory that (rightly!) recognizes that unforeseeable events still matter.

Utilitarianism as a moral theory can be understood as combining (i) aggregative impartial welfarism as an account of the correct moral goals (i.e., what matters or what we should care about), and (ii) the teleological principle that our reasons for action are given by applying *instrumental rationality* to the *correct moral goals*. This means that a misguided action must stem from either misguided moral goals or pursuing moral goals in an ineffective way.

A genuinely threatening objection to utilitarianism must then undermine one of these two sub-claims. Most commonly, critics challenge the utilitarian account of what matters, for example by suggesting that we should also care independently about rights, equality, or our nearest and dearest. But the cluelessness objection gives us no reason to doubt that future people genuinely matter, and hence that moral agents ought to care about the well-being of future people.[17]

---

17. Strikingly, even Lenman grants that "the invisible consequences of action very plausibly matter too," but he adds that "there is no clear reason to suppose this mattering to be a matter of moral significance any more than the consequences, visible or otherwise, of earthquakes or meteor impacts (although they may certainly matter enormously) need be matters of, in particular, moral concern. There is nothing particularly implausible here. It is simply to say, for example, that the crimes of Hitler, although they were a terrible thing, are not something we can sensibly raise in discussion of the moral failings or excellences of [someone who saved the life of Hitler's distant ancestor]." This is a strange use of "moral significance." Moral agents clearly ought to care about earthquakes, meteor strikes, and future genocidal dictators. (At a minimum, we ought to prefer that there be fewer of such things, as part of our beneficent concern for others generally.) An agent who was truly *indifferent* to these things would not be a virtuous agent; their indifference reveals a callous disregard for future people. So, it could certainly constitute a "moral failing" to fail to care about such harmful events.

On the other hand, if Lenman really just means to say that *which unforeseeable consequences actually occur* shouldn't affect our assessment of a person's "moral failings or excellences," then this seems a truism that in no way threatens consequentialism. It's a familiar point that many forms of agential assessment (e.g., rationality, virtue, etc.) are "internalist"—supervening on intrinsic properties of the agent, and not what happens in the external world, beyond their ⊃l. Hybrid utilitarians comfortably combine such internalism about agential assessments ꞇilitarian account of our reasons for action. Lenman, "Consequentialism and Clueless-

It may just be a sad fact about the world that we truly cannot know how to achieve our moral goals.

For example, suppose you must pull a magic lever either to the left or the right and are told only that the fate of the world hangs on the lever's resulting position. You have no way of knowing which option will save the world. But it would be strange to conclude from this that the fate of the world does not morally matter. It would seem more reasonable to conclude that you're in a rough spot, and (in the absence of further evidence about which option is more likely to save the world) morality can offer you no useful guidance in these particular circumstances.

So, premise 3 appears mistaken.[18] It's always possible that agents may be unable to know how to achieve their moral goals. In such a case, the true moral theory may fail to be action-guiding. But that does not undermine its truth. There's no principled reason to prefer an alternative theory that offers extra "guidance" without actually helping you to achieve the right moral goals.

All plausible theories should agree that overall consequences are *among* the considerations that matter (even if they diverge from consequentialism in claiming that other factors matter in addition). Moderate deontologists, for example, posit extra deontic constraints but allow that they may be overridden when the stakes are sufficiently high. This suggests that the cluelessness objection should be addressed to all moral theorists, not just consequentialists. These theorists may similarly reply that cluelessness is (at most) a practical difficulty and not an objection to the *truth* of a moral theory.[19]

---

18. Unless interpreted in such a way as to no longer demand guidance where none is possible. While it's surely fine to have fact-relative reasons that outstrip our epistemic grasp, a more compelling version of the premise might just claim that evidence-relative reasons must be within our epistemic grasp. But then it risks collapsing into mere tautology: by definition, the "evidence-relative reasons" posited by any theory—including consequentialism—will be epistemically accessible (assuming that "evidence" and "epistemic access" go together). The question instead becomes what (if any) evidence-relative reasons the theory implies that we have.

19. Though there's some reason to think that the practical difficulties may be even worse for non-consequentialists. See Andreas Mogensen and William MacAskill, "The Paralysis Argument," *Philosophers' Imprint* 21, no. 15 (2021): 1–17, http://hdl.handle.net/2027/spo .3521354.0021.015.

Conclusion

There is reason to doubt whether concerns about cluelessness really present an *objection* to utilitarianism at all. Cluelessness may just be a sad implication of the circumstances in which we find ourselves. But considerations of expected value, mediated via plausible heuristics, may continue to guide us nonetheless. We might reasonably take near-term expected value at face value, even if we've no idea about the long-term consequences of the acts in question. Moreover, even if long-term cluelessness swamps near-term expected value, there may still be some options—like working to reduce existential risk—that have appreciably positive long-run expected value. So utilitarianism does not leave us entirely clueless about how to act, after all (see Chapter 7).

For additional resources
and study aids, see
https://utilitarianism.net/

The Abusability Objection

Introduction

As a consequentialist theory, utilitarianism directs us to promote good outcomes. When we can't be certain of the consequences of our actions, it tells us to promote *expected value*. Because it gives no intrinsic weight to commonsense constraints or rights, some worry that utilitarian ethics is too easily abusable, allowing people to construct false justifications for horrifically harmful actions. Blindly following the results of their expected value (mis-)calculations might lead even well-meaning individuals into disaster. As a result, many have claimed that utilitarianism is *self-effacing* or recommends against its own acceptance.

To evaluate this objection, we must clarify two things. First, what practical guidance does utilitarianism actually offer? Expected value provides a *criterion* against which actions can be evaluated rather than a *decision procedure* to use in all circumstances. This distinction is crucial for understanding the relation between utilitarian theory and practice, as it turns out that utilitarians should still give significant weight to commonsense constraints on instrumental grounds.

Second, what (if anything) is objectionable about self-effacing moral theories? As we'll see, there are strong reasons to think that all reasonable moral views are at least sometimes self-effacing. So, a view's self-effacement is not evidence that it is false.

How Utilitarianism Could Be Misused

It's a common trope that only villains endorse the consequentialist principle that "the ends justify the means." The idea that it's okay to trample human rights for the "greater good" is something we hear from the likes of Thanos, not from the good guys.[1] And there are reasons why we tell this kind of morality tale: though none of them were plausibly utilitarians, the real-world examples of Hitler, Stalin, and Mao demonstrate the danger of imposing a totalizing ideology in a way that's completely unhinged from ordinary moral constraints.[2]

This is all to say that ordinary moral constraints have immense instrumental value, and we generally expect wholesale disregard of them to result in disaster. It's plainly contrary to utilitarian principles to disregard immense instrumental value. To do great harm while falsely claiming the mantle of the "greater good" would be a clear misuse of utilitarian theory, and one that it's worth guarding against. Utilitarians thus have strong reason to agree that we should regard a person's villainous-seeming claims about the "greater good" with sharp suspicion.

Utilitarianism implies that if an act *really were* to produce the best consequences for overall well-being, then it would be worth it. But we should be suspicious of the further claim that villainous means actually serve this end in practice. Historically, such claims have most often proven to be disastrously false.

Is Utilitarianism Self-Effacing?

As explained in Chapter 6 (Utilitarianism and Practical Ethics), a plausible utilitarian decision procedure might direct us to

1. pursue any "low-hanging fruit" for effectively helping others while avoiding harm;
2. inculcate virtues for real-world utilitarians (including respect for commonsense moral norms); and
3. in a calm moment, reflect on how we could better prioritize and allocate our moral efforts, including by seeking out expert cost-benefit analyses and other evidence to better inform our overall judgments of expected value.

---

1. It's also notable that superheroes are depicted as putting so little effort into cause prioritization, often fighting local crime when they could (more helpfully, but far less dramatically) use their powers in more scalable ways to do good on a global scale—as this comic on the SMBC website satirically illustrates: http://smbc-comics.com/comic/2011-07-14 (posted July 14, 2011).

2. In particular, it doesn't seem plausible to suppose they were primarily driven by impartial beneficence.

Notably, whatever decision procedure utilitarianism *actually* recommends can't predictably yield worse outcomes than an available alternative. If it did, utilitarianism would instead recommend that better alternative. Agents who genuinely do as utilitarianism recommends will, by definition, do better (in expectation) than if they did otherwise. The same cannot be said of non-consequentialist theories, which risk sometimes *actually justifying* doing (or allowing) more harm than good.[3]

But a residual objection remains for two reasons. First, sincerely *trying* to follow a moral theory doesn't mean that you'll *succeed* in doing as it recommends; inept agents, inspired by utilitarianism, could still do great harm. Second, not all agents are morally sincere. Some may intentionally do harm while invoking the "greater good" to rationalize their actions. Accordingly, critics may worry that widespread acceptance of utilitarian justifications would make it easier for bad actors to get away with committing atrocities.[4]

Neither of these residual objections speaks to the *truth* of utilitarianism. Sometimes, true claims can be misunderstood or misused in harmful ways.[5] The question is what should be done about this risk.

One possibility would be to embrace some non-utilitarian moral theory as a "noble lie."[6] Many philosophers have speculated that consequentialist ethics may be *self-effacing* and direct us to believe some other theory instead.[7] For example,

---

3. That is, less demanding views may justify selfish (in)actions, such as neglecting the needs of the global poor, non-human animals, and future generations. So it's worth considering how competing views fare against their own versions of the abusability objection.

4. Though again, it's interesting to consider how competing views fare against this objection. Many are so vague that they leave plenty of room for self-serving interpretations, and so would also seem easily exploitable by bad actors.

5. As John Stuart Mill writes, "There is no difficulty in proving any ethical standard whatever to work ill, if we suppose universal idiocy to be conjoined with it." Mill, "What Utilitarianism Is," chap. 2 in *Utilitarianism* (London, 1863; Utilitarianism.net), https://www.utilitarianism .net/books/utilitarianism-john-stuart-mill/2/.

6. Or perhaps as a simplified "lie-to-children." See Wikipedia, s.v. "Lie-to-Children," last modified April 1, 2024, 14:55, https://en.wikipedia.org/wiki/Lie-to-children.

7. Most famously, Bernard Williams wrote, "Utilitarianism's fate is to usher itself from the scene." Williams, "A Critique of Utilitarianism," in *Utilitarianism: For and Against*, J. J. C. Smart and Bernard Williams (Cambridge: Cambridge University Press, 1973), 134. The idea of "esoteric morality" is found in Henry Sidgwick's (1874) *The Methods of Ethics* and was

one might speculate that people have a psychological tendency to underweight "merely" instrumental considerations. So, we would be better protected against atrocities if people generally believed human rights to have *non-instrumental* moral significance. But in light of the general instrumental value of truth-seeking,[8] it's worth first checking whether the risks can be mitigated without resorting to deception.

A more honest option would be to make clear the utilitarian case for moral constraints in practice, as we've done throughout this text.[9] If commonsense norms have high instrumental value, and explicit calculations to the contrary are more likely to be mistaken than correct, then real-life violations of common-sense norms *cannot easily be justified on utilitarian grounds.*[10] Crucially, if more people come to appreciate this fact, then it will be harder for bad actors to abuse utilitarian ideas. Interestingly, this suggests that the abusability objection may *itself* be self-effacing, as explained in the following note.[11]

---

subsequently criticized (for its elitist vibes) as "government house utilitarianism." But only implausibly absolutist views can strictly rule out the possibility that esotericism may sometimes be justified. Sidgwick, *The Methods of Ethics*, ed. Jonathan Bennett (London, 1874; Early Modern Texts, 2017), https://www.earlymoderntexts.com/authors/sidgwick. For broader discussion, see Katarzyna de Lazari-Radek and Peter Singer, "Secrecy in Consequentialism: A Defence of Esoteric Morality," *Ratio* 23, no. 1 (January 2010): 34–58, https://doi.org/10.1111/j.1467-9329.2009.00449.x.

8. Stefan Schubert and Lucius Caviola, "Virtues for Real-World Utilitarians, section 5: Truth-seeking," accessed April 10, 2023, https://www.utilitarianism.net/guest-essays/virtues-for-real-world-utilitarians/.

9. For a famous historical example, see John Stuart Mill's (1859) *On Liberty*, which argues for the utilitarian importance of respecting others' freedom. See also Schubert and Caviola, "Virtues for Real-World Utilitarians."

10. Moral uncertainty is also relevant here, as one needn't have *most* confidence in deontological views for them to still exert an additional tempering effect.

11. In spreading the false idea that utilitarianism easily justifies abuses, proponents of the abusability objection are, ironically enough, contributing to the very problem they worry about. Given the strong theoretical case for utilitarianism, it's inevitable that many reflective people will be drawn to the view. If you start telling them that their view justifies real-life atrocities, some of them might believe you. That would be bad because the claim is both harmful and false. As a result, we do better to promote a more sophisticated understanding of the relation between utilitarian theory and practice—emphasizing the value of generally reliable rules and

To this end, it's worth noting that utilitarian underpinnings can justify "moral rules" in different senses of the term. Most obviously, utilitarianism can support treating rules as *heuristics*, or "rules of thumb," for more reliably identifying the best option and avoiding harm. Heuristics are typically understood as overridable, allowing for exceptions when one can secure more reliable information without undue cost. Utilitarianism can also justify *policies*, such as committing to follow a simple rule without exceptions, if adopting such a policy would prove better than failing to do so. (Such a policy might sometimes result in one acting suboptimally, but it could still be worth adopting if any alternative policy—including a policy of trying to act upon expected value calculations—would realistically result in even *worse* suboptimality.)[12] An important example might be the exceptionless *enforcement* of (social and legal) sanctions against those who violate human rights or other generally good rules.

Consider a Ticking Time Bomb scenario, where one supposedly can only prevent a nuclear detonation by illegally torturing a suspect. If millions of lives are on the line, the argument goes, we should accept that torture could be justified. But given the risk of abuse, we might also want anyone who commits torture to suffer strict legal sanctions. If millions of lives are really on the line, the agent should be willing to go to jail. If someone wants to torture others but isn't willing to go to jail for it, this raises serious questions about their moral integrity—and the likely consequences of letting them run loose. Accordingly, there's no inconsistency in utilitarians holding *both* that (i) violating human rights could be justified in the most extreme circumstances, and yet (ii) anyone who violates human rights should be strictly held to account.

In these ways, utilitarianism can go a fair way toward accommodating commonsense norms, mitigating the risk of abuse, without resorting to full-blown moral deception or self-effacement.

---

heuristics, and the unreliability of crude calculations when these conflict with more reliable heuristics.

12. For discussion of related issues, see Derek Parfit, *Reasons and Persons* (Oxford: Clarendon Press, 1984), part 1.

Are Self-Effacing Theories Objectionable?

We should generally be averse to lying, including about the moral truth itself. But it's ultimately an empirical question as to what the consequences would be of any particular individual coming to believe any given moral theory.[13] In cases where the results of true beliefs would be bad, we may have practical reasons not to draw attention to those truths, or—in extreme cases—even to outright lie.[14] But that doesn't make the truth inherently objectionable; the problem instead lies with those who would misunderstand or otherwise misuse it.[15]

Every sensible (non-absolutist) moral theory is *possibly* self-effacing: if an evil demon will torture everyone for eternity unless you agree to be brainwashed into having false moral views, you surely ought to agree to the brainwashing. Moreover, ethical theory is generally regarded as non-contingent: whichever moral theory is true, this isn't an accident—the same fundamental moral theory must be true in all possible worlds.[16] That means that the actually correct moral theory, whichever one it is, remains true in some possible worlds where it's self-effacing. Perhaps our world is one of them, or perhaps not. The truth of the matter does not turn on this, either way. So, a theory's being self-effacing is irrelevant to philosophical assessments of its correctness.

---

13. Whether a certain belief has good or bad effects may vary across different individuals and contexts. There may be good reasons not to teach kindergarteners about the possibility of rare exceptions to moral rules, for example.

14. Compare the case of the Murderer at the Door, inquiring as to the whereabouts of their intended victim. Kant notoriously denied that lying is *ever* permissible, but few have found his response to this case remotely plausible. Cf. Immanuel Kant, "On the Supposed Right to Lie From Benevolent Motives," accessed May 25, 2024, http://www.sophia-project.org/uploads/1/3/9/5/13955288/kant_lying.pdf.

15. That is, if we must withhold the truth—from ourselves or others—that may be a reason to think less of the relevant people, rather than to think poorly of the relevant true claim.

16. When philosophers speak of "possible worlds," they just mean a possible *scenario*, or *way the world could have been*. A proposition p is said to be "true in" a possible world w if and only if, *were w to be actual, p would be true*. The (non-contingent) fundamental ethical theory combines with (contingent) facts about a world to yield the (contingent) applied moral claims or verdicts that are true in a world.

Conclusion

To understand utilitarianism, one must understand the distinction between the theory's *criterion* and recommended *decision procedures*. Canonical statements of utilitarianism state its criterion or moral goal: what makes an act worth doing is that it promotes (expected) value or well-being. When some imagine that this entails constantly calculating utilities, they are making a mistake. We cannot immediately "read off" a decision procedure from the theory alone, for how to pursue utilitarian goals in an instrumentally rational way depends on contingent facts about our cognitive capabilities and broader psychology.

Sometimes, a little knowledge can be a dangerous thing, and this seems plausibly true of utilitarianism. Someone who endorses the utilitarian criterion without thinking clearly about our epistemic limitations might end up acting in ways that are (predictably) very bad by utilitarian lights. In theory, one might try to avoid this problem either by depriving people of *any* knowledge of utilitarianism or by striving to convey the *full* picture. In practice, there are obvious reasons to prefer the latter, as true beliefs—especially about morality—can generally be expected to guide people toward better actions. So we can best protect against the risk of abuse by being clear that utilitarianism does *not* easily justify atrocities.

Still, at the end of the day, there's no guarantee that true beliefs will be socially optimal. It's always possible that any reasonable, non-absolutist moral theory may turn out to be self-effacing. This possibility is not an objection to those views.

Conclusion

In this book, we've (i) laid out the core elements of utilitarian moral theory, (ii) offered arguments in support of the view, (iii) highlighted the key practical implications for how we should live our lives, and (iv) critically explored the most significant objections, and how utilitarians might respond.

Utilitarianism is all about beneficence: making the world a better place for sentient beings without restriction.

As a *consequentialist* view, it endorses rules *only* when those rules serve to better promote overall well-being. Utilitarianism has no patience for rules that exist only to maintain the privilege of those better off under the status quo. If a change in the distribution of well-being *really would* be for the better overall, those who stand to lose out have no veto right against such moral progress. Many find this feature of the view objectionable. We think the opposite. Still, we recognize the *instrumental* importance of many moral rules and constraints for promoting overall well-being. The best rules achieve this by encouraging cooperation, maintaining social stability, and preventing atrocities. In principle, it could sometimes be worth breaking even the best rules, on those rare occasions when doing so would truly yield better overall outcomes. But in practice, people are not sufficiently reliable at identifying the exceptions. So, for practical purposes, we wholeheartedly endorse following reliable rules (like most commonsense moral norms)—precisely for their good utilitarian effects.

As a *welfarist* view, utilitarianism assesses consequences purely in terms of well-being for sentient beings: positive well-being is the sole intrinsic good, and negative well-being is the sole intrinsic bad. Everything else is good or bad only instrumentally through its effects on well-being. And as an *impartial* view, it gives *equal moral weight* to each individual's interests, no matter where, when, who, or what species they might be. For those who find utilitarianism's focus on impartial well-being too narrow, we saw that there are many "near-utilitarian views" that expand the theory of value (or add a moderate degree of partiality) while continuing to share utilitarianism's most important practical implications.

Many of those implications stem from the *aggregative* nature of the theory. However good it is to save one life, it's twice as good to save two. So, given that we have limited time and resources, it's important that we use these *effectively*—to do more good rather than less. Rather than settling for whatever half-decent idea first springs to mind, utilitarian beneficence directs us to *prioritize* between competing causes and interventions with an eye to getting the best moral return on our efforts. Like most reasonable theories, it implies that we would do well to engage in *effective altruism*—finding the best ways to help others and putting them into practice. This might involve donating, working, or conducting outreach to effectively improve the well-being of the global poor, factory-farmed animals, and future generations.

We saw that there are powerful arguments in favor of utilitarianism. Some draw upon concrete intuitions about what fundamentally matters; others upon abstract principles like *ex ante Pareto*, made vivid by the Veil of Ignorance thought experiment. Yet other arguments seek to undermine non-consequentialist alternatives, highlighting disturbing structural features of deontology such as its built-in status quo bias, its reliance on the doubtful distinction between "doing" and "allowing," and its tendency to require acts that diverge from what an ideal observer would *want* to see done.

Finally, in Part II of this book, we surveyed the challenges to utilitarian theory. We saw that many powerful objections have been levied against utilitarianism over the years. But we also saw that none were decisive, or left utilitarians with nothing plausible to say in response. We shared a "toolkit" of strategies that can be employed, time and again, to help utilitarians defang various objections. The force of these responses may help to explain utilitarianism's enduring influence and appeal to many, long after critics predicted its demise.

That's not to say that everyone will be convinced. Philosophy is not a discipline that lends itself to universal assent or convergence, and moral philosophy least of all. We trust that debates over the plausibility and appeal of utilitarianism will continue to rage. But we hope that this text helps shed light on the current state of the debates and will help even staunchly anti-utilitarian partisans to at least better understand the utilitarian moral perspective. And if some who were previously undecided come to share our sense that there are important moral insights to be found in utilitarian ethics—especially when it comes time to put our ethics into practice—all the better!

We close this text by offering (in the appendix) a *study guide* to Peter Singer's 1972 essay, *Famine, Affluence, and Morality*. Singer's famous paper nicely illustrates our key theme that the most important practical implications of utilitarian beneficence can be shared by many other views. While written from a broadly utilitarian perspective, the actual premises of Singer's argument are much more modest and prove notoriously difficult for *any* moral agent to deny. We hope our readers enjoy and benefit from grappling with Singer's ideas, as we ourselves have.

—Richard, Darius, and Will

Readers can find additional resources at **utilitarianism.net**, including study guides, a glossary of key terms, brief biographies of key Utilitarian thinkers, as well as guest essays by leading academics on specific topics relating to utilitarianism, and more.

Study Guide: Peter Singer's "Famine, Affluence, and Morality"

Introduction

Peter Singer's "Famine, Affluence, and Morality"[1] is widely regarded as one of the most important and influential texts in applied ethics. This study guide explains Singer's central argument, explores possible objections, and clarifies common misunderstandings.

The Argument

Singer argues that most of us in affluent societies are making a terrible moral mistake. When we look at distant suffering—such as results from global poverty, famine, or disease—we tend to think that helping is morally *optional* or what philosophers call "supererogatory." Even if we could very easily give more to effective charities to help, we think doing so would go "above and beyond the call of duty." It would be *generous* to give more, we think, but hardly *required*. We assume it's perfectly fine to spend our money on expensive clothes, travel, entertainment, or other luxuries instead. But Singer argues that this assumption is mistaken. Instead, he argues, it is seriously morally wrong to live high while others die.[2]

---

1. Singer, "Famine, Affluence, and Morality," *Philosophy and Public Affairs* 1, no. 3 (Spring 1972): 229–43, https://www.jstor.org/stable/2265052.
2. See also Peter Unger, *Living High and Letting Die: Our Illusion of Innocence* (Oxford: Oxford University Press, 1996).

Singer's argument for this conclusion is straightforward, resting largely on a key moral principle that we will call Singer's *rescue principle*. The argument may be summarized as follows:[3]

> P1. Suffering and death from lack of food, shelter, or medical care are very bad.
>
> P2. We can prevent such suffering and death by donating to effective charities (in place of consumer purchases).
>
> P3. Many of our consumer purchases are morally insignificant: we could give them up without thereby sacrificing anything morally significant.
>
> P4. The *rescue principle*: If it is in our power to prevent something very bad from happening, without thereby sacrificing anything morally significant, we ought, morally, to do it.[4]
>
> Therefore,
>
> C. We ought, morally, to donate to effective charities rather than make morally insignificant consumer purchases.[5]

Note that although Singer is a utilitarian, this argument does not rely on utilitarianism as a premise. P1–P4 are all claims that non-utilitarians (and even non-consequentialists) could accept.

This is a really striking argument. The four premises each seem perfectly plausible. The conclusion logically follows. Yet the conclusion is radically at odds with how almost all of us live our lives. *Every* time we purchase something unnecessary,

---

3. P1 and P4 are quoted (with minor edits for clarity) from Singer's text. See "Famine, Affluence, and Morality," 231. P2, P3, and C are our own extrapolations.

4. Singer advocates a stricter version of the rescue principle, where we are required to sacrifice even some genuinely morally significant things, so long as they are not *comparably* significant to the harms thereby prevented. We focus here on the less demanding version of the rescue principle since (as Singer notes) it's sufficient for practical purposes while being more difficult to reject. But the stronger version is also plausible and entailed by utilitarianism (while also compatible with other moral theories).

5. Note that this conclusion leaves open that there may be some third option that you ought to do that is *even better* than donating to effective charities. It's just making the *contrastive* normative claim that, *between the two specified options*, you ought to donate rather than make morally insignificant consumer purchases.

Singer's argument implies that we not only *could* but also *should* do better. When you think about how this would apply to your own life, it could well turn out that the majority of the purchases you make in your everyday life would be considered morally wrong. Most of us could probably live significantly more frugally without sacrificing anything morally significant and use the savings to relieve suffering or even prevent several untimely deaths. According to Singer's argument, that is then precisely what we are morally required to do.[6] (Note that similar arguments could also apply to one's choice of career.)[7]

Could such a radical conclusion really be true? You are probably already thinking of ways to dismiss it. But it's not enough to simply reject the conclusion. To reject it, you must show one (or more) of the premises to be false.

Assessing the Premises

Premise 1: Badness

The first premise claims that *suffering and death are very bad*. That is hard to deny. Any plausible ethical theory—whether utilitarianism, deontology, virtue ethics,

---

6. Unless, again, there is some other option that would do *even more* good, in which case we may be required to do that instead!

7. The career-focused version of Singer's argument might look like this (with P1 unchanged):

P2*: We can prevent suffering and death by working in an impactful job rather than spending our time on a career that does not help others.

P3*: We can work in an impactful job without significant uncompensated sacrifice.

P4*: If it is in our power to prevent something very bad from happening, without significant uncompensated sacrifice, we ought, morally, to do it.

Therefore,

C*: We ought, morally, to work in an impactful job rather than spend our time on a career that does not help others.

Note that P3 and P4 are worded in terms of significant *uncompensated* sacrifice because one's career choice is a major life decision that is likely to involve significant trade-offs. If one passes up becoming an artist (say), there may be something morally significant about that loss, even if one is overall happier with an alternate career. If you receive benefits commensurate with what you sacrificed, we can say that your sacrifice was *compensated* and so not costly to you, all things considered.

etc., will agree that, all else being equal, suffering and death are bad,[8] especially suffering that is extreme, involuntary, and uncompensated.

Premise 2: Preventability

The second premise is similarly secure: *We can prevent suffering and death by donating to effective charities.* Some "aid skeptics" are critical of foreign aid programs. This might suggest that we just do not know whether a given charity actually does any good. Some charitable interventions, on closer examination, even turn out to be counterproductive. However, while many charities have little impact, the most *effective* charities do a remarkable amount of good. Fortunately, finding effective charities is easy by consulting reputable sources such as GiveWell's in-depth charity evaluations. Even prominent aid skeptics do not deny that GiveWell's top-rated charities are genuinely effective.[9] So there is no real question that well-targeted

---

8. Someone who is sufficiently desperate to escape the argument might reject the first premise by claiming that *overpopulation* is such a problem that we should not seek to save lives after all (because lives saved add to overpopulation, thus increasing overall suffering). But there are a number of reasons why this is badly misguided. First, this claim is a myth: empirically, saving lives in poor countries does not lead to overpopulation. See Melinda Gates, "Saving Lives Does Not Lead to Overpopulation," The Breakthrough Institute, January 30, 2014, https://thebreakthrough.org/issues/conservation/saving-lives-does-not-lead-to-overpopulation; and Hans Rosling, "Will Saving Poor Children Lead to Overpopulation?" Gapminder Foundation, video 3:35, https://www.gapminder.org/answers/will-saving-poor-children-lead-to-overpopulation/. Second, someone who really believed this claim would also need to advocate for shutting down hospitals, letting serial killers go free, etc. Few would be willing to consistently hold the view that there is no point in saving innocent lives. Letting people die unnecessarily seems an atrocious way to attempt to counteract overpopulation. Third, there are obviously better alternatives, such as empowering women in ways that predictably lower birth rates. Examples of this include global family planning charities or girls' education. See Singer, "Famine, Affluence, and Morality," 240. Finally, note that it's increasingly disputed whether we should be more concerned about overpopulation or underpopulation, and that none of these concerns touch on the importance of reducing suffering, which increases the quality rather than quantity of life. See Ord, "Overpopulation or Underpopulation?" chap. 3 of *Is the Planet Full?* ed. Ian Goldin (Oxford: Oxford University Press, 2014).
9. "The Lack of Controversy over Well-Targeted Aid," GiveWell, updated July 26, 2016, https://blog.givewell.org/2015/11/06/the-lack-of-controversy-over-well-targeted-aid/.   .

donations can be expected to prevent a lot of suffering and death. (Of course, the argument will not apply to anyone who lacks the resources to be able to make any such donations. It's exclusively directed at those of us who do, at least sometimes, make unnecessary purchases.)

Premise 3: Insignificant Sacrifice

The third premise claims that we could give up many of our consumer purchases *without thereby sacrificing anything morally significant*. Could one reasonably deny this? One could insist that all interests are morally significant in the sense that they count for *something*, so you always have at least *some* reason to make any consumer purchase that would bring you the slightest bit of extra happiness. But of course Singer does not mean to deny this. His use of "significant" here is not meant to distinguish interests from non-interests (that count for literally zero) but rather to distinguish especially *weighty* or important interests from relatively trivial ones. And it cannot plausibly be denied that some of our consumer purchases are relatively trivial or not especially important to our lives.

It's an interesting question precisely how to distinguish significant interests from comparatively trivial ones. The two extremes seem intuitively clear enough: luxury goods like designer clothes seem fairly unimportant while providing a good life for one's own child is obviously of genuine importance. In intermediate cases where it's unclear whether an interest qualifies as deeply "morally significant," it will be similarly unclear whether Singer's argument requires us to be willing to sacrifice that interest in order to prevent grave harm.[10] But it's important to note that an argument can be sound and practically important even if it is sometimes unclear how to apply it.

Premise 4: Singer's Rescue Principle

Finally, we come to Singer's rescue principle: *If it is in our power to prevent something very bad from happening, without thereby sacrificing anything morally significant, we*

---

10. Though, as we'll see below, the Drowning Child scenario might help to illuminate the boundaries of morality's demands here.

ought, morally, to do it. If we are to reject the argument's conclusion, we must reject this premise. But can you really believe that it's morally okay to just sit back and watch something terrible happen when you could *easily* (without sacrificing anything important) prevent it?

Some may claim that our only duty is to *do no harm*.[11] On this view, it would be wrong to steal from the global poor, and it would be *generous* to help them, but we have no *obligation* to help in any way—it's never wrong to simply mind one's own business. This minimal view of morality (as limited to the duty not to harm others) meshes nicely with common views about charity. But it turns out to be unacceptable when we consider a broader range of cases, as Singer brings out with his famous Drowning Child thought experiment.

The Drowning Child

Singer writes:

> If I am walking past a shallow pond and see a child drowning in it, I ought to wade in and pull the child out. This will mean getting my clothes muddy, but this is insignificant, while the death of the child would presumably be a very bad thing.[12]

In a case like this, when you can *easily* prevent something very bad (like a child's death), it seems clear that doing so is not only morally praiseworthy but morally *required*. That remains true even if saving the child comes at a cost to yourself, as long as the cost is insignificant in comparison to the value of the child's life. Since the cost of ruining your clothes (even an expensive suit that costs several thousand dollars to replace) is insignificant compared to the child's life, you ought to wade into the pond to save the child.

What does the minimal "do no harm" view of morality imply about the right way to act in the thought experiment? Well, it's not your fault that the child is

---

11. Or, even more minimally, to simply *not violate anyone's rights*. Either way, philosophers call this a *negative* duty—a duty to *not* do a certain action—in contrast to *positive* duties to *do* a certain action.

12. Singer, "Famine, Affluence, and Morality," 231.

drowning; you did not push them in. If you were to walk by and let the child drown, you would not be causing any *additional* harm—they would be just as badly off if you were not there in the first place. So the minimal view implies that it would be morally fine for you to just walk by (or even sit and eat some popcorn while watching the child drown). But that strikes most people as obscenely immoral. So the minimalist's response to Singer's rescue principle fails.

If applied consistently, Singer's principle has radical implications in the real world. He writes:

> We are all in that situation of the person passing the shallow pond: we can all save lives of people, both children and adults, who would otherwise die, and we can do so at a very small cost to us: the cost of a new . . . shirt or a night out at a restaurant or concert, can mean the difference between life and death to more than one person somewhere in the world.[13]

If you accept that saving the drowning child is morally required, even at the cost of ruining your expensive suit, then morality may equally require you to donate an equivalent amount of money to save a child's life via other means. And you *can* save a child's life just by donating a few thousand dollars to GiveWell's top charities. (Or you can save a *quality-adjusted life year* by donating $100 or so.) If you would not think it's okay to let a child drown when you have the ability to prevent it, moral consistency requires that you likewise refuse to let children die unnecessarily from poverty or preventable disease.

Aside from helping to address objections to Singer's rescue principle, the Drowning Child thought experiment clarifies which of our interests are sufficiently "insignificant" that we may be called to sacrifice them to prevent grave harm to others. For example, someone might initially think that wearing designer clothes is a vital part of their identity, but if pressed on whether they would sooner watch a child drown than give up this expensive lifestyle, they might change their mind.[14]

---

13. Singer, "The Drowning Child and the Expanding Circle," *New Internationalist*, April 5, 1997, https://newint.org/features/1997/04/05/peter-singer-drowning-child-new-internationalist.
14. Of course, the relevant question is not the psychological one of what someone would be willing to choose but the moral one of what choice is truly justifiable. But it's often by thinking

Objections

Not everyone accepts Singer's radical conclusion about our moral obligations to donate to those in need. Yet, Singer's conclusion is difficult to avoid since the standard objections no longer seem plausible when applied to corresponding variations of the pond case.[15] For example:

1. You may believe charitable donations are *uncertain* to help. Would that remove the moral requirement to donate? But suppose you are similarly uncertain whether the child in the pond is truly drowning (maybe they are just playing a game). Even so, mere uncertainty does not justify doing nothing. So long as the chance that your actions would help is sufficiently high (relative to the costs or any associated risks from attempting aid), you may still be required to wade in and offer assistance, just in case. Similarly, uncertainty about the impacts of your donations does not justify keeping the money to yourself, as long as the expected value of your donations is sufficiently high (relative to the costs).

2. What if *other*, wealthier people could give more instead? Surely, they are under an even greater moral obligation to give since doing so is less of a sacrifice for them. But suppose that other people stand around the pond, watching the child drown but refusing to help. They *ought* to help, so ideally, your help would not be needed. But given that they *are not* helping, so your help *is* needed, it sure seems like it would still be wrong for you to do nothing and let the child drown. Likewise, it would be wrong not to save others' lives by donating, even if there are more affluent people who could help but refuse to do so. (The "bystander effect" suggests that waiting for others to help first could easily result in no one helping at all.)

3. What about geographical proximity as a factor? Does it make a moral difference that the drowning child is *right in front of you*, whereas the

---

through such a choice from the inside that we form our moral beliefs about which choices are morally permissible.

15. See also Singer, "Common Objections to Giving," in *The Life You Can Save: Acting Now to End World Poverty*, 2nd ed. (Bainbridge Island, WA: The Life You Can Save), available free at https://www.thelifeyoucansave.org/the-book/.

beneficiaries of your donations are *far away*? Imagine that the pond with the drowning child was actually located far away from you, say, in another country, and you could rescue the child's life by simply pressing a button. Surely, you would be required to press the button, even if you had to pay some money to do so. What matters morally is your ability to prevent the child from dying at a low cost to yourself, so that is what you should do—regardless of how far away the child is. Many moral theories (including utilitarianism) explicitly deny that geographical proximity is inherently morally relevant.[16]

4. Or, perhaps you think it's enough to do your "fair share": to just give as much as would be needed if everyone else did the same (perhaps 5 percent of one's income). But suppose that after saving one child from drowning, you notice three other drowning children. Two bystanders are just watching the children drown, though you are relieved that one other adult is on track to save two of the remaining three children. Would it be okay to watch the last child drown on the grounds that you have already done the "share" (saving one out of four) that *would* have sufficed if everyone had done likewise? Or should you step up and do the share that is required to *actually* save all the children, given what others are—and are not—doing?

It is unfair when some do not do their share. It's unfairly demanding on us to have to do more than our ideal share would have been. But it would be *even more* unfair on the child to just let them drown. Losing their life would be a far greater burden than the extra cost to us of helping more. So, while some unfairness is inevitable when some do not do their share, concern to minimize unfairness should still lead us to step up and do more when needed.

None of these responses seems successful in establishing a morally important difference between the Drowning Child thought experiment and charitable giving. But considerations of salience, repeatability, or emergency may prove more significant. We address these in the next three sections.

---

16. Though for a competing view, see F. M. Kamm, "Famine Ethics: The Problem of Distance in Morality and Singer's Ethical Theory," in *Singer and His Critics*, ed. Dale Jamieson (Oxford: Blackwell, 1999), 174–203.

Salience

Although geographical distance by itself does not seem to make a moral difference, it may make a psychological difference to us by affecting the *salience* of the different needs at stake. The visible suffering of a child right before our eyes has a very different emotional impact than merely abstract knowledge of distant suffering. This difference in emotional impact plausibly explains why most of us would be so much more strongly motivated to save the drowning child than to relieve distant suffering by donating to charity. But what is the moral significance of this difference in psychological salience?

Plausibly, greater salience can help bring to our attention genuine reasons to act that are there regardless but that we might otherwise mistakenly neglect. After all, it's not as though a suffering child suddenly becomes objectively more important once they enter our visual field. But we certainly become more *aware* of them (and how vital it is to help them). If this is right, it seems there is just as much moral reason to help those in need who are far away; we just tend not to *notice* this so much, and so we (understandably) make the moral mistake of failing to do as much as is objectively warranted in order to aid them.[17]

On this analysis, the difference in salience does not affect the strength of our moral reasons—it's just as *important* to save a distant child as it is to save one right before our eyes. But it does make an important difference to how we should evaluate the failure to act. Intuitively, failing to save the child from drowning would be morally *monstrous*, whereas failing to donate does not reflect *so* badly on you, even if it's a serious moral mistake. We can explain this difference in terms of one's *quality of will*. One is blameworthy to the extent that one acts from malicious motivations or acts in a way that reveals an egregious lack of concern for others. To neglect more salient suffering reveals a greater absence of altruistic concern, even holding fixed the magnitude of the suffering in each case. So, it is more blameworthy. As Richard Y. Chappell and Helen Yetter-Chappell put it: "A child drowning before our eyes shocks us out of complacency, activating whatever altruistic concern we may have, whereas the constant suffering of the global poor

---

17. Though for a competing view, which takes normal empathetic responses to determine what is right, see Michael Slote, "Famine, Affluence, and Virtue," in *Working Virtue: Virtue Ethics and Contemporary Moral Problems*, ed. Rebecca L. Walker and Philip J. Ivanhoe (Oxford: Clarendon Press, 2007): 279–96.

is easier to ignore, meaning that inaction does not necessarily imply [such] an egregious lack of concern."[18]

We can thus accommodate the intuition that failing to donate to effective charities is not as *blameworthy* as watching a child drown (since only the latter reveals an extreme lack of altruistic concern), without this providing any reason to deny that aid in either case may be equally morally *important*.

Repeatability

A notable difference between the two cases is that it's very rare to come across drowning children, whereas the needs of the global poor are constant and unrelenting. The significance of this fact is that a policy of *helping those nearby in need of direct rescue* would not be expected to prove especially costly. But a policy of *helping anyone in the world in desperate need of aid* would soon take over your life. A better analogy would then seem to be a limitless line of ponds containing drowning children. And when we consider such a case, it may no longer seem so wrong to at least *sometimes* take a break and thereby let a child drown.[19]

Of course, to save as many lives as possible over the long term, it would likely be optimal to take strategic breaks for self-care. At a minimum, you need to eat and sleep. But you may also save more lives in the long run if you take care to avoid burnout, taking extra breaks to spend time with friends and pursue hobbies that help you to de-stress. If so, taking such strategic breaks is morally justified by Singer's principles. (There is no virtue in being counter-productively self-sacrificial in one's altruism.) So, this is not yet a counterexample to Singer's view.

Still, this optimal route is highly demanding since it involves significant personal sacrifice. Suppose that in order to save the most lives, you had to forsake your plans to become a parent, and cut down time spent with friends and hobbies to the bare minimum required to maintain your sanity and productivity. That is a big ask and one that involves the loss of many morally significant goods in life.

---

18. Chappell and Yetter-Chappell, "Virtue and Salience," *Australasian Journal of Philosophy* 94, no. 3 (2016): 453, https://doi.org/10.1080/00048402.2015.1115530.
19. Travis Timmerman, "Sometimes There Is Nothing Wrong with Letting a Child Drown," *Analysis* 75, no. 2 (April 2015): 204–12, https://doi.org/10.1093/analys/anv015.

If Singer's principle required us to pursue this optimal route, it might not seem so plausible after all.

But *does* it require this? Unlike maximizing utilitarianism, P4 only asks us to give up things that are not morally significant. Since the above sacrifices are clearly morally significant, it seems that they would be excluded from the list of P4's possible demands.[20]

One difficulty is that it's not immediately clear how to apply the rescue principle to cases of *repeated* actions. Consider: giving up any *one* second of life might seem trivial. But repeated enough times, you would eventually give up your *entire life*, which is certainly significant. This suggests that repeatedly making an insignificant sacrifice might add up to an extremely significant sacrifice. To apply the rescue principle sensibly, then, it's not enough to ask whether the immediate sacrifice *in isolation* is morally significant. We must further ask whether it's part of a pattern that, in context, *adds up* to a morally significant sacrifice. If interpreted in this way, Singer's rescue principle would seem to allow broad leeway for reserving substantial time and resources to pursue the personal projects that are most important to us.[21]

Still, the conclusion of Singer's argument remains strikingly revisionary. Even if we may reserve the majority of our spare time and resources for personal projects, we are still required to do much more for others than almost any of us *actually* do. Even when we need not entirely give up some expensive (or time-intensive) pastime, we may be morally required to economize—if by doing so we could

---

20. Notably, Singer's stricter *comparable sacrifice principle* might require those sacrifices, if none of the personal losses were *comparable* in significance to the extra lives saved. Singer himself endorses the utilitarian thought that we ought (in principle) to give to the point of *marginal utility*, where the cost to us of giving any more would equal or outweigh the gain to others. But non-utilitarians might, of course, take a different view of what counts as being of comparable moral significance. And the weaker rescue principle (P4) that our main text focuses on is certainly less demanding.

21. This interpretation brings Singer's rescue principle much closer to Richard W. Miller's *Principle of Sympathy*, according to which: "One's underlying disposition to respond to neediness as such ought to be sufficiently demanding that giving which would express greater underlying concern would impose a significant risk of worsening one's life, if one fulfilled all further responsibilities; and it need not be any more demanding than this." Miller, "Beneficence, Duty and Distance," *Philosophy and Public Affairs* 32, no. 4 (October 2004): 359, https://doi .org/10.1111/j.1088-4963.2004.00018.x.

(perhaps over several years) save many lives without significant lifetime loss to our own well-being. Many hobbies plausibly exhibit diminishing marginal utility: the more time and money we plow into them, the less additional value we gain from further investment. In such cases, we may be able to cut our personal investment by, say, half while still retaining most of the well-being we gain from the hobby. And of course many of us also spend time and money on entirely frivolous things that, on reflection, do not significantly contribute to our lives at all. If we reflect carefully and honestly, most of us would likely find significant opportunities to do more to help others without needing to sacrifice anything truly important. If Singer's rescue principle is right—and it seems hard to deny—then we really ought to pursue these opportunities.

Emergencies

The last major challenge to Singer's argument comes from the idea that special ethical norms apply in *emergency* cases that cannot be broadly generalized. The drowning child scenario is a paradigmatic emergency. So perhaps common sense could be restored by combining a minimal view of our everyday obligations with ambitious positive obligations to assist in cases of emergency.

The difficulty for this view is to provide it with a principled basis. Why should emergency deaths be treated as inherently more important than equally preventable deaths from ongoing causes?

Sterri and Moen propose to explain this in terms of an "informal insurance model."[22] Their basic idea is that emergency ethics can be understood as a mutually beneficial agreement among all in the moral community to informally insure each other against rare, unexpected risks of grave harm. That is, we undertake to help others in emergency situations on the understanding that they would do the same for us. Since emergencies are rare, the comfortably off can agree to participate in such a scheme without expecting to be bled dry by all the world's needs. And since emergency situations can befall anyone, it's in their enlightened self-interest to do so. We are all better off informally insuring each other against disaster in this way than if we all were left to fend for ourselves.

---

22. Aksel Braanen Sterri and Ole Martin Moen, "The Ethics of Emergencies," *Philosophical Studies* 178, no. 8 (August 2021): 2621–34.

This line of argument faces two significant problems common to efforts to ground ethics in enlightened self-interest. Firstly, the underlying logic of mutual benefit excludes from the moral community not just the global poor but also others (including infants, non-human animals, future generations, and the severely disabled) who are not in a position to reciprocate. But surely you still ought to rescue a drowning paraplegic, for example, even if he could not do the same for you.

The second problem is that even when the informal insurance model gets the right result (requiring that you help), it does so for the wrong reasons. It implies that you should help for the sake of *playing your part in a cooperative scheme of mutual benefit*, which does not seem remotely the right reason to save a child from drowning.

To see this, imagine extending the logic of the informal insurance model to a society that includes water-phobic robots who just want to collect paper clips but occasionally drop them in puddles. In order to secure the assistance of the robots in helping to free us from getting our feet caught on railroad tracks (or other non-water-related emergencies), we might reciprocate by rescuing their lost paper clips from puddles. If the informal insurance account of emergency ethics were correct, then your moral reason to save a drowning child would be of *exactly the same kind* as your reason to "save" a paper clip from a puddle in the imagined scenario. But this is clearly wrong. We have moral reasons to save lives and avert great harms for the sake of the affected individuals. These moral reasons are distinct from (and more important than) our reasons to participate in mutual-benefit schemes.

Conclusion

Singer identifies a logical tension in our ordinary moral thought. We tend not to think much about our power to prevent great suffering (and even save lives). Even when this fact is brought to our attention, we tend to assume that it's morally okay for us not to act on it or to do very little. Helping would be generous, we think, but not required.

However, Singer's rescue principle seems undeniable: if we can *easily* prevent something very bad—that is, without giving up anything morally significant—it sure seems that we ought to do so. And the Drowning Child scenario verifies this principle: we would not think it okay to just watch a child drown when you could easily save them at no risk to yourself. Differences in salience may explain why we find it easier to ignore more distant suffering, but it would also seem to suggest that we are morally mistaken to do so.

Considering repeatability means that we need to take our overall patterns of response into account: sacrifices that are small in isolation may add up to extreme sacrifices that are more than Singer's principle would require. But even so, there are likely to be many changes we could make to our lives in order to help others more without overall causing any significant loss to our own well-being. If Singer is right, we are morally required to make these changes. It's no less important than saving a child who is drowning right before our eyes.

Discussion Questions

* Many effective altruists now believe that you can do more good through pursuing a high-impact career than by donating (even generously) while working at a less impactful job. How does that affect your view of Singer's argument? Could you be morally required to consider a career change? Should someone in a high-impact career be expected to donate to charity in addition?

* This study guide focuses on the more moderate version of Singer's rescue principle. But he also defends a stronger version, according to which we are morally required to prevent bad things from happening whenever we can do so without sacrificing anything of *comparable* moral significance. How much difference do you see between these two versions of the principle? Do you think the stronger principle is correct?

* What would a scalar utilitarian think of Singer's principles? If there is no such thing as obligation, just better and worse actions, how would that affect Singer's argument? Would saving lives become any less important or worthwhile if it was no longer "obligatory" in addition? What do you think is added by saying that an act is (not only good but also) "obligatory"?

- Imagine that you are going to donate money to an effective charity—enough to save *two* lives. But along the way, you see a child drowning in a pond. There is no time to set aside the cash in your pockets: if you jump in, the money will be destroyed, so you will be unable to make the donation after all. Should you still save the drowning child? Why or why not?

- We tend to just think about the money or resources that people already have. But suppose that you could easily earn *more*, say by working overtime (or shifting to a more lucrative job). Might it be wrong not to earn more money (in order to then donate more)? How would you apply Singer's principles to this case?

- Suppose a wealthy friend tends to get defensive when confronted with moral challenges. Currently, they donate a little bit to help others, but you know that if you told them about Singer's argument, they would clam up and stop donating altogether.

  - Would it be wrong for you to tell them about Singer's argument?

  - If so, would that mean that Singer's conclusion is *false*, and they are not obliged to donate more after all? Or could a moral claim be true even if it was not always a good idea to tell people about it?

Essay Tips

Your professor will explain their general expectations or what they are looking for in a good philosophy paper. You can find other helpful general guidelines online.[23] If writing on Singer's "Famine, Affluence, and Morality" in particular, you should take care to avoid the following common pitfalls:

- Do not get hung up on empirical disputes, such as those surrounding aid skepticism. The interesting philosophical question is whether Singer's moral *principles* are correct. So, just suppose we are in a

---

23. For example, see Jim Pryor, "Guidelines on Writing a Philosophy Paper," JimPryor.net, updated September 6, 2012, http://www.jimpryor.net/teaching/guidelines/writing.html.

position where we could help others. The fundamental philosophical question here is: How much *could* morality, in principle, require us to give up in order to help others? Aid skepticism does not answer this question but merely dodges it. (Further, as William MacAskill emphasizes: "There are thousands of pressing problems that call out for our attention and that we could make significant inroads on with our resources."[24] Global health charities are far from the only way that our money could be productively used to help others.)

- Do not get distracted by the sociological question of whether we could hope to *convince* most of society to act on Singer's recommendations. The question is what we, as individuals, *ought to do*. It's not about what we can *convince* others of. That would, again, be to dodge the fundamental moral question.

- Although Singer is a utilitarian, his argument in this paper does not rely on utilitarianism as a premise. Look again at the premises. These are all claims that even non-utilitarians could (and arguably should) accept. Alternatively, if you think that non-utilitarians ought to reject one or more of these premises, your essay should offer an argument to this effect.

- If you are having trouble coming up with an original "take" on the argument, reading published responses can often be helpful until you find one that you disagree with. (You might start with our suggestions in Resources and Further Reading.) You can then write about why you disagree, diagnosing where you think the other author's argument or objection goes wrong. Or, if you disagree with Singer's original argument, you could explain why, while also showing how you think others' *defenses* of his argument (as found, for example, in this very study guide) go wrong.

Good luck! And remember to cite your sources.

---

24. MacAskill, "Aid Scepticism and Effective Altruism," *Journal of Practical Ethics* 7, no. 1: 46–60, http://www.jpe.ox.ac.uk/papers/aid-scepticism-and-effective-altruism/.

Resources and Further Reading

Chapter 1: Introduction to Utilitarianism

Introduction

Appiah, Kwame Anthony. "What Is Utilitarianism?" 15-Minute Masterclass. Royal Institute of Philosophy, posted July 18, 2022. YouTube video, 17:44. https://www.youtube.com/watch?v=wd_peZ-zNwo.

Bykvist, Krister. *Utilitarianism: A Guide for the Perplexed*. London: Continuum, 2010.

de Lazari-Radek, Katarzyna, and Peter Singer. *Utilitarianism: A Very Short Introduction*. Oxford: Oxford University Press, 2017.

"Utilitarianism: Crash Course Philosophy #36." CrashCourse Philosophy, posted November 21, 2016. YouTube video, 10:00. https://youtube/-a739VjqdSI.

The Classics

Bentham, Jeremy. *An Introduction to the Principles of Morals and Legislation*. Edited by Jonathan Bennett. London, 1789; Early Modern Texts, 2017. https://www.earlymoderntexts.com/assets/pdfs/bentham1780.pdf.

Mill, John Stuart. *Utilitarianism*. London, 1863; Utilitarianism.net, 2023. https://www.utilitarianism.net/books/utilitarianism-john-stuart-mill/1.

Sidgwick, Henry. *The Methods of Ethics*. Edited by Jonathan Bennett. London, 1874; 7th ed. Indianapolis, IN: Hackett Publishing, 1981.

Further Reading

Crimmins, James, ed. *The Bloomsbury Encyclopedia of Utilitarianism*. London: Bloomsbury, 2017.

Driver, Julia. "The History of Utilitarianism." *The Stanford Encyclopedia of Philosophy*, edited by Edward N. Zalta. Winter 2014 Edition. https://plato.stanford.edu/entries/utilitarianism-history/.

Ng, Yew-Kwang. "Welfarism and Utilitarianism: A Rehabilitation." *Utilitas* 2, no. 2 (1990): 171–93. https://doi.org/10.1017/S0953820800000650.

Parfit, Derek. *On What Matters*. Oxford: Oxford University Press, 2017.

Schultz, Bart. *The Happiness Philosophers: The Lives and Works of the Great Utilitarians.* Princeton, NJ: Princeton University Press, 2017.

Chapter 2: Elements and Types of Utilitarianism

Consequentialism

Driver, Julia. *Consequentialism.* New Problems of Philosophy, edited by José Luis Bermúdez. Abingdon: Routledge, 2011.

Scheffler, Samuel. *The Rejection of Consequentialism: A Philosophical Investigation of the Considerations Underlying Rival Moral Conceptions.* Oxford: Clarendon Press, 1994.

Sinnott-Armstrong, Walter. "Consequentialism." *Stanford Encyclopedia of Philosophy*, edited by Edward N. Zalta. Winter 2015 Edition. https://plato.stanford.edu/entries/consequentialism/.

Welfarism and Theories of Well-Being

Crisp, Roger. "Well-Being." *The Stanford Encyclopedia of Philosophy*, edited by Edward N. Zalta. Fall 2017 Edition. https://plato.stanford.edu/entries/well-being/.

Holtug, Nils. "Welfarism—The Very Idea." *Utilitas* 15, no. 2 (July 2003): 151–74. doi:10.1017/S0953820800003927.

Kagan, Shelly. "The Limits of Well-Being." *Social Philosophy and Policy* 9, no. 2 (Summer 1992): 169–89. https://doi.org/10.1017/S0265052500001461.

Impartiality

Goodin, Robert. "What Is So Special about Our Fellow Countrymen?" *Ethics* 98, no. 4 (July 1988): 663–86. https://doi.org/10.1086/292998.

Jollimore, Troy. "Impartiality." *The Stanford Encyclopedia of Philosophy*, edited by Edward N. Zalta. Winter 2018 Edition. https://plato.stanford.edu/entries/impartiality/.

Aggregationism

Broome, John Broome. *Weighing Goods: Equality, Uncertainty, and Time*, chaps. 4 and 10. London: Wiley-Blackwell, 1991.

Bykvist, Krister. "Utilitarian Aggregation." Chap. 5 in *Utilitarianism: A Guide for the Perplexed.* London: Continuum, 2010.

Norcross, Alastair. "Comparing Harms: Headaches and Human Lives." *Philosophy and Public Affairs* 26, no. 2 (Spring 1997): 135–67. https://spot.colorado.edu/~norcross/Comparingharms.pdf.

Hedonism

Crisp, Roger. "Hedonism Reconsidered." *Philosophy and Phenomenological Research* 73, no. 3 (2006): 619–45. https://doi.org/10.1111/j.1933-1592.2006.tb00551.x.

Feldman, Fred. *Pleasure and the Good Life: Concerning the Nature, Varieties and Plausibility of Hedonism.* Oxford: Oxford University Press, 2004.

Kagan, Shelly. "The Limits of Well-Being." *Social Philosophy and Policy* 9, no. 2 (Summer 1992): 169–89. https://doi.org/10.1017/S0265052500001461.

Moen, Ole Martin. "An Argument for Hedonism." *The Journal of Value Inquiry* 50 (June 2016): 267–81. https://doi.org/10.1007/s10790-015-9506-9.

Moore, Andrew. "Hedonism." *The Stanford Encyclopedia of Philosophy*, edited by Edward N. Zalta. Winter 2019 Edition. https://plato.stanford.edu/archives/win2019/entries/hedonism/.

Population Ethics

Arrhenius, Gustaf. "Future Generations: A Challenge for Moral Theory." PhD diss., Uppsala University, 2000. http://www.diva-portal.org/smash/get/diva2:170236/FULLTEXT01.pdf.

Arrhenius, Gustaf, Jesper Ryberg, and Torbjörn Tännsjö. "The Repugnant Conclusion." *The Stanford Encyclopedia of Philosophy*, edited by Edward N. Zalta. Spring 2017 Edition. https://plato.stanford.edu/entries/repugnant-conclusion/.

Greaves, Hilary. "Population Axiology." *Philosophy Compass* 12, no. 11 (November 2017). https://doi.org/10.1111/phc3.12442.

Gustafsson, Johan E. "Our Intuitive Grasp of the Repugnant Conclusion." In *The Oxford Handbook of Population Ethics*, edited by Gustaf Arrhenius, Krister Bykvist, Tim Campbell, and Elizabeth Finneron-Burns. Oxford: Oxford University Press, 2022.

Huemer, Michael Huemer. "In Defence of Repugnance." *Mind* 117, no. 468 (October 2008): 899–933. https://www.jstor.org/stable/20532700.

Parfit, Derek. *Reasons and Persons.* Oxford: Clarendon Press, 1984.

Maximizing, Satisficing, and Scalar Utilitarianism

Bradley, Ben. "Against Satisficing Consequentialism." *Utilitas* 18, no. 2 (June 2006): 97–108. https://doi.org/10.1017/S0953820806001877.

Chappell, Richard Y. "Deontic Pluralism and the Right Amount of Good." In *The Oxford Handbook of Consequentialism*, edited by Douglas W. Portmore, 498–512. Oxford: Oxford University Press.

———. "Willpower Satisficing." *Noûs* 53, no. 2 (June 2019): 251–65. https://doi.org/10.1111/nous.12213.

Norcross, Alastair. *Morality by Degrees: Reasons without Demands.* New York: Oxford University Press, 2020.

———. "The Scalar Approach to Utilitarianism." In *The Blackwell Guide to Mill's Utilitarianism*, edited by Henry West, 217–32. Wiley-Blackwell, 2006.

Sinhababu, Neil. "Scalar Consequentialism the Right Way. *Philosophical Studies* 175 (2018): 3131–44. https://philarchive.org/archive/SINSCT-3.

Expectational Utilitarianism versus Objective Utilitarianism

Crisp, Roger. *Routledge Philosophy Guidebook to Mill on Utilitarianism*. 99–101. Abingdon: Routledge, 1997.

Graham, Peter A. *Subjective Versus Objective Moral Wrongness*. Cambridge: Cambridge University Press, 2021.

Jackson, Frank Jackson. "Decision-Theoretic Consequentialism and the Nearest and Dearest Objection." *Ethics* 101, no. 3 (1991): 461–82. https://doi.org/10.1086/293312.

Multi-Level Utilitarianism versus Single-Level Utilitarianism

Crisp, Roger. *Routledge Philosophy Guidebook to Mill on Utilitarianism*. 105–12. Abingdon: Routledge, 1997.

Hare, Richard M. *Moral Thinking: Its Levels, Method, and Point*. Oxford: Oxford University Press, 1981.

Railton, Peter. "Alienation, Consequentialism, and the Demands of Morality." *Philosophy and Public Affairs* 13, no. 2 (Spring 1984): 134–71. https://www.jstor.org/stable/2265273.

Global Utilitarianism and Hybrid Utilitarianism

Chappell, Richard Y. "Fittingness: The Sole Normative Primitive." *Philosophical Quarterly* 62, no. 249 (June 2012): 684–704. https://doi.org/10.1111/j.1467-9213.2012.00075.x.

———. "Consequentialism: Core and Expansion." In *The Oxford Handbook of Normative Ethics*, edited by David Copp, Connie Rosati, and Tina Rulli. Oxford: Oxford University Press, forthcoming.

McElwee, Brian. "The Ambitions of Consequentialism." *Journal of Ethics and Social Philosophy* 17, no. 2 (2020). https://doi.org/10.26556/jesp.v17i2.528.

Ord, Toby. "Beyond Action: Applying Consequentialism to Decision Making and Motivation." DPhil thesis, University of Oxford, 2009. http://files.tobyord.com/beyond-action.pdf.

Pettit, Philip, and Michael Smith. "Global Consequentialism." In *Morality, Rules and Consequences: A Critical Reader*, edited by Brad Hooker, Elinor Mason, and Dale Miller. Edinburgh: Edinburgh University Press, 2000.

Chapter 3: Arguments for Utilitarianism

Broome, John. "Utilitarianism and Expected Utility." *The Journal of Philosophy* 84, no. 8 (August 1987): 405–22. https://doi.org/10.2307/2026999.

———. *Weighing Goods: Equality, Uncertainty, and Time*. London: Wiley-Blackwell, 1991.

Bykvist, Krister. *Utilitarianism: A Guide for the Perplexed*. London: Continuum, 2010.

de Lazari-Radek, Katarzyna, and Peter Singer. "Justifications." Chap. 2 in *Utilitarianism: A Very Short Introduction*. Oxford: Oxford University Press, 2017.

Goodin, Robert. *Utilitarianism as a Public Philosophy*. Cambridge: Cambridge University Press, 1995.

Gustafsson, Johan E. "Utilitarianism without Moral Aggregation." *Canadian Journal of Philosophy* 51, no. 4 (May 2021): 256–69. https://doi.org/10.1017/can.2021.20.

Hare, Caspar. "Should We Wish Well to All?" *Philosophical Review* 125, no. 4 (2016): 451–72. http://doi.org/10.1215/00318108-3624764.

Harsanyi, John C. "Cardinal Welfare, Individualistic Ethics, and Interpersonal Comparisons of Utility." *The Journal of Political Economy* 63, no. 4 (August 1955): 309–21. https://www.jstor.org/stable/1827128.

———. *Rational Behavior and Bargaining Equilibrium in Games and Social Situations*. Cambridge: Cambridge University Press, 1977.

Smart, J. J. C. "An Outline of a System of Utilitarian Ethics." In *Utilitarianism: For and Against*, J. J. C. Smart and Bernard Williams. Cambridge University Press, 1973.

Chapter 4: Theories of Well-Being

Introduction

Crisp, Roger. "Well-Being." *The Stanford Encyclopedia of Philosophy*, edited by Edward N. Zalta. Fall 2017 Edition. https://plato.stanford.edu/entries/well-being/.

Kagan, Shelly. "The Limits of Well-Being." *Social Philosophy and Policy* 9, no. 2 (Summer 1992): 169–89. https://doi.org/10.1017/S0265052500001461.

Lin, Eden. "Well-Being, Part 1: The Concept of Well-Being." *Philosophy Compass* 17, no. 2 (February 2022). https://doi.org/10.1111/phc3.12812.

———. "Well-Being, Part 2: Theories of Well-Being." *Philosophy Compass* 17, no. 2 (February 2022). https://doi.org/10.1111/phc3.12813.

Parfit, Derek. "What Makes Someone's Life Go Best." Appendix I to *Reasons and Persons*. Oxford: Clarendon Press, 1984.

Welfarism

Holtug, Nils. "Welfarism—The Very Idea." *Utilitas* 15, no. 2 (July 2003): 151–74. doi:10.1017/S0953820800003927.

Moore, Andrew, and Roger Crisp. "Welfarism in Moral Theory." *Australasian Journal of Philosophy* 74, no. 4 (June 1996): 598–613. https://doi.org/10.1080/00048409612347551.

Hedonism

Crisp, Roger. "Hedonism Reconsidered." *Philosophy and Phenomenological Research* 73, no. 3 (November 2006): 619–45. https://doi.org/10.1111/j.1933-1592.2006.tb00551.x.

Feldman, Fred. *Pleasure and the Good Life: Concerning the Nature Varieties and Plausibility of Hedonism*. Oxford: Oxford University Press, 2004.

Labukt, Ivar. "Hedonic Tone and the Heterogeneity of Pleasure." *Utilitas* 24, no. 2 (June 2012): 172–99. https://doi.org/10.1017/S0953820812000052.

Moen, Ole Martin. "An Argument for Hedonism." *The Journal of Value Inquiry* 50 (June 2016): 267–81. https://doi.org/10.1007/s10790-015-9506-9.

Moore, Andrew. "Hedonism." *The Stanford Encyclopedia of Philosophy*, edited by Edward N. Zalta. Winter 2019 Edition. https://plato.stanford.edu/entries/hedonism/.

Desire Theories

Heathwood, Chris. "Desire Satisfactionism and Hedonism." *Philosophical Studies* 128 (April 2006): 539–63. https://doi.org/10.1007/s11098-004-7817-y.

———. "Desire-Fulfillment Theory." In *The Routledge Handbook of Philosophy of Well-Being*, edited by Guy Fletcher. London: Routledge, 2015.

Murphy, Mark. "The Simple Desire-Fulfillment Theory." *Noûs* 33, no. 2 (December 2002): 247–72. https://doi.org/10.1111/0029-4624.00153.

Rabinowicz ,Wlodek, and Jan Österberg. "Value Based on Preferences: On Two Interpretations of Preference Utilitarianism." *Economics and Philosophy* 12, no. 1 (April 1996): 1–27. https://doi.org/10.1017/S0266267100003692.

Singer, Peter. "About Ethics." Chap. 1 in *Practical Ethics*, 3rd ed. Cambridge: Cambridge University Press, 2011.

Objective List Theories

Fletcher, Guy. "A Fresh Start for an Objective List Theory of Well-Being." *Utilitas* 25, no. 2 (2013): 206–20. https://doi.org/10.1017/S0953820812000453.

Griffin, James. *Well-Being: Its Meaning, Measurement and Moral Importance*. Oxford: Clarendon Press, 1986.

Lin, Eden. "Pluralism about Well-Being." *Philosophical Perspectives* 28, no. 1 (2014): 127–54. https://doi.org/10.1111/phpe.12038.

Chapter 5: Population Ethics

General Discussions of Population Ethics

Arrhenius, Gustaf. "Future Generations: A Challenge for Moral Theory." PhD diss., Uppsala University, 2000. http://www.diva-portal.org/smash/get/diva2:170236/FULLTEXT01.pdf.

Chappell, Richard Y. "Population Ethics." Section 7 in *Parfit's Ethics*. Cambridge: Cambridge University Press, 2021.

Greaves, Hilary. "Population Axiology." *Philosophy Compass* 12, no. 11 (November 2017). https://doi.org/10.1111/phc3.12442.

Parfit, Derek. "Future Generations." Part 4 in *Reasons and Persons*. Oxford: Clarendon Press, 1984.

The Total View and Repugnant Conclusion

Arrhenius, Gustaf. "The Very Repugnant Conclusion." In *Logic, Law, Morality: Thirteen Essays in Practical Philosophy in Honour of Lennart Åqvist*, edited by Krister Segerberg and Ryszard Sliwinski, 29–44. Uppsala: Uppsala University, 2003.

Arrhenius, Gustaf, Jesper Ryberg, and Torbjörn Tännsjö. "The Repugnant Conclusion." *The Stanford Encyclopedia of Philosophy*, edited by Edward N. Zalta. Winter 2022. https://plato.stanford.edu/entries/repugnant-conclusion/.

Gustafsson, Johan E. "Our Intuitive Grasp of the Repugnant Conclusion." In *The Oxford Handbook of Population Ethics*, edited by Gustaf Arrhenius, Krister Bykvist, Tim Campbell, and Elizabeth Finneron-Burns. New York: Oxford University Press, 2022.

Huemer, Michael. "In Defence of Repugnance." *Mind* 117, no. 468 (October 2008): 899–933. https://www.jstor.org/stable/20532700.

Spears, Dean, and Mark Budolfson. "Repugnant Conclusions." *Social Choice and Welfare* 57 (2021): 567–88. https://doi.org/10.1007/s00355-021-01321-2.

Tännsjö, Torbjörn. "Why We Ought to Accept the Repugnant Conclusion." *Utilitas* 14, no. 3 (November 2002): 339–59. https://doi.org/10.1017/S0953820800003642.

Zuber, Stéphane, Nikhil Venkatesh, Torbjörn Tännsjö, Christian Tarsney, H. Orri Stefánsson, Katie Steele, Dean Spears, et al. "What Should We Agree on about the Repugnant Conclusion?" *Utilitas* 33, no. 4 (April 2021): 379–83. https://doi.org/10.1017/S095382082100011X.

Variable Value Theories

Hurka, Thomas. "Value and Population Size." *Ethics* 93, no. 3 (April 1983): 496–507. https://doi.org/10.1086/292462.

Sider, Theodore. "Might Theory X Be a Theory of Diminishing Marginal Value?" *Analysis* 51, no.4 (1991): 265–71. https://doi.org/10.1093/analys/51.4.265.

Critical Level and Critical Range Theories

Blackorby, Charles, Walter Bossert, and David J. Donaldson. "Intertemporal Population Ethics: Critical-Level Utilitarian Principles." *Econometrica* 63, no. 6 (November 1995): 1303–20. https://doi.org/10.2307/2171771.

———. *Population Issues in Social Choice Theory, Welfare Economics, and Ethics*. Cambridge: Cambridge University Press, 2005.

Broome, John. *Weighing Lives.* Oxford: Oxford University Press, 2004.

Gustafsson, Johan E. "Population Axiology and the Possibility of a Fourth Category of Absolute Value." *Economics and Philosophy* 36, no. 1 (March 2020): 81–110. https://doi.org/10.1017/S0266267119000087.

Neutrality Intuition

Broome, John. "Should We Value Population?" *The Journal of Political Philosophy* 13, no. 4 (December 2005): 399–413. https://doi.org/10.1111/j.1467-9760.2005.00230.x.

Bykvist, Kryster. "The Benefits of Coming into Existence." *Philosophical Studies* 135, no. 3 (September 2007): 335–62. https://doi.org/10.1007/s11098-005-3982-x.

Harman, Elizabeth. "Can We Harm and Benefit in Creating?" *Philosophical Perspectives* 18 (2004): 89–113. https://www.jstor.org/stable/3840929.

McMahan, Jeff. "Causing People to Exist and Saving People's Lives." *The Journal of Ethics* 17 (June 2013): 5–35. https://doi.org/10.1007/s10892-012-9139-1.

Rabinowicz, Wlodek. "Broome and the Intuition of Neutrality." *Philosophical Issues* 19, no. 1 (October 2009): 389–411. https://doi.org/10.1111/j.1533-6077.2009.00174.x.

Person-Affecting Views and the Asymmetry

Arrhenius, Gustaf. "Can the Person Affecting Restriction Solve the Problems in Population Ethics?" In *Harming Future Persons*, edited by Melissa A. Roberts and David T. Wasserman. Vol. 35 of *International Library of Ethics, Law, and the New Medicine.* Dordrecht: Springer, 2009.

Cohen, Daniel. "An Actualist Explanation of the Procreation Asymmetry." *Utilitas* 32, no. 1 (March 2020): 70–89. https://doi.org/10.1017/S0953820819000293.

Frick, Johann. "Conditional Reasons and the Procreation Asymmetry." *Philosophical Perspectives* 34, no. 1 (December 2020): 53–87. https://doi.org/10.1111/phpe.12139.

———. "Making People Happy, Not Making Happy People': A Defense of the Asymmetry Intuition in Population Ethics." Doctoral diss., Harvard University, 2014. http://nrs.harvard.edu/urn-3:HUL.InstRepos:13064981.

Hare, Caspar. "Voices from Another World: Must We Respect the Interests of People Who Do Not, and Will Never, Exist?" *Ethics* 117, no. 3 (April 2007): 498–523. https://doi.org/10.1086/512172.

Narveson, Jan. "Moral Problems of Population." *The Monist* 57, no. 1 (January 1973): 62–86. https://doi.org/10.5840/monist197357134.

Parsons, Josh. "Axiological Actualism." *Australasian Journal of Philosophy* 80, no. 2 (2002): 137–47. https://www.tandfonline.com/doi/abs/10.1093/ajp/80.2.137?journalCode=rajp20.

Roberts, Melinda A. "A New Way of Doing the Best That We Can: Person-Based Consequentialism and the Equality Problem." *Ethics* 112, no. 2 (January 2002): 315–50. https://doi.org/10.1086/324321.

Practical Implications of Population Ethics

Althaus, David, and Lukas Gloor. "Reducing Risks of Astronomical Suffering: A Neglected Priority." Center on Long-Term Risk. Last updated August 2019. https://longtermrisk.org/reducing-risks-of-astronomical-suffering-a-neglected-priority/.

Beckstead, Nick. "On the Overwhelming Importance of Shaping the Far-Future." PhD diss., Rutgers University, 2013. https://drive.google.com/file/d/0B8P94pg6WYCIc0lXSUVYS1BnMkE/view?resourcekey=0-nk6wM1QIPl0qWVh2z9FG4Q.

MacAskill, William. *What We Owe the Future.* New York: Basic Books, 2022.

Ord, Toby. *The Precipice: Existential Risk and the Future of Humanity.* London: Bloomsbury Publishing, 2020.

Impossibility Theorems in Population Ethics

Arrhenius, Gustaf. "An Impossibility Theorem for Welfarist Axiologies." *Economics and Philosophy* 16, no. 2 (November 2000): 247–66. https://doi.org/10.1017/S0266267100000249.

Carlson, Erik. "Mere Addition and Two Trilemmas of Population Ethics." *Economics and Philosophy* 14, no. 2 (October 1998): 283–306. https://doi.org/10.1017/S0266267100003862.

Kitcher, Philip. "Parfit's Puzzle." *Noûs* 34, no. 4 (December 2000): 550–77. https://doi.org/10.1111/0029-4624.00278.

Ng, Yew-Kwang. "What Should We Do about Future Generations? Impossibility of Parfit's Theory X." *Economics and Philosophy* 5, no. 2 (October 1989): 235–53. https://doi.org/10.1017/S0266267100002406.

Chapter 6: Utilitarianism and Practical Ethics

Is There a Difference between Doing and Allowing Harm?

Bennett, Jonathan. *The Act Itself.* Oxford University Press, 1995.

Woolard, Fiona, and Frances Howard-Snyder. "Doing vs. Allowing Harm." *The Stanford Encyclopedia of Philosophy,* edited by Edward N. Zalta. Winter 2016 Edition. https://plato.stanford.edu/entries/doing-allowing/.

The Expanding Moral Circle

Singer, Peter. "The Drowning Child and the Expanding Circle." *New Internationalist.* April 5, 1997. https://newint.org/features/1997/04/05/peter-singer-drowning-child-new-internationalist.

———. *The Expanding Circle: Ethics, Evolution, and Moral Progress.* Princeton, NJ: Princeton University Press, 2011.

Cosmopolitanism: Expanding the Moral Circle across Geography

"Poverty and Our Response to It #44." CrashCourse Philosophy, posted January 30, 2017. YouTube video, 8:53. https://youtube/D5sknLy7Smo.

Scheffler, Samuel. "Conceptions of Cosmopolitanism." *Utilitas* 11, no. 3 (1999): 255–76. https://doi.org/10.1017/S0953820800002508.

Singer, Peter. "Famine, Affluence, and Morality." *Philosophy and Public Affairs* 1, no. 3 (Spring 1972): 229–43. https://www.jstor.org/stable/2265052.

———. *The Life You Can Save: Acting Now to End World Poverty*. 2nd ed. Bainbridge Island, WA: The Life You Can Save, 2019. Available free at http://www.thelifeyou cansave.org/the-book/.

Anti-Speciesism: Expanding the Moral Circle across Species

"Non-Human Animals #42." CrashCourse Philosophy, posted January 16, 2017. YouTube video, 9:46. https://youtube/y3-BX-jN_Ac.

McMahan, Jeff. "Animals." In *The Blackwell Companion to Applied Ethics*, edited by R. G. Frey and Christopher Wellman, 525–36. Oxford: Blackwell, 2002.

Sebo, Jeff. "A Utilitarian Case for Animal Rights." Effective Altruism Global, posted December 18, 2019. YouTube video, 25:43. https://www.youtube.com/watch?v=vELWCTgA9oA.

Singer, Peter. *Animal Liberation*. New York: HarperCollins, 2017.

Longtermism: Expanding the Moral Circle across Time

Beckstead, Nick."On the Overwhelming Importance of Shaping the Far-Future." PhD diss., Rutgers University, 2013. https://drive.google.com/file/d/0B8P94pg6WYCIc0lXSUVYS1BnMkE/view?resourcekey=0-nk6wM1QIPl0qWVh2z9FG4Q.

Bostrom, Nick. "Astronomical Waste: The Opportunity Cost of Delayed Technological Development." *Utilitas* 15, no. 3 (November 2003): 308–14. https://doi.org/10.1017/S0953820800004076.

Greaves, Hilary, and William MacAskill. "The Case for Strong Longtermism." GPI Working Paper 5-2021, *Global Priorities Institute*, 2019. https://globalprioritiesinsti tute.org/hilary-greaves-william-macaskill-the-case-for-strong-longtermism/.

MacAskill, William. *What We Owe the Future*. New York: Basic Books, 2022.

Ord, Toby. *The Precipice: Existential Risk and the Future of Humanity*. London: Bloomsbury Publishing, 2020.

Respecting Commonsense Moral Norms

Gibbard, Allan. "Utilitarianism and Human Rights." *Social Philosophy and Policy* 1, no. 2 (Spring 1984): 92–102. https://doi.org/10.1017/s0265052500003897.

Hare, Richard M. *Moral Thinking: Its Levels, Method, and Point.* Oxford: Oxford University Press, 1981.

Mackie, J. L. "Rights, Utility, and Universalization." In *Utility and Rights*, edited by R. G. Frey. Oxford: Basil Blackwell, 1985.

Pettit, Philip, and Geoffrey Brennan. "Restrictive Consequentialism." *Australasian Journal of Philosophy* 64, no. 4 (1986): 438–55. https://doi.org/10.1080/00048408612342631.

Chapter 7: Acting on Utilitarianism

General

de Lazari-Radek, Katarzyna, and Peter Singer. "Utilitarianism in Action." Chap. 6 in *Utilitarianism: A Very Short Introduction.* Oxford: Oxford University Press, 2017.

Singer, Peter. *Practical Ethics.* 3rd ed. Cambridge: Cambridge University Press, 2011.

Effective Altruism

Chappell, Richard Y. "Why Not Effective Altruism?" *Public Affairs Quarterly* 38. no. 1 (2024): 3-21. https://philpapers.org/rec/CHAWNE

MacAskill, William. *Doing Good Better: Effective Altruism and How You Can Make a Difference.* New York: Penguin Random House, 2015.

———. "Effective Altruism." Forthcoming in *The Norton Introduction to Ethics*, edited by Elizabeth Harman and Alex Guerrero. https://www.williammacaskill.com/s/MacAskill_Effective_Altruism-1.pdf.

———. "What Are the Most Important Moral Problems of Our Time?" Posted April 2018. TED video, 11:45. https://www.ted.com/talks/will_macaskill_what_are_the_most_important_moral_problems_of_our_time.

Singer, Peter. "The Why and How of Effective Altruism." Filmed March 2013. TED video, 17:02. https://www.ted.com/talks/peter_singer_the_why_and_how_of_effective_altruism.

Websites and organizations relevant to effective altruism:

- 80,000: Research non-profit aiming to help talented individuals maximize the social impact of their careers. https://80000hours.org/.

- EffectiveAltruism.org: Website providing online resources about effective altruism. https://www.effectivealtruism.org/.

- Giving What We Can: Community of people having pledged to give 10 percent of their lifetime earnings to effective charities. https:// www.givingwhatwecan.org/.

- GiveWell: Charity evaluator aiming to find outstanding giving opportunities. https://www.givewell.org/.

- Charity Entrepreneurship: Charity incubator helping start multiple high-impact charities annually. https://www.charityentrepreneurship .com/.

Podcasts on effective altruism and utilitarianism:
- *80,000 Hours Podcast.* "Effective Altruism: An Introduction." 10 episodes. https://80000hours.org/podcast/effective-altruism-an-introduction/.

- MacAskill, William. "Doing Good: A Conversation with William MacAskill." *Making Sense Podcast with Sam Harris*, December 14, 2020. 02:14:43. https://samharris.org/podcasts/228-doing-good/.

- Singer, Peter. What Is Moral Progress?: A Conversation with Peter Singer." *Making Sense Podcast with Sam Harris*, October 21, 2016. 47:31. https://samharris.org/podcasts/what-is-moral-progress/.

- Singer, Peter, and Kasia de Lazari Radek. *Lives Well Lived*. Apple Podcasts. https://podcasts.apple.com/us/podcast/lives-well-lived/ id1743702376.

Global Health and Development

Ord, Toby. "The Moral Imperative toward Cost-Effectiveness in Global Health." In *Effective Altruism: Philosophical Issues*, edited by Hilary Greaves and Theron Pummer. Oxford: Oxford University Press, 2019.

Singer, Peter. *The Life You Can Save: Acting Now to End World Poverty*. 2nd ed. Bainbridge Island, WA: The Life You Can Save, 2019. Available free at http://www.thelifeyoucansave .org/the-book/.

Unger, Peter. *Living High and Letting Die: Our Illusion of Innocence*. Oxford: Oxford University Press, 1996.

Farm Animal Welfare

Bollard, Lewis. "Lewis Bollard on Big Wins against Factory Farming and How They Happened." *80,000 Hours Podcast with Rob Wiblin*, February 15, 2021. 02:33:16.

https://80000hours.org/podcast/episodes/lewis-bollard-big-wins-against
-factory-farming/.

John, Tyler M., and Jeff Sebo. "Consequentialism and Nonhuman Animals." In *The Oxford Handbook of Consequentialism*, edited by Douglas W. Portmore. Oxford: Oxford University Press, 2020.

Whittlestone, Jess. "Animal Welfare." *Effective Altruism*. 2017 https://www.effectivealtru ism.org/articles/cause-profile-animal-welfare/.

Existential Risks

Bostrom, Nick. "Existential Risk Prevention as Global Priority." *Global Policy* 4, no 1 (February 2013): 15–31. http://www.existential-risk.org/concept.pdf.

Ord, Toby. *The Precipice: Existential Risk and the Future of Humanity*. London: Blooms-bury Publishing, 2020.

Chapter 8: Near-Utilitarian Alternatives

Beyond Welfarism

Anderson, Elizabeth S. What Is the Point of Equality? *Ethics* 109, no. 2 (January 1999): 287–337. https://doi.org/10.1086/233897.

Parfit, Derek. "Equality and Priority." *Ratio* 10, no. 3 (December 1997): 202–21. https://doi .org/10.1111/1467-9329.00041.

Routley, Richard. "Is There a Need for a New, an Environmental, Ethic?" *Proceedings of the XVth World Congress of Philosophy* 1 (1973): 205–10. https://doi.org/10.5840/ wcp151973136.

Prioritarianism

Greene, Joshua, and Jonathan Baron. "Intuitions about Declining Marginal Utility." *Journal of Behavioral Decision Making* 14 (June 2000): 243–55. https://dx.doi .org/10.2139/ssrn.231183.

Gustafsson, Johan E. "Ex-Ante Prioritarianism Violates Sequential Ex-Ante Pareto." *Utilitas* 34, no. 2 (2022): 167–77. https://doi.org/10.1017/S0953820821000303.

Parfit, Derek. "Equality and Priority." *Ratio* 10, no. 3 (December 1997): 202–21. https://doi.org/10.1111/1467-9329.00041.

Desert-Adjusted Views

Feldman, Fred. "Adjusting Utility for Justice: A Consequentialist Reply to the Objection from Justice." *Philosophy and Phenomenological Research* 55, no. 3 (September 1995): 567–85. https://doi.org/10.2307/2108439.

Egoism and Partialism

Goodin, Robert. "What Is So Special about Our Fellow Countrymen?" *Ethics* 98, no. 4 (July 1988): 663–86. https://doi.org/10.1086/292998.

Jollimore, Troy. "Impartiality." *The Stanford Encyclopedia of Philosophy*, edited by Edward N. Zalta. Winter 2018 Edition. https://plato.stanford.edu/entries/impartiality/.

Keller, Simon. *Partiality*. Princeton, NJ: Princeton University Press, 2013.

Mogensen, Andreas. "The Only Ethical Argument for Positive δ?" *Philosophical Studies* 179 (2022): 2731–50. https://globalprioritiesinstitute.org/andreas-mogensen-the-only-ethical-argument-for-positive-delta-2/.

Parfit, Derek. "Rationality and Time." Part 2 in *Reasons and Persons*. Oxford: Clarendon Press, 1984.

Beyond Consequentialism

Ashford, Elizabeth. "The Demandingness of Scanlon's Contractualism." *Ethics* 113, no. 2 (January 2003): 273–302. https://doi.org/10.1086/342853.

Taurek, John M. "Should the Numbers Count?" *Philosophy and Public Affairs* 6, no. 4 (Summer 1977): 293–316. https://www.jstor.org/stable/2264945.

Ross, David. *The Right and the Good*. Oxford: Clarendon Press, 1930.

Part II: Objections to Utilitarianism and Responses

General

de Lazari-Radek, Katarzyna, and Peter Singer. "Objections." Chap. 4 in *Utilitarianism: A Very Short Introduction*. Oxford: Oxford University Press, 2017.

Smart, J. J. C., and Bernard Williams. *Utilitarianism: For and Against*. Cambridge: Cambridge University Press, 1973.

The Rights Objection

Bykvist, Krister. "Is Utilitarianism Too Permissive?" Chap. 8 in *Utilitarianism: A Guide for the Perplexed*. London: Continuum, 2010

de Lazari-Radek, Katarzyna, and Peter Singer. "Objections: Does Utilitarianism Tell Us to Act Immorally?" Section in chap 4 in *Utilitarianism: A Very Short Introduction*. Oxford: Oxford University Press, 2017.

Kagan, Shelly. *The Limits of Morality*. New York: Oxford University Press, 1989.

———. *Normative Ethics*, chap. 3. Boulder, CO: Westview Press, 1998.

Rivera-López, Eduardo. "The Moral Murderer: A (More) Effective Counterexample to Consequentialism." *Ratio* 25, no. 3 (September 2012): 307–25. https://doi.org/10.1111/j.1467-9329.2012.00544.x.

Thomson, Judith Jarvis. "Killing, Letting Die, and the Trolley Problem." *The Monist* 59, no. 2 (April 1976): 204–17. https://doi.org/10.5840/monist197659224.

Woodcock, Scott. "When Will a Consequentialist Push You in Front of a Trolley?" *Australasian Journal of Philosophy*. 95, no. 2 (2017): 299–316. https://doi.org/10.1080/00048402.2016.1212909.

The Mere Means Objection

Kerstein, Samuel. "Treating Persons as Means." *The Stanford Encyclopedia of Philosophy*, edited by Edward N. Zalta. Summer 2019 Edition. https://plato.stanford.edu/archives/sum2019/entries/persons-means/.

Parfit, Derek. "Merely as a Means." Chap. 9 in vol. 1 of *On What Matters*. Oxford: Oxford University Press, 2011.

The Separateness of Persons Objection

Brink, David O. "Consequentialism, the Separateness of Persons, and Aggregation." In *The Oxford Handbook of Consequentialism*, edited by Douglas W. Portmore. New York: Oxford University Press, 2020.

Chappell, Richard Y. *Parfit's Ethics*, section 3.2. Cambridge: Cambridge University Press, 2021.

———. "Value Receptacles." *Noûs* 49, no. 2 (June 2015): 322–32. https://doi.org/10.1111/nous.12023.

Cohen, G. A. "Rescuing Conservatism: A Defense of Existing Value." Chap. 9 in *Reasons and Recognition: Essays on the Philosophy of T. M. Scanlon*, edited by R. Jay Wallace, Rahul Kumar, and Samuel Freeman. Oxford: Oxford University Press, 2011.

Dickert, Stephan, Daniel Västfjäll, Janet Kleber, and Paul Slovic. "Scope Insensitivity: The Limits of Intuitive Valuation of Human Lives in Public Policy." *Journal of Applied Research in Memory and Cognition* 4, no. 3 (2015): 248–55. http://doi.org/10.1016/j.jarmac.2014.09.002.

Nozick, Robert. *Anarchy, State, and Utopia*. New York: Basic Books, 1974.

Parfit, Derek. "Justifiability to Each Person." *Ratio* 16, no. 4 (December 2003): 368–90. https://doi.org/10.1046/j.1467-9329.2003.00229.x.

Paul, Ellen Frankel, Fred D. Miller Jr., and Jeffrey Paul, eds. *Utilitarianism: The Aggregation Question*. Cambridge: Cambridge University Press, 2010.

Rawls, John. *A Theory of Justice*. Rev. ed. Cambridge, MA: Belknap Press, 1999.

Scanlon, T. M. *What We Owe to Each Other*. Cambridge, MA: Belknap Press, 1998.

The Demandingness Objection

Berkey, Brian. "The Demandingness of Morality: Toward a Reflective Equilibrium." *Philosophical Studies* 173, no. 11 (November 2016): 3015–35. https://doi.org/10.1007/s11098-016-0648-9.

Bykvist, Krister. "Is Utilitarianism Too Demanding? Chap. 7 in *Utilitarianism: A Guide for the Perplexed*. London: Continuum, 2010.

de Lazari-Radek, Katarzyna, and Peter Singer. *The Point of View of the Universe: Sidgwick and Contemporary Ethics*, 317–36. Oxford: Oxford University Press, 2014.

Kagan, Shelly. "Does Consequentialism Demand Too Much? Recent Work on the Limits of Obligation." *Philosophy and Public Affairs*. 13, no. 3 (Summer 1984): 239–54. https://www.jstor.org/stable/2265413.

Mogensen, Andreas. "Moral Demands and the Far Future." *Philosophy and Phenomenological Research* 103, no. 3 (September 2020): 567–85. https://doi.org/10.1111/phpr.12729.

Singer, Peter. "Famine, Affluence, and Morality." *Philosophy and Public Affairs* 1, no. 3 (Spring 1972): 229–43. https://www.jstor.org/stable/2265052.

Sobel, David. "The Impotence of the Demandingness Objection." *Philosophers' Imprint* 7, no. 8 (September 2007): 1–17. https://hdl.handle.net/2027/spo.3521354.0007.008.

Wolf, Susan. "Moral Saints." *The Journal of Philosophy* 79, no 8 (August 1982): 419–34. https://www.jstor.org/stable/2026228.

The Alienation Objection

Chappell, Richard Y. "The Right Wrong-Makers." *Philosophy and Phenomenological Research* 103, no. 2 (2020): 426–40. https://doi.org/10.1111/phpr.12728.

Maguire, Barry, and Calvin Baker. "The Alienation Objection to Consequentialism." In *The Oxford Handbook of Consequentialism*, edited by Douglas W. Portmore. Oxford University Press, 2020.

Pettit, Philip, and Geoffrey Brennan. "Restrictive Consequentialism." *Australasian Journal of Philosophy* 64, no. 4 (1986): 438–55. https://doi.org/10.1080/00048408612342631.

Railton, Peter. "Alienation, Consequentialism, and the Demands of Morality." *Philosophy and Public Affairs* 13, no. 2 (Spring 1984): 134–71. https://www.jstor.org/stable/2265273.

Stocker, Michael. "The Schizophrenia of Modern Ethical Theories." *Journal of Philosophy* 73, no. 14 (August 1976): 453–66. https://doi.org/10.2307/2025782.

Williams, Bernard. "Persons, Character and Morality." In *Moral Luck: Philosophical Papers, 1973–1980*. Cambridge: Cambridge University Press, 1981.

The Special Obligations Objection

de Lazari-Radek, Katarzyna, and Peter Singer. "The Objectivity of Ethics and the Unity of Practical Reason." *Ethics* 123, no. 1 (October 2012): 9–31. https://doi.org/10.1086/667837.

Everett, Jim A. C., Nadira S. Faber, Julian Savulescu, and Molly J. Crockett. "The Costs of Being Consequentialist: Social Inference from Instrumental Harm and Impartial Beneficence." *Journal of Experimental Social Psychology* 79 (November 2018): 200–216. https://doi.org/10.1016/j.jesp.2018.07.004.

Goodin, Robert. "What Is So Special about Our Fellow Countrymen?" *Ethics* 98, no. 4 (July 1988): 663–86. https://doi.org/10.1086/292998.

Jackson, Frank. "Decision-Theoretic Consequentialism and the Nearest and Dearest Objection." *Ethics* 101, no. 3 (1991): 461–82. https://doi.org/10.1086/293312.

Parfit, Derek. *Reasons and Persons*. Oxford: Clarendon Press, 1984.

The Equality Objection

Crisp, Roger. "Equality, Priority, and Compassion." *Ethics* 113, no. 4 (July 2003): 745–63. https://doi.org/10.1086/373954.

Ord, Toby. "A New Counterexample to Prioritarianism." *Utilitas* 27, no. 3 (2015): 298–302. http://amirrorclear.net/files/a-new-counterexample-to-prioritarianism.pdf.

Parfit, Derek. "Equality and Priority." *Ratio* 10, no. 3 (December 1997): 202–21. https://doi.org/10.1111/1467-9329.00041.

Temkin, Larry. "Equality, Priority or What?" *Economics and Philosophy* 19, no. 1 (April 2003): 61–87. https://doi.org/10.1017/S0266267103001020.

———. *Inequality*. New York: Oxford University Press, 1993.

The Cluelessness Objection

Burch-Brown, Joanna. "Clues for Consequentialists." *Utilitas* 26, no. 1 (January 2014): 105–19. https://doi.org/10.1017/S0953820813000289.

Greaves, Hilary. "Cluelessness." *Proceedings of the Aristotelian Society* 116, no. 3 (October 2016): 311–39. https://doi.org/10.1093/arisoc/aow018.

Lenman, James. "Consequentialism and Cluelessness." *Philosophy and Public Affairs* 29, no. 4 (October 2000): 342–70. https://doi.org/10.1111/j.1088-4963.2000.00342.x.

Mogensen, Andreas. "Maximal Cluelessness." *The Philosophical Quarterly* 71, no. 1 (January 2021): 141–62. https://doi.org/10.1093/pq/pqaa021.

Mogensen, Andreas, and William MacAskill. "The Paralysis Argument." *Philosophers' Imprint* 21, no. 15 (2021): 1–17. http://hdl.handle.net/2027/spo.3521354 .0021.015.

Thorstad, David, and Andreas Mogensen. "Heuristics for Clueless Agents: How to Get Away with Ignoring What Matters Most in Ordinary Decision-Making." GPI Working Paper 2-2020, Global Priorities Institute, 2020. https://globalprioritiesinstitute .org/david-thorstad-and-andreas-mogensen-heuristics-for-clueless-agents-how-to-get -away-with-ignoring-what-matters-most-in-ordinary-decision-making/.

The Abusability Objection

de Lazari-Radek, Katarzyna, and Peter Singer. "Secrecy in Consequentialism: A Defence of Esoteric Morality, *Ratio* 23, no. 1 (January 2010): 34–58. https://doi .org/10.1111/j.1467-9329.2009.00449.x.

Gibbard, Allan. "Utilitarianism and Human Rights." *Social Philosophy and Policy* 1, no. 2 (Spring 1984): 92–102. https://doi.org/10.1017/s0265052500003897.

Hare, Richard M. *Moral Thinking: Its Levels, Method, and Point.* Oxford: Oxford University Press, 1981.

Mackie, J. L. "Rights, Utility, and Universalization." In *Utility and Rights*, edited by R. G. Frey. Oxford: Basil Blackwell, 1985.

Parfit, Derek. "Self-Defeating Theories." Part 1 in *Reasons and Persons*. Oxford: Clarendon Press, 1984.

Pettit, Philip, and Geoffrey Brennan. "Restrictive Consequentialism." *Australasian Journal of Philosophy* 64, no. 4 (1986): 438–55. https://doi.org/10.1080/00048408612342631.

Williams, Bernard. "A Critique of Utilitarianism." In *Utilitarianism: For and Against*, J. J. C. Smart and Bernard Williams. Cambridge University Press, 1973.

Peter Singer's "Famine, Affluence, and Morality"

Resources for Study Guide: Peter Singer's "Famine, Affluence, and Morality"

Chappell, Richard Y., and Helen Yetter-Chappell. "Virtue and Salience." *Australasian Journal of Philosophy* 94, no. 3 (2016): 449–63. https://doi.org/10.1080/00048402.2 015.1115530.

Forcehimes, Andrew T., and Luke Semrau. "Beneficence: Does Agglomeration Matter?" *Journal of Applied Philosophy* 36, no. 1 (2019): 17–33. https://doi.org/10.1111/ japp.12276.

Kamm, F. M. "Famine Ethics: The Problem of Distance in Morality and Singer's Ethical Theory." In *Singer and His Critics*, 174–203, edited by Dale Jamieson. Oxford: Blackwell: 174–203.

MacAskill, William. "Aid Scepticism and Effective Altruism." *Journal of Practical Ethics* 7, no. 1 2019): 49–60. http://www.jpe.ox.ac.uk/papers/aid-scepticism-and -effective-altruism/.

Miller, Richard. "Beneficence, Duty and Distance." *Philosophy and Public Affairs* 32, no. 4 (October 2004): 357–83. https://doi.org/10.1111/j.1088-4963.2004.00018.x.

Pummer, Theron. *The Rules of Rescue: Cost, Distance, and Effective Altruism.* Oxford: Oxford University Press, 2023.

Sin, William. "Trivial Sacrifices, Great Demands." *Journal of Moral Philosophy* 7, no. 1 (2010): 3–15. https://doi.org/10.1163/174046809X12551571293172.

Singer, Peter. "Famine, Affluence, and Morality." *Philosophy and Public Affairs* 1, no. 3 (Spring 1972): 229–43. https://www.jstor.org/stable/2265052.

———. *The Life You Can Save: Acting Now to End World Poverty*. 2nd ed. Bainbridge Island, WA: The Life You Can Save, 2019. Available free at https://www.thelifeyou cansave.org/the-book/.

Slote, Michael. "Famine, Affluence, and Virtue." In *Working Virtue: Virtue Ethics and Contemporary Moral Problems*, 279–96, edited by Rebecca L. Walker and Philip J. Ivanhoe. Oxford: Clarendon Press, 2007.

Sterri, Aksel Braanen, and Ole Martin Moen. "The Ethics of Emergencies." *Philosophical Studies* 178, no. 8 (August 2021): 2621–34. https://doi.org/10.1007/s11098-020-01566-0.

Thomson, Jordan Arthur. "Relief from Rescue." *Philosophical Studies* 179, no. 4 (2021): 1221–39. https://doi.org/10.1007/s11098-021-01705-1.

Timmerman, Travis. "Sometimes There Is Nothing Wrong with Letting a Child Drown." *Analysis* 75, no. 2 (April 2015): 204–12. https://doi.org/10.1093/analys/anv015.

Unger, Peter. *Living High and Letting Die: Our Illusion of Innocence*. Oxford: Oxford University Press.

Index